The Great Indian Political Leaders

The Great Indian Political Leaders

Kailash Puri

CYBER TECH PUBLICATIONS
4264/3, Ansari Road, Daryaganj, New Delhi-110002 (India)
Ph.: 011-23244078. Fax: 011-23280028
E-Mail: cyberpublicationsdelhi@yahoo.com

THE GREAT INDIAN POLITICAL LEADERS

Kailash Puri

First Edition 2009

Published by :

G.S. Rawat for **Cyber Tech Publications**
4264/3, Ansari Road, Daryaganj, New Delhi-110002 (India)
Ph.: 011-23244078. Fax: 011-23280028
E-Mail: cyberpublicationsdelhi@yahoo.com

Printed at . Asian Offset Printers (0878184)

Preface

Real national executive power is centered in the Council of Ministers, the Union Cabinet, led by the Prime Minister of India, who is the Head of Government. The President appoints the Prime Minister, who is the designated leader of the political party or coalition commanding parliamentary majority. All Central Government decisions are nominally taken in the name of the President. The Ministers may be of 3 types - Cabinet Minister, Minister of State (Independent Charge) and deputy ministers, in order of seniority. Cabinet Ministers and Ministers of State with independent charge may usually attend Cabinet meetings.

The North Block situated at Raisina Hill, Delhi houses Finance and Home Ministries and Department of Personnal and Training (Ministry of Personnel, Public Grievances and Pensions). The day-to-day enforcement and administration of national laws lies in the hands of the various federal Union Ministries and Departments, created by the Indian Parliament to deal with specific areas of national and international affairs. In matters delegated to the States, Ministries act in advisory and funding capacity.

Since a long time India is governed by political leaders. This book tells about a few great and eminent political leaders.

— *Author*

CONTENTS

1

Time and Life of Mahatma

In January 1948, before three pistol shots put an end to his life, Gandhi had been on the political stage for more than fifty years. He had inspired two generations of India, patriots, shaken an empire and sparked off a revolution which was to change the face of Africa and Asia. To millions of his own people, he was the Mahatma-the great soul-whose sacred glimpse was a reward in itself. By the end of 1947 he had lived down much of the suspicion, ridicule and opposition which he had to face, when he first raised the banner of revolt against racial exclusiveness and imperial domination. His ideas, once dismissed as quaint and utopian, had begun to strike answering chords in some of the finest minds in the world. "Generations to come, it may be", Einstein had said of Gandhi in July 1944, "will scarcely believe that such one as this ever in flesh and blood walked upon earth."

Though his life had been continual unfolding of an endless drama, Gandhi himself seemed the least dramatic of men. It would be difficult to imagine a man with fewer trappings of political eminence or with less of the popular image of a heroic figure. With his loin cloth, steel-rimmed glasses, rough sandals, a toothless smile and a voice which rarely rose above a whisper, he had a disarming humility. He used a stone instead of soap for his bath, wrote his letters on little bits of paper with little stumps of pencils which he could hardly hold between his fingers, shaved with a crude country razor and ate with a wooden spoon from a prisoner's bowl. He was, if one were to use the famous words of the Buddha, a man who had "by rousing himself, by earnestness, by restraint and control, made for himself an island which no flood could overwhelm."

Gandhi's, deepest strivings were spiritual, but he did not-as had been the custom in his country-retire to a cave in the Himalayas to seek his salvation. He carried his cave within him. He did not know, he said, any religion apart from human activity; the spiritual law did not work in a vacuum, but expressed itself through the ordinary activities of life. This aspiration to relate the spirit-not the forms-of religion to the problems of everyday life runs like a thread through Gandhi's career; his uneventful childhood, the slow unfolding and the near-failure of his youth, reluctant plunge into the politics of Natal, the long, unequal struggle in South Africa, and the vicissitudes of the Indian struggle for freedom, which under his leadership was to culminate in a triumph not untinged with tragedy.

CHILDHOOD

Mohandas Gandhi was born on October 2,1869, at Porbandar, on the western coast of India. His grandfather Uttamchand Gandhi and father Karamchand Gandhi occupied the high office of the diwan (Chief Minister) of Porbandar. To be Diwan of one of the princely states was on sinecure. Porbandar was one of some three hundred 'native' states in western India which were ruled by princes whom the accident of birth and the support of the British kept on the throne. To steer one's course safely between wayward Indian princes, the overbearing British 'Political Agent' of the suzerain power and the long-suffering subjects required a high degree of patience, diplomatic skill and commonsense. Both Uttamchand and Karamchand were good administrators. But they were also upright and honourable men. Loyal to their masters, they did not flinch from offering unpalatable advice. They paid the price for the courage of their convictions. Uttamchand Gandhi had his hose besieged and shelled by the ruler's troops and had to flee the State; his son Karamchand also preferred to leave Porbandar, rather than compromise with his principles.

Karamchand Gandhi was, in the words of his son, "a lover of his clan, truthful, brave, generous." The strongest formative influence on young Mohandas, however, was that of his mother Putlibai. She was a capable woman who made herself felt in court circles through her friendship with the ladies of the palace, but her chief interest was in the home. When there was sickness in the family, she wore herself out in days and nights of nursing. She had little of the weaknesses, common to women of her age and class, for finery or jewellery. Her life was an endless chain of fasts and vows through which her frame seemed to be borne only by the strength of her faith. The children clung to her as she divided her day between the home and the temple. Her fasts and vows puzzled and fascinated them. She was not versed in the scriptures; indeed except for a smattering of Gujarati, she was practically unlettered. But her abounding lover, her endless austerities and her iron will, left a permanent impression upon Mohandas, her youngest son. The image of woman he imbibed from his mother was one of love and sacrifice. Something of her maternal love he came to possess himself, and as he grew, it flowed out in an ever-increasing measure, bursting the bonds of family and community, until it embraced the whole of humanity. To his mother, he owed not only a passion for nursing which later made him wash leper's sores in his Ashram, but also an inspiration for his techniques of appealing to the heart through self-suffering-a technique which wives and mothers have practised from time immemorial.

Young Mohandas' school career was undistinguished. He did not shine in the classroom or in the playground. Quiet, shy and retiring, he was tongue-tied in company. He did not mind being rated as a mediocre student, but he was exceedingly jealous of his reputation. He was proud of the fact that he had never told a lie to his teachers or classmates; the slightest aspersion on his character drew his tears. Like most growing children he passed through a rebellious phase, but contrary to the impression fostered by his autobiography, Gandhi's adolescence was no stormier than that of many of his contemporaries. Adventures into the forbidden land of meat-eating and smoking and petty pilfering were, and are not uncommon among boys of his age. What was extraordinary was the way his adventures ended. In every case when he had gone astray, he posed for himself a problem for which he sought a solution by framing a proposition in moral algebra. 'Never again' was his promise to himself after each escapade. And he kept the promise.

OFF TO ENGLAND

Mohan passed the matriculation examination of Bombay University in 1887. His father's death a year earlier had strained the means of the family. Being the only boy in the family who had persevered in his studies, its hopes rested on him and he was sent to Bhavnagar, the nearest town with a college. Unfortunately for Mohan the teaching was in English. He was unable to follow the lectures and despaired of making any progress. Meanwhile, Mavji Dave, a friend of the family, suggested that Mohan should go to English to qualify at the bar. Mohan jumped at the idea of going abroad.

His elder brother had no doubt that the proposal was attractive but wondered how they could afford it. His mother was reluctant to let her youngest boy sail to an alien land to face unknown temptations and dangers. The Modh Bania caste to which the Gandhis belonged, threatened to excommunicate the whole family if its injunction against foreign travel was infringed. All these hurdles were, however, successfully overcome by Mohan's determination to go abroad, and in September 1888, at the age of 18, he sailed for England.

From the rural surroundings of Rajkot to the cosmopolitan atmosphere of a steamship was a tremendous change for Mohan. Adaptation to Western food, dress and etiquette was a painful process. Both on board the ship and in London in the first few weeks, Mohan could not help feeling that he was making a fool of himself. He had promised his mother before leaving India that he would not "touch wine, woman or meat". The vegetarian vow became a continual source of embarrassment to him. His friends feared that his food fads would ruin his health, and make of him, socially, a square peg. To disarm his critics and to prove that, vegetarianism apart, he was not impervious to the new environment, he decided to put on a thick veneer of 'English culture'. Having made up his mind to become an 'English Gentleman', he spared neither time nor money. Whatever the cost, the veneer had to be the best in the market. New suits were ordered from the most fashionable tailors in London; the watch was adorned with a double gold chain from India; under expert tuition, lessons began in elocution, dancing and music.

Gandhi could not, however, throw himself into this experiment with complete self-abandon. The habit of introspection had never deserted him. English dancing and music did nit come easy to him. He began to see that drapers and dance halls could turn him into an English gentleman, but only an English gentleman about town. After a brief three months' excursion, the introvert returned to his shell.

There was a rebound from extreme extravagance to meticulous economy. He began to keep an account of every farthing he spent. He changed his rooms, cooked his own breakfast and, to save bus fares, walked eight to ten miles daily. He was able to pare down his expenses to £2 a month. He began to feel keenly the obligations to his family and was glad that he had reduced the calls on his brother for funds. Simplicity harmonized his inward and outward life; the dandyism of the first three months had been only a defensive armour against those who considered him a misfit in English society.

Vegetarianism, which had been a source of embarrassment to him, soon became an asset. He came across a book entitled Plea for Vegetarianism by Henry S. Salt, whose arguments went home. A meatless diet had been hitherto a matter of sentiment to him; henceforth, it was one of reasoned conviction. Vegetarianism was no longer an inconvenient obligation to his parents; it became a mission, the starting point of a discipline of body and mind which was to transform his life. With the zeal of a new convert, Gandhi devoured books on developed an interest in cooking, outgrew the taste for condiments, and came to the sensible conclusion that the seat of taste is not in the tongue but in the mind. The control of the palate was one of the first steps in that discipline which was to culminate many years later in total sublimation.

The immediate effect of vegetarianism was to give a new poise to young Gandhi, and to draw him out of his shell. He made his first venture into journalism by contributing nine articles to the Vegetarian. These articles, largely descriptive, and had occasional flashes of humour. That he should have sent these articles for publication at all is a notable achievement, if we recall that back home in Bhavnagar College he had been unable to follow lectures in English. He became a member of the Executive committee of the London Vegetarian Society. In Bays water where he stayed for a short time, he formed a vegetarian club. He came into contact with at least one eminent vegetarian, Sir Edwin Arnold, the author of the Light of Asia and The song Celestial, the two books which moved him deeply. He was stirred by the life if the Buddha and the message of the Gita. In the vegetarian restaurants and boarding houses of London he came across not only food faddists but also a few devout men of religion. He owed his introduction to the Bible to one such contact.

The New Testament, particularly the Sermon on the Mount went straight to his heart. The verses, "But I say unto you that ye resist not evil; but whosoever shall thee at the law and take away thy coat, let him have thy cloak also" reminded him of the lines of the Gujarati poet, Shamal Bhatt, which he used to hum as a child:

For a bowl of water give a goodly meal;

For a kindly greeting bow thou down with zeal;

For a single penny pay thou back with gold;

If the life be rescued, life do not withhold.

Thus the words and actions of the wise regard;

Every little service tenfold they reward.

But the truly noble know all men as one,

And return with gladness good for evil done.

The teachings of the Bible, the Buddha and Bhatt fused in his mind. The idea of returning love for hatred, and good for evil, captivated him; he did not yet comprehend it full, but it continued to ferment in his impressionable mind.

In 1891 Gandhi passed the law examination successfully, but was assailed by doubts and anxieties. He had read the law, but could he practise it? He found it hard enough to speak to strangers in a small party. How would he be able to cross swords with his rivals in the courtroom? He had hard of legal luminaries like Sir Pherozeshah Mehta of Bombay and could well imagine the sorry figure he would cut in comparison. It was thus "with just a little leaven of hope mixed with despair" that he sailed for India. A great shock lay in store for him when he landed at Bombay. His mother had died while he was in England. It was only natural that he should have been anxious to justify the hopes of his family which had invested so much on his foreign education. His elder brother frankly expected rich dividends in the form of "wealth, and name and fame". The barrister's degree, however, was not an open sesame to the top of the bar. Gandhi noticed that the home-bred Vakils of Rajkot knew more of Indian law and charged lower fees than England sure ridicule; Gandhi, therefore, accepted the advice of friends to go to Bombay to study India law and to secure what briefs he could.

His experience in Bombay was no happier than in Rajkot. After waiting unconscionably, he got his first brief for the modest fee of thirty rupees. As he rose to cross-examine a witness, he was unable to collect his thoughts, collapsed into his chair and refunded the fee to his client. This was a disgraceful debut, which filled the young barrister with black despair as to his future in a profession he had entered at such a heavy cost.

The straits to which he had been reduced may be surmised from the fact that he applied and was turned down for a part time job as a teacher in a Bombay high school with the modest salary of seventy rupees (£5 1/2) a month. It was with some relief that he discovered that he had a flair for drafting memorials and petitions. He wound up his little establishment in Bombay and returned to Rajkot where petition-writing brought him an income of three hundred rupees a month. He might have settled down as a barrister scribe if he had not incurred the displeasure of the British Political Agent in Rajkot in whose court most of his work lay. So, when an offer of a job came to him from South Africa, he gladly accepted it.

The contract was for a year in connection with a civil suit; the remuneration was £105, a first-class return fare and actual expenses. The fee was modest and it was not quite clear whether he was engaged as counsel or as a clerk, but he was in no position to pick and choose. He could hardly have imagined the new vistas of maturity and public service which the South African adventure was to open to him.

In 1891 Gandhi passed the law examination successfully, but was assailed by doubts and anxieties. He had read the law, but could he practise it? He found it hard enough to speak to strangers in a small party. How would he be able to cross swords with his rivals in the courtroom? He had hard of legal luminaries like Sir Pherozeshah Mehta of Bombay and could well imagine the sorry figure he would cut in comparison. It was thus "with just a little leaven of hope mixed with despair" that he sailed for India.

A great shock lay in store for him when he landed at Bombay. His mother had died while he was in England. It was only natural that he should have been anxious to justify the hopes of his family which had invested so much on his foreign education. His elder brother frankly expected rich dividends in the form of "wealth, and name and fame". The barrister's degree, however, was not an open sesame to the top of the bar. Gandhi noticed that the home-bred Vakils of Rajkot knew more of Indian law and charged lower fees than England sure ridicule; Gandhi, therefore, accepted the advice of friends to go to Bombay to study India law and to secure what briefs he could.

His experience in Bombay was no happier than in Rajkot. After waiting unconscionably, he got his first brief for the modest fee of thirty rupees. As he rose to cross-examine a witness, he was unable to collect his thoughts, collapsed into his chair and refunded the fee to his client. This was a disgraceful debut, which filled the young barrister with black despair as to his future in a profession he had entered at such a heavy cost.

The straits to which he had been reduced may be surmised from the fact that he applied and was turned down for a part time job as a teacher in a Bombay high school with the modest salary of seventy rupees (£5 1/2) a month. It was with some relief that he discovered that he had a flair for drafting memorials and petitions. He wound up his little establishment in Bombay and returned to Rajkot where petition-writing brought him an income of three hundred rupees a month. He might have settled down as a barrister scribe if he had not incurred the displeasure of the British Political Agent in Rajkot in whose court most of his work lay. So, when an offer of a job came to him from South Africa, he gladly accepted it. The contract was for a year in connection with a civil suit; the remuneration was £105, a first-class return fare and actual expenses. The fee was modest and it was not quite clear whether he was engaged as counsel or as a clerk, but he was in no position to pick and choose. He could hardly have imagined the new vistas of maturity and public service which the South African adventure was to open to him.

IN THE 'DARK CONTINENT'

Gandhi landed at Durban in May 1893. His employer Dada Abdulla, one of the wealthiest Indian merchants in Natal, took him to see the Durban court. When the European magistrate ordered Gandhi to take off his turban, he refused, left the courtroom and wrote a letter of protest in the local press in which he was mentioned "as an unwelcome visitor". The experience in Durban, however, was nothing compared with what befell him in the course of his journey from Durban to Pretoria. When his train reached Maritzburg late in the evening, he was ordered to leave the first class compartment and shift to the van compartment. He refused, but was unceremoniously turned out of the carriage. It was a bitterly cold night as he crept into the unlit waiting-room of Maritzburg station and brooded over what had happened. His client had given him no warning of the humiliating conditions under which Indians lived in South Africa. Should he not call off the contract and return to India? Should he accept these affronts as part of the bargain?

So far Gandhi had not been conspicuous for assertiveness; on the contrary he had been pathologically shy and retiring. But something happened to him in that wind-swept waiting-room of Maritzburg railway station as he smarted under the insult inflicted on him. The iron entered his soul. In retrospect, this incident seemed to him as one of the most creative experiences of his life. From that hour, he refused to accept injustice as a part of the natural-or unnatural-order in South Africa. He would reason, he would plead; he would appeal to the better judgment and the latent humanity of the ruling race; he would resist, but he would never be a willing victim of racial arrogance. It was not so much a question of redeeming his own self-respect as that of his community, his country, even of humanity.

The helpless resignation of the mass of Indian settlers, the fact that they were illiterate, had few rights and did not know how to assert the rights they had. All this had the miraculous effect of dissipating young Gandhi's own diffidence. The feeling of inferiority which had dogged him as a student in England and as a budding lawyer in India vanished. In Bombay he had been unable to face a small cause court but one of the first things he did on arrival at Pretoria was to convene a meeting of the Indian residents "to present to them a picture of their condition in Transvaal".

During the next twelve months, Gandhi was busy with the civil suit which had brought him to Pretoria. In June 1894, he returned to Durban to sail for India. At the farewell party which his grateful client Dada Abdulla gave him at Sydenham, a pleasant suburb of Durban, Gandhi happened to glance through the pages of the Natal Mercury, and learnt that a bill was being introduced into the Natal Legislature to disfranchise India settlers. Gandhi's host and other Indian merchants present at the party were unable to throw any light on this measure. They knew enough English to be able to converse with their white customers, but few of them could read newspapers, much less follow the proceedings of the Natal Legislature. They had come to Natal for trade, and politics did not interest them. They had not yet realized that politics could affect their trade. "This is the first nail into our coffin", was Gandhi's comment. The Indian merchants pleaded with him to stay on in Natal to take up the fight on their behalf. Gandhi agreed to defer his stay for a month.

Gandhi lost no time in settling down to work; the farewell party converted itself into a political committee to plan Indian opposition to the bill. A sound instinct seems to have guided the young barrister in organizing his first political campaign. He infused a spirit of solidarity into the heterogeneous elements composing the Indian community, and brought home the implications of the disfranchising measures not only to his own people, but to the saner section of the European public opinion and the Natal Government Most important of all, he gave the widest publicity to his campaign to quicken the conscience of the peoples and Governments of India and Great Britain; through petitions to the legislatures, statements in newspapers, letters to prominent persons in Natal, Britain and India, and through public meeting, Gandhi stressed the justice of the Indians, case. All this created a great stir but the disfranchising bill was nevertheless passed by the Natal Legislature. On the insistence of his Indian friends in Durban, Gandhi agreed to prolong his stay in Natal, and was enrolled as an advocate to the Supreme Court. Since he retaining fees to produce a minimum 300 a year which he reckoned enough to pay his way in Durban.

THE YOUNG POLITICIAN

The first experience of political agitation into which Gandhi had been pitch forked cured him of what once had seemed an incorrigible self-consciousness. Not that he had a sudden attack of egotism; he was conscious of his limitations, and in a letter dated July 5, 1894 to Dadabhai Naoroji, the eminent leader of the Indian National Congress, wrote: "A word for myself and I have done. I am inexperienced and young and, therefore, quite liable to make mistakes. The responsibility undertaken is quite out of proportion to my ability. So, you will see that I have not taken the matter up, which is beyond my ability, in order to enrich myself at the expense of the Indians. I am the only available person who can handle the question." The concept of inferiority is a relative one; in a community looking to him for leadership, Gandhi forgot his own limitations. As the only available person, he undertook a task from which elsewhere he would have shrunk.

Gandhi had come to South Africa in 1893 for a year. He could hardly have imagined that he would have to stay on for the best part of two decades. The struggle of the Indian immigrants for elementary civic rights was to be long and hard The disfranchising of the Indians which had been the immediate cause of Gandhi's intervention in the politics of Natal was only a symptom of the racial malaise that had begun to afflict the Dark Continent.

"The Asiatics", wrote Lord Milner, "are strangers forcing themselves upon a community reluctant to receive them." In fact, the Indian emigration to South Africa in the eighteen-sixties started at the instance of the European settlers who were in possession of vast virgin lands ideal for tea, coffee and sugar plantations, but lacked man-power. The Negro could not be compelled to work after the abolition of slavery. Recruiting agents of the European planters toured some of the poorest and most congested districts of India and painted rosy prospects of work in Natal. Free passage, board and lodging; a wage of ten shillings a month for the first year rising by one shilling every year; and the right to a free return passage to India after five years' 'indenture' (or alternatively, the option to settle in the land of their adoption) drew thousands of poor and illiterate Indians to distant Natal.

The European planters and merchants did not relish the idea of Indian Labourers settling down as free citizens at the end of the five year' 'indenture'. A tax of £3 was therefore levied on every member of the family of an ex-indentured labourer even though he was merely exercising his right to settle in Natal in terms of the agreement which had governed his emigration from India. It was a crippling tax for the poor wretches whose wages ranged between ten and twelve shillings month.

The Indian merchant who had followed the Indian labourer to Natal had disabilities of his own. No one could trade without a licence, which a European could have for the asking and Indian only after much effort and expense, if at all. And since an educational test in a European language was made a sine quanon for an immigrant from India, except of course the semi-slave indentured labourers who continued to be imported.

The legal disabilities on Indians were bad enough, but the daily humiliations they suffered were worse. They were commonly described as "Asian dirt to be heartily curse, chokeful of vice, that live upon rice and the black vermin". They were not allowed to walk on footpaths. First and second class tickets were not issued to them. If a white passenger objected, they could be unceremoniously bundled out of a railway compartment; they had sometimes to travel on footboards of trains. European hotels would not admit them. Gandhi realized that what the India urgently needed was a permanent organization to look after their interests. Out of deference to Dadabhai Naoroji, Who had presided over the Indian National Congress in 1893, he called the new organization Natal Indian Congress. He was not conversant with the constitution and functions of the Indian National Congress. This ignorance proved an asset, as he fashioned the Natal Congress in his own way to suit the needs of the Natal Indians, as a live body functioning throughout the year and dedicated not only to politics but to the moral and social uplift of its members.

Though it served a community which had very little political experience, it was not a one-man show. An indefatigable secretary though he was, Gandhi enlisted popular interest and enthusiasm at every step. He made the enrolment of members and the collection of subscriptions into something more than a routine. He employed a gently but irresistible technique for exerting moral pressure on halfhearted supporters. Once in a small village, he sat through the night and refused to take his dinner until at dawn his host, an Indian merchant, agreed to raise his subscription for the Natal Indian Congress from three to six pounds.

In these early years of his politics apprenticeship, Gandhi formulated his own code of conduct for a politician. He did not accept the popular view that in politics one must fight for one's; arty, right or wrong. He avoided exaggeration and discouraged it in his colleagues. The Natal Indian Congress was not merely an instrument for the defence of political and economic rights for the Indian minority, but also a lever for its internal reform and unity. He did not spare his own people and roundly criticized them for their shortcomings. He was not only the stoutest champion of the Natal Indians, but also their severest critic.

Under his leadership, the Indian community in Natal endeavoured to secure the repeal of discriminatory laws and vexatious regulations and stave off further oppressive measures. Gandhi was in touch with Naoroji and other members of the British committee of the Indian National Congress in London. He sought their advice and support in representing the South African Indian Indian's case to the Secretary of State for India, and British Colonial Secretary.

He was an indefatigable correspondent, bombarding his friends, opponents, newspaper editors and men in authority in three continents, with telegrams, letters and memoranda on the grievances of the India in South Africa. It is a measure of Gandhi's success as a publicist that the Indian National Congress Recorded its protest against the disabilities imposed upon the Indian settlers in South Africa, and the London Times devoted several leading articles to this problem. In 1896 he paid a brief visit to India to canvass public support for the cause he had made his own. On return to Natal from this trip on January 10,1897, he was nearly lynched in the streets Durban by a mob of Europeans who had been infuriated by Press reports of Gandhi's advocacy of the Indian cause in his native land.

On the outbreak of the Boer War in 1899, Gandhi organized an Indian Ambulance Corps of 1100 men. Vere Stent, the editor of the Pretoria News, has left a fascinating pen-portrait of Gandhi in the battlefield: "After a night's work which had shattered men with much bigger frames, I came across Gandhi in the early morning sitting by the roadside-eating a regulation biscuit. Every man in (General) Buller's force was dull and depressed, and damnation was heartily invoked on everything. But Gandhi was stoic in his bearing, cheerful and confident in his conversation and had a kindly eye."

It must be recognised that Gandhi's ideas on non-violence had not yet fully matured. His argument at this time was that Indian settlers in British colonies, while demanding all the privileges of citizenship must also accept all its obligations, which included participation in the defence of the country of adoption. Gandhi's gesture in raising an ambulance corps on behalf of a minority which was denied elementary rights was a fine one, but it was wasted. The end of the Boer War brought no relief to the Indians. Their grievances remained unredressed. Indeed, new chains were forged for them in the former Boer Colonies.

SATYAGRAHA STRUGGLE IN SOUTH AFRICA

It was the passage of the Asiatic Registration Act in Transvaal in 1907 which convinced Gandhi that the method of protest, petition and prayer which he had sedulously pursued for nearly fourteen years had failed. It was at this juncture that he evolved a new technique, which came to be known as Passive Resistance;

but as it ruled out both verbal and physical violence, it differed in important respects from the campaign waged on behalf of the suffragettes in England. The principles and techniques of Gandhi's movement were to evolve gradually in the ensuing months ant years; its author was a man for whom theory was the handmaid of action.

It is not possible here to give a detailed account of the Satyagraha struggle which Gandhi led in South Africa for seven years. It required great courage, patience and organizing ability to persuade the small Indian community to pit itself against the government. Gandhi had to reckon with the immense political and economic power wielded by the dominant European community, the stubbornness of the local government in South Africa, the reluctance of the British Colonial Office to antagonize the Union Government in Pretoria, the apathy of the Government of India and the limited resources of the small India minority fighting for its survival on an alien soil. Gandhi himself worked under terrific pressure. In January 1908, he was arrested for breach of the registration law and clapped into prison. The following month he was released after an understanding seemed to have been reached with the government. A few days later, he was beaten up and severely injured by a compatriot, who accused him of betraying the Indian cause.

The truce with the Transvaal Government did not last long. The Satyagraha campaign had to be renewed. There were acts of defiance by the Indians and punitive measures by the authorities. Gandhi set up a small colony-Tolstoy Farm-at an 1100 acre site, 21 miles from Johannesburg where his colleagues in the Satyagraha struggle and their families could support a frugal and hard existence-which was in fact harder than life in jail-by-running a cooperative farm. "We had all become labourers," Gandhi recalled later, "put on labourer's dress, but in the European style, *viz.*, Workman's trousers and shirts which were imitated from prisoner's uniform". Those who went to Johannesburg on private errands had to walk. Gandhi himself, though past forty and living only on fruits, did not think much of walking forty miles a day; he once did 55 miles without feeling any the worse for it. All residents of Tolstoy Farm including children had their quota of manual labour.

Those who had known this austere discipline could have little fear of goal.

In 1912, Gokhale, one-of the most eminent Indian politicians of the day, paid a visit to South Africa and discussed the problems of the Indian community with General Smuts and other members of the South African Government. He returned to India with the impression that the Asiatic Registration Act and the hated £3 tax on the ex-indentured labourers would be abolished. When this did not happen, and an additional provocation was given by Supreme Court Judgment invalidating marriages of non-Christians in South Africa, Gandhi launched what turned out to be the final phase of his struggle in South Africa.

A party of eleven Indian women, including Gandhi's wife Kasturba, courted imprisonment by crossing from Natal into Transvaal without a permit. The Indian labourers in the coal mines at New Castle went on a sympathetic strike. The mine-owners retaliated by cutting off water and electric connection to the areas where the labourers lived. Gandhi had no option but to take charge of the miners and their families, 2037 men, 127 women and 57 children. He decided to walk them from New Castle to Tolstoy Farm, but was arrested on the way. In Volksrust jail he was make to dig stones and sweep the compound. Later he was transferred to Pretoria jail and lodged in a dark cell ten feet long and seven feet wine, which was lit up at night only to check up on the prisoner. He was denied a bench, refused permission to walk in the cell and subjected to numberless pinpricks. Summoned for evidence in a case, he was marched to the court with hand-cuffs on his hands and manacles on his feet. Meanwhile, the Indian labourers had been put into special trains, and taken back to New Castle mines where they were forced to go underground by mounted military police.

The 'blood and iron' policy of the South African Government stirred India deeply. Gokhale sent two earnest Christian young men, C.F. Andrews and Pearson, to assist Gandhi. Lord Hardinge, the viceroy of India, courageously denounced the high-handed policies of the South African Government. Negotiations began between Gandhi and the South African Government under pressure from Delhi and London. Eventually an agreement was reached. Some of the major points on which the Satyagraha struggle had been waged were conceded to the Indians. The tax on the ex-indentured labourers was abolished; marriages performed according to Indian rites were legalized, and a domicile certificate bearing the holder's thumb-imprint was too a sufficient evidence of the right to enter South Africa.

In 1939, a quarter of a century after the conclusion of the Satyagraha campaign, General Smuts, Gandhi's chief antagonist in South Africa, recalled: "Gandhi himself received-what no doubt he desired-a short period of rest and quiet in goal. For him everything went according to plan. For me-the defender of law and order-there was the usual trying situation, the odium of carrying out a law which had no strong public support, and finally the discomfiture when the law had to be repealed. For him it was a successful coup."

In goal Gandhi had prepared a pair of sandals for General Smuts, who wrote that there was no hatred and personal ill-feeling, and when the fight was over, "there was the atmosphere in which decent peace would be concluded.

THE MAKING OF MAHATMA

In 1914 Gandhi left South Africa. He had gone there as a junior counsel of a commercial firm for £105 a year; he had stayed on to command, and then voluntarily to give up a peak practice of £5000 a year. In Bombay as a young lawyer he had a nervous break-down while cross-examining witnesses in a petty civil suit; in the South Africa, he had founded a new political organization with the sure touch of a seasoned politician. The hostility of the European politicians and officials and the helplessness of the Indian merchants and labourers had put him on his mettle.

No glittering rewards for him; the perils ranged from professional pinpricks to lynching. Nevertheless, it was a piece of good fortune that he began his professional and political career in South Africa. Dwarfed as he had felt by the great lawyers and leader of India, it is unlikely that he would have developed much initiative in his homeland. When he founded the Natal Indian Congress at the age of twenty-five, he was writing on a tabula rasa: he could try out ideas which in an established political organization would have been laughed out court. What had truth and vows to do with politics? It was a question which often recurred in Indian politics, and if Gandhi was not confounded by it, it was because, far back in South Africa, he had observed and confirmed the connection. For a man who was no doctrinaire, and whose theory often lagged behind practice, it was a decided advantage that the scene of his early activities should have been one where he was unfettered by political precedents or professionals. Natal and Transvaal were no bigger than some of the smallest provinces of India. The struggle for Indian independence was conducted Gandhi on much larger scale and on much bigger issues, but there were not a few occasions when he derived inspiration from his experience in South Africa.

Not only his politics, but his personality took shape in South Africa. The most formative years of his life had been spent there. His interest in moral and religious questions dated back to his early childhood. But it was only in South Africa that he had an opportunity of studying them systematically. His Quaker friends in Pretoria failed to convert him to Christianity, but they whetted his innate appetite for religious studies. He delved deep into Christianity and other religions, including his own. In his first year in South Africa he read 'quite eighty books', most of them on religion. One of these was Tolstoy's Kingdom of God is Within You. Tolstoy became his favourite author and in the coming years he read the Gospels in Brief, What to do? The Slavery of Our Times, How Shall We Escape? Letters to a Hindoo and The First Step. Tolstoy's bold idealism and fearless candour gripped him, his Christian anarchism dissipated the spell of institutional religion. Tolstoy's emphasis on the necessity of an accord between moral principles and daily life confirmed his own strivings for self-improvement.

Few men read so little to so much profit as Gandhi did. A book was for Gandhi not a mere diversion for the hour, it was embodied experience, which had to be accepted or rejected. Ruskin's Unto The Last drove him with compelling urgency from the capital of Natal to the wilderness of Zululand to practise a life of voluntary poverty, and literally to live by the sweat of his brow. It was in Tolstoy's books that we may seek one of the strongest influences on Gandhi. He was, of course, not given to indiscriminate imitation. But in Tolstoy he found a writer whose views elaborated his own inchoate beliefs. It was not only on the organized or covert violence of the modern state and the right of the citizen to civil disobedience that Gandhi found support in Tolstoy.

There were innumerable subjects, ranging from modern civilization and industrialism to sex and schools, on which he tended to agree with Tolstoy's analysis. There was an exchange of letters between the two which gives an impression of gratitude and reverence by the young Indian on the threshold of his career, and of delightful surprise by the aged Tolstoy. "And so your activity in Transvaal," wrote Tolstoy to Gandhi, "as it seems to us, at the end of the world, is the most essential work, the most important of all the work now being done in the world, and in which not only the nations of the Christian, but of all the world will undoubtedly take part."

While books on Christianity and Islam were easily available in South Africa, Gandhi had to send for books on Hinduism from India. He corresponded with his friend Raychandbhai, whose influence in favour of Hinduism was decisive at a time when Gandhi's Quaker friends believed him to be on the way to baptism. The study of comparative religion, the browsing on theological works, the conversations and correspondence with the learned, brought Gandhi to the conclusion that true religion was more a matter of the heart than of the intellect, and that genuine beliefs were those which were literally lived.

Gandhi's style of life was also transformed during these years. From the Gita which he described as his "spiritual dictionary", he had imbibed the ideal of "non-possession" which set him on the road to voluntary poverty, and of "selfless action " which equipped him with an extraordinary stamina for his public life. He trained himself as a dispenser in a charitable hospital in order to be able to attend on the 'indentured' labourers, the poorest Indians in South Africa. At Phoenix near Durban, and at Tolstoy Farm near Johannesburg, he set up little colonies, where he and those who shared his ideals, could find a haven from the heat and dust of towns, and men's greed and hatred, A pen-portrait of Gandhi as he was in his late thirties has been left by his first biographer Rev.

Joseph J. Doke of Johannesburg: "A small, lithe, spare figure stood before me, and a refined earnest face looked into mine.

The skin was dark, the eyes dark, but the smile which lighted up the face, and that direct fearless glance simply took one's heart by storm. I judged him to be some thirty-eight years of age, which proved correct. He spoke English perfectly and was evidently a man of culture. There was a quite assured strength about him, a greatness of heart, a transparent honesty that attracted me at once to the Indian leader. Our Indian friend lives on a higher plane than most men do. His actions, like the actions of Mary of Bethany, are often counted eccentric, and not infrequently misunderstood. Those who do not know him think there is some unworthy motive behind, some Oriental 'slimness' to account for such profound unworldliness. But those who know him well are ashamed of themselves in his presence. Money, I think has no charm for him. His compatriots...wonder at him, grow angry at his strange unselfishness, and love him with the love of pride and trust. He is one of those outstanding characters with whom to walk is a liberal education...whom to know is to love."

RETURN TO INDIA

A hero's welcome awaited Gandhi when he landed on January 9, 1915, at the Apollo Bunder in Bombay. Three days later he was honoured by the people of Bombay at a magnificent reception in the palatial house of a Bombay magnate Jehangir Petit. The Government of India joined with the people of India in showering honours on Gandhi. He received a "Kaiser-I-Hind" gold medal in the King's birthday honours list of 1915. His association with Gokhale was guarantee enough of his being a safe politician. Of course, he had led an extra-constitutional movement in South Africa, defied laws and filled goals, but the cause for which he had fought appeared as much humanitarian as political, dear to all Indian as and all Englishmen whose sense of humanity had not been blunted by racial arrogance or political expediency. Lord Hardinge's open support of the Satyagraha movement had in any case removed the stigma of rebellion from South Africa's Indian movement. Gandhi was in no hurry to plunge into politics. His political mentor on the Indian scene was Gokhale. One of the first things Gokhale did was to extract a promise from Gandhi that he would not express himself upon public questions for a year, which was to be a "year of probation". Gokhale was very keen that Gandhi should join the Servants of India Society in Poona. Gandhi was only too willing to fall in with the wishes of Gokhale, but several members of the Society feared that there was too great a gap between the ideals and methods of the Society and those of Gandhi. While the question of his admission as a 'Servant of India' was being debated, Gandhi visited his home towns of Porbandar and Rajkot and went on to Santiniketan in West Bengal, the cosmopolitan University of the Poet Rabindranath Tagore.

The trip to Santiniketan ended abruptly with a telegram from Poona that Gokhale was dead. Gandhi was stunned. He mourned Gokhale by going barefoot for a year, and out of respect for the memory of his mentor, made another effort to seek admission to the Servants of India Society. Finding a sharp division of opinion in the Society on this point, he withdrew his application for admission.

During 1915-the year of probation-Gandhi eschewed politics severely. In his speeches and writings he confined himself to the reform of the individual and the society and avoided the issues which dominated Indian politics. His restraint was partly due to self-imposed silence and partly to the fact that he was still studying conditions in India and making up his mind.

Mahatma Gandhi

Mohandas Karamchand Gandhi (October 2, 1869-January 30, 1948) was a major political and spiritual leader of the Indian Independence Movement. He was the pioneer of satyagraha-resistance through mass civil disobedience strongly founded upon ahinsa (non-violence) becoming one of the strongest philosophies of freedom struggles worldwide. Gandhi is commonly known and spoken of worldwide as Mahatma Gandhi and is fondly called Bapu.

Gandhi first employed his ideas of civil disobedience in the Indian struggle for civil rights in South Africa. Upon his return to India, Gandhi helped lead poor farmers and labourers to protest oppressive taxation and widespread discrimination.

Leading the Indian National Congress, Gandhi worked for the alleviation of poverty, the liberation of women, brotherhood, an end to untouchability and caste discrimination and for the economic self-sufficiency of the nation. However, Gandhi's work focused upon the goal of Swaraj-self-rule for India. Gandhi famously led Indians in the disobedience to the salt tax through the 400 kilometre (248 miles) Dandi March, and in an open call for the British to Quit India in 1942.

Gandhi remained committed to non-violence even in the most extreme situations. Gandhi was a student of Hindu philosophy and lived simply, organizing an Ashram that was self-sufficient in its needs. He made his own clothes and lived on a simple vegetarian diet. He used rigorous fasts for self-purification as well as a means of protest. Gandhi's teachings have inspired civil rights leaders such as Dr. Martin Luther King, Jr., Steve Biko, Nelson Mandela and Aung San Suu Kyi. Gandhi is honoured as the Father of the Nation in India. His birthday on October 2nd is annually commemorated as Gandhi Jayanti, a national holiday.

Early Life: Mohandas Karamchand Gandhi was born into the Hindu Modh family in Porbandar, India, in 1869. He was the son of Karamchand Gandhi, the diwan (Prime Minister) of Porbandar, and Putlibai, Karamchand's fourth wife, a Hindu of the Pranami Vaishnava order. Karamchand's first two wives, who each bore him a daughter, died from unknown reasons (rumored to be in childbirth). His third wife was deemed incapacitated and permitted Karamchand to marry again. Growing up with a devout mother and surrounded by the Jain influences of Gujarat, Gandhi learned from an early age the tenets of non-injury to living beings, vegetarianism, fasting for self-purification, and mutual tolerance between members of various creeds and sects. He was born into the vaishya, or business, caste.

Gandhi and his Wife Kasturba (1902)

In May 1883, at the age of 13, Gandhi was married through his parents' arrangements to Kasturba Makhanji (also spelled "Kasturbai" or known as "Ba"), who was his age. They had four sons: Harilal Gandhi, born in 1888; Manilal Gandhi, born in 1892; Ramdas Gandhi, born in 1897; and Devdas Gandhi, born in 1900.

Gandhi was a mediocre student in his youth at Porbandar and later Rajkot. He barely passed the matriculation exam for Samaldas College at Bhavanagar, Gujarat. He was also unhappy at the college, because his family wanted him to become a barrister.

At the age of 18 on September 4, 1888, Gandhi went to University College London to train as a barrister. His time in London, the Imperial capital, was influenced by a vow he had made to his mother in the presence of the Jain monk Becharji, upon leaving India, to observe the Hindu precepts of abstinence from meat, alcohol, and promiscuity. Although Gandhi experimented with adopting "English" customs-taking dancing lessons for example-he could not stomach his landlady's mutton and cabbage.

She pointed him towards one of London's few vegetarian restaurants. Rather than simply go along with his mother's wishes, he read about, and intellectually embraced vegetarianism. He joined the Vegetarian Society, was elected to its executive committee, and founded a local chapter. He later credited this with giving him valuable experience in organizing institutions. Some of the vegetarians he met were members of the Theosophical Society, which had been founded in 1875 to further universal brotherhood, and which was devoted to the study of Buddhist and Hindu Brahmanistic literature. They encouraged Gandhi to read the Bhagavad Gita. Not having shown a particular interest in religion before, he read works of and about Hinduism, Christianity, Buddhism, Islam and other religions.

He returned to India after being admitted to the bar of England and Wales, but had limited success establishing a law practice in Bombay, later applying and being turned down for a part-time job as a high school teacher.

He ended up returning to Rajkot to make a modest living drafting petitions for litigants, but was forced to close down that business as well when he ran afoul of a British officer. In his autobiography, he describes this incident as a kind of unsuccessful lobbying attempt on behalf of his older brother. It was in this climate that (in 1893) he accepted a year-long contract from an Indian firm to a post in Natal, South Africa.

Civil Rights Movement in South Africa (1893-1914)

Gandhi in South Africa (1895): Gandhi read his first newspaper at the age of 18, and was prone to stage fright while speaking in court. South Africa changed him dramatically, as he faced the discrimination commonly directed at blacks and Indians. One day in court at Durban, the magistrate asked him to remove his turban. Gandhi refused and stormed out of the courtroom. He was thrown off a train at Pietermaritzburg, after refusing to move from the first class to a third class coach while holding a valid first class ticket. Travelling further on by stagecoach, he was beaten by a driver for refusing to travel on the foot board to make room for a European passenger.

He suffered other hardships on the journey as well, including being barred from many hotels. These incidents have been acknowledged by several biographers as a turning point in his life, explaining his later social activism. It was through witnessing firsthand the racism, prejudice and injustice against Indians in South Africa that Gandhi started to question his people's status, and his own place in society. However, these events by no means explain why he inculcated non-violence instead of aggressive revolution.

At the end of his contract, Gandhi prepared to return to India. However, at a farewell party in his honour in Durban, he happened to glance at a newspaper and learned that a bill was being considered by the Natal Legislative Assembly to deny the right to vote to Indians. When he brought this up with his hosts, they lamented that they did not have the expertise necessary to oppose the bill, and implored Gandhi to stay and help them. He circulated several petitions to both the Natal Legislature and the British Government in opposition to the bill.

Though unable to halt the bill's passage, his campaign was successful in drawing attention to the grievances of Indians in South Africa. Supporters convinced him to remain in Durban to continue fighting against the injustices levied against Indians in South Africa. He founded the Natal Indian Congress in 1894, with himself as the Secretary. Through this organization, he molded the Indian community of South Africa into a homogeneous political force, publishing documents detailing Indian grievances and evidence of British discrimination in South Africa. Gandhi returned briefly to India in 1896 to bring his wife and children to live with him in South Africa. When he returned in January 1897, a white mob attacked and tried to lynch him. In an early indication of the personal values that would shape his later campaigns, he refused to press charges on any member of the mob, stating it was one of his principles not to seek redress for a personal wrong in a court of law. At the onset of the South African War, Gandhi argued that Indians must support the war effort in order to legitimize their claims to full citizenship, organizing a volunteer ambulance corps of 300 free Indians and 800 indentured labourers called the Indian Ambulance Corps, one of the few medical units to serve wounded black South Africans. He himself was a stretcher-bearer at the Battle of Spion Kop, and was decorated. At the conclusion of the war, however, the situation for the Indians did not improve, but continued to deteriorate. In 1906, the Transvaal government promulgated a new Act compelling registration of the colony's Indian population.

At a mass protest meeting held in Johannesburg on September 11th that year, Gandhi adopted his methodology of satyagraha (devotion to the truth), or non-violent protest, for the first time, calling on his fellow Indians to defy the new law and suffer the punishments for doing so, rather than resist through violent means. This plan was adopted, leading to a seven-year struggle in which thousands of Indians were jailed (including Gandhi himself on many occasions), flogged, or even shot, for striking, refusing to register, burning their registration cards, or engaging in other forms of non-violent resistance. While the government was successful in repressing the Indian protesters, the public outcry stemming from the harsh methods employed by the South African government in the face of peaceful Indian protesters finally forced South African General Jan Christian Smuts to negotiate a compromise with Gandhi.

In May 1915, Gandhi founded an Ashram on the outskirts of Ahmedabad, India and called it Satyagrah Ashram (also known as Sabarmati Ashram). There lodged twenty five men and women who took vows of truth, celibacy, ahinsa, non-possession, control of the palate, and service of the Indian people.

Struggle for Indian Independence (1916-1945)

As he had done in the South African War, Gandhi urged support of the British in World War I and was active in encouraging Indians to join the army. His rationale, opposed by many others, was that if he desired the full citizenship, freedoms and rights in the Empire, it would be wrong not to help in its defence. He spoke at the conventions of the Indian National Congress, but was primarily introduced to Indian issues, politics and the Indian people by Gopal Krishna Gokhale, at the time one of the most respected leaders of the Congress Party.

CHAMPARAN AND KHEDA

Gandhi's first major achievements came in 1918 with the Champaran agitation and Kheda Satyagraha, although in the latter it was indigo and other cash crops instead of the food crops necessary for their survival. Suppressed by the militias of the landlords (mostly British), they were given measly compensation, leaving them mired in extreme poverty. The villages were kept extremely dirty and unhygienic; and alcoholism, untouchability and purdah were rampant. Now in the throes of a devastating famine, the British levied an oppressive tax which they insisted on increasing in rate. The situation was desperate. In Kheda in Gujarat, the problem was the same. Gandhi established an Ashram there, organizing scores of his veteran supporters and fresh volunteers from the region. He organized a detailed study and survey of the villages, accounting the atrocities and terrible episodes of suffering, including the general state of degenerate living. Building on the confidence of villagers, he began leading the clean-up of villages, building of schools and hospitals and encouraging the village leadership to undo and condemn many social evils, as accounted above.

But his main assault came as he was arrested by police on the charge of creating unrest and was ordered to leave the province. Hundreds of thousands of people protested and rallied outside the jail, police stations and courts demanding his release, which the court reluctantly granted. Gandhi led organized protests and strikes against the landlords, who with the guidance of the British government, signed an agreement granting more compensation and control over farming for the poor farmers of the region, and cancellation of revenue hikes and collection until the famine ended. It was during this agitation, that Gandhi was addressed by the people as Bapu (Father) and Mahatma (Great Soul). In Kheda, Patel represented the farmers in negotiations with the British, who suspended revenue collection and granted relief. All of the prisoners were released. Gandhi's resulting fame spread all over the nation. Also he had loads of enemies in South Africa, one of them is called Laurence Message.

Non-cooperation: This was Gandhiji's answer to any act of injustice, which is still valid and practical in today's scenario as well, this approach to oppose actually complements his other teachings as such questions may get raised in our minds like "is it actually possible to practice Truth, Non violence, Respect to all etc. and also fight for the right?"

Non cooperation gave the answer and history confirms it as how effective this 'weapon' was. In Punjab, the Jallianwala Bagh massacre of civilians by British troops caused deep trauma to the nation, and increased public anger and acts of violence. Gandhi criticized both the actions of the British, and the retaliatory violence of Indians. He authored the resolution offering condolences to British civilian victims and condemning the riots, which after initial opposition in the party, was accepted after Gandhi made an emotional speech pushing forth his principle that all violence was evil and could not be justified. But it was after the massacre and violence that Gandhi's mind focused upon obtaining complete self-government and control of all Indian government institutions, maturing soon into Swaraj or complete individual, spiritual, political independence. Gandhi was invested with executive authority on behalf of the Indian National Congress in December 1921. Under Gandhi's leadership, the Congress was reorganized with a new constitution, with the goal of Swaraj. Membership in the party was opened to anyone prepared to pay a token fee. A hierarchy of committees was set up to improve discipline, transforming the party from an elite organization to one of mass national appeal.

Gandhi expanded his non-violence platform to include the swadeshi policy-the boycott of foreign-made goods, especially

British goods. Linked to this was his advocacy that khadi (homespun cloth) be worn by all Indians instead of British-made textiles. Gandhi exhorted Indian men and women, rich or poor, to spend time each day spinning khadi in support of the independence movement. This was a strategy to inculcate discipline and dedication to weed out the unwilling and ambitious, and include women in the movement at a time when many thought that such activities were not "respectable" for women. In addition to boycotting British products, Gandhi urged the people to boycott British educational institutions and law courts, to resign from government employment, and to forsake British titles and honours.

"Non-cooperation" enjoyed wide-spread appeal and success, increasing excitement and participation from all strata of Indian society, yet just as the movement reached its apex, it ended abruptly as a result of a violent clash in the town of Chauri Chaura, Uttar Pradesh, in February 1922. Fearing that the movement was about to take a turn towards violence, and convinced that this would be the undoing of all his work, Gandhi called off the campaign of mass civil disobedience. Gandhi was arrested on March 10, 1922, tried for sedition, and sentenced to six years. Beginning on March 18, 1922, he only served about two years of the sentence, being released in February 1924 after an operation for appendicitis. Without Gandhi's uniting personality, the Indian National Congress began to splinter during his years in prison, splitting into two factions, one led by Chitta Ranjan Das and Motilal Nehru favouring party participation in the legislatures, and the other led by Chakravarti Rajagopalachari and Sardar Vallabhbhai Patel, opposing this move. Furthermore, cooperation among Hindus and Muslims, which had been strong at the height of the nonviolence campaign, was breaking down. Gandhi attempted to bridge these differences through many means, including a three-week fast in the autumn of 1924, but with limited success.

SWARAJ AND THE SALT SATYAGRAHA

Gandhi stayed out of the limelight for most of the 1920s, preferring to resolve the wedge between the Swaraj Party and the Indian National Congress, and expanding initiatives against untouchability, alcoholism, ignorance and poverty. He returned to the fore in 1928. The year before, the British government had appointed a new constitutional reform commission under Sir John Simon, numbering not a single Indian in its ranks. The result was a boycott of the commission by Indian political parties. Gandhi pushed through a resolution at the Calcutta Congress in December 1928 calling on the British government to grant India dominion status or face a new campaign of non-violence with complete independence for the country as its goal. Gandhi had moderated the views of younger men like Subhas Chandra Bose and Jawaharlal Nehru, who sought a demand for immediate independence, but also modified his own call to a one year wait, instead of two.

The British did not respond. On December 31, 1929, the flag of India was unfurled in Lahore. January 26, 1930 was celebrated by the Indian National Congress, meeting in Lahore, as India's Independence Day. This day was commemorated by almost every other Indian organization. Making good on his word in March 1930, he launched a new satyagraha against the tax on salt, highlighted by the famous Salt March to Dandi from March 12 to April 6, 1930, marching 400 kilometres (248 miles) from Ahmedabad to Dandi, Gujarat to make salt himself. Thousands of Indians joined him on this march to the sea. This campaign was one of his most successful, resulting in the imprisonment of over 60,000 people.

The government, represented by Lord Edward Irwin, decided to negotiate with Gandhi. The Gandhi-Irwin Pact was signed in March 1931. In it, the British Government agreed to set all political prisoners free in return for the suspension of the civil disobedience movement. Furthermore, Gandhi was invited to attend the Round Table Conference in London as the sole representative of the Indian National Congress. The conference was a disappointment to Gandhi and the nationalists, as it focused on the Indian princes and Indian minorities rather than the transfer of power. Furthermore, Lord Irwin's successor, Lord Willingdon, embarked on a new campaign of repression against the nationalists. Gandhi was again arrested, and the government attempted to destroy his influence by completely isolating him from his followers.

This tactic was not successful. In 1932, through the campaigning of the Dalit leader B. R. Ambedkar, the government granted untouchables separate electorates under the new constitution. In protest, Gandhi embarked on a six-day fast in September 1932, successfully forcing the government to adopt a more equitable arrangement via negotiations mediated by the Dalit cricketer turned political leader Palwankar Baloo. This began a new campaign by Gandhi to improve the lives of the untouchables, whom he named Harijans, the children of God. On May 8, 1933 Gandhi began a 21-day fast of self-purification to help the Harijan movement. In the summer of 1934, three unsuccessful attempts were made on his life.

When the Congress Party chose to contest elections and accept power under the Federation scheme, Gandhi decided to resign from party membership. He did not at all disagree with the party's move, but felt that if he resigned, his popularity with Indians would cease to stifle the party's membership, that actually varied from communists, socialists, trade unionists, students, religious conservatives, to those with pro-business convictions. Gandhi also did not want to prove a target for Raj propaganda by leading a party that had temporarily accepted political accommodation with the Raj.

Gandhi returned to the head in 1936, with the Nehru presidency and the Lucknow session of the Congress. Although Gandhi desired a total focus on the task of winning independence and not speculation about India's future, he did not restrain the Congress from adopting socialism as its goal. Gandhi had a clash with Subhas Bose, who had been elected to the presidency in 1938. Gandhi's main issues with Bose were his lack of commitment to democracy, and lack of faith in non-violence. Bose won his second term despite Gandhi's criticism, but left the Congress when the All-India leaders resigned en masse in protest of his abandonment of principles introduced by Gandhi.

WORLD WAR II AND QUIT INDIA

World War II broke out in 1939 when Nazi Germany invaded Poland. Initially, Gandhi had favoured offering "non-violent moral support" to the British effort, but other Congress leaders were offended by the unilateral inclusion of India into the war, without consultation of the people's representatives. All Congressmen elected to office resigned en masse. After lengthy deliberations, Gandhi declared that India could not be party to a war ostensibly being fought for democratic freedom, while that freedom was denied in India herself. As the war progressed, Gandhi increased his demands for independence, drafting a resolution calling for the British to Quit India. This was Gandhi's and the Congress Party's most definitive revolt aimed at securing the British exit from Indian shores.

Gandhi was criticized by some Congressmen and other Indian political groups, both pro-British and anti-British. Some felt that opposing Britain in its life-death struggle was immoral, and others felt that Gandhi wasn't doing enough. Quit India became the most forceful movement in the history of the struggle, with mass arrests and violence on an unprecedented scale. Thousands of freedom fighters were killed or injured by police gunfire, and hundreds of thousands were arrested.

Gandhi and his supporters made it clear they would not support the war effort unless India was granted immediate independence. He even clarified that this time the movement would not be stopped if individual acts of violence were committed, saying that the "ordered anarchy" around him was "worse than real anarchy". He called on all Congressmen and Indians to maintain discipline in ahinsa, and Karo Ya Maro (Do or Die) in the cause of ultimate freedom. Gandhi and the entire Congress Working Committee were arrested in Bombay by the British on August 9, 1942.

Gandhi was held for two years in the Aga Khan Palace in Pune. It was here that Gandhi suffered two terrible blows in his personal life-his 42 year old secretary Mahadev Desai died of a heart attack 6 days later, then his wife Kasturba died after 18 months imprisonment in February 1944 (six weeks later Gandhi suffered a severe malaria attack). He was released before the end of the war on May 6, 1944 because of his failing health and necessary surgery; the Raj did not want him to die in prison and enrage the nation. Although Quit India somewhat succeeded in its objective, the ruthless suppression of the movement brought order to India by the end of 1943. At the end of the war, the British gave clear indications that power would be transferred to Indian hands, and Gandhi called off the struggle, and the Congress leadership and around 100,000 political prisoners were released.

FREEDOM AND PARTITION OF INDIA

Gandhi advised the Congress to reject the proposals the British Cabinet Mission offered in 1946, as he was deeply suspicious of the grouping proposed for Muslim-majority states-Gandhi viewed this as a precursor to partition. However, this became one of the few times the Congress broke from Gandhi's advice (though not his leadership), as Nehru and Patel knew that if the Congress did not approve the plan, the control of government would pass to the Muslim League. Between 1946 and 1947, over 5,000 people were killed in violence. Gandhi was vehemently opposed to any plan that partitioned India into two separate countries.

An overwhelming majority of Muslims living in India, side by side with Hindus and Sikhs, were in favour of Partition. Additionally Muhammad Ali Jinnah, the leader of the Muslim League, commanded widespread support in West Punjab, Sindh, NWFP and East Bengal. The partition plan was approved by the Congress leadership as the only way to prevent a wide-scale Hindu-Muslim civil war. Congress leaders knew that Gandhi would viscerally oppose partition, and it was impossible for the Congress to go ahead without his agreement, for Gandhi's support in the party and throughout India was strong. Gandhi's closest colleagues had accepted partition as the best way out, and Sardar Patel endeavoured to convince Gandhi that it was the only way to avoid civil war. A devastated Gandhi gave his assent.

On the day of the transfer of power, Gandhi did not celebrate independence with the rest of India, but was alone in Calcutta, mourning the partition and working to end the violence. After India's independence, Gandhi focused on Hindu-Muslim peace and unity. He conducted extensive dialogue with Muslim and Hindu community leaders, working to cool passions in northern India, as well as in Bengal. Despite the Indo-Pakistani War of 1947, he was troubled when the Government decided to deny Pakistan the Rs. 55 crores due as per agreements made by the Partition Council. Leaders like Sardar Patel feared that Pakistan would use the money to bankroll the war against India. Gandhi was also devastated when demands resurged for all Muslims to be deported to Pakistan, and when Muslim and Hindu leaders expressed frustration and an inability to come to terms with one another.

He launched his last fast-unto-death in Delhi, asking that all communal violence be ended once and for all, and that the payment of Rs. 55 crores be made to Pakistan. Gandhi feared that instability and insecurity in Pakistan would increase their anger against India, and violence would spread across the borders. He further feared that Hindus and Muslims would renew their enmity and precipitate into an open civil war.

After emotional debates with his life-long colleagues, Gandhi refused to budge, and the Government rescinded its policy and made the payment to Pakistan. Hindu, Muslim and Sikh community leaders, including the Rashtriya Swayamsevak Sangh and Hindu Mahasabha assured him that they would renounce violence and call for peace. Gandhi thus broke his fast by sipping orange juice.

Assassination: On January 30, 1948, on his way to a prayer meeting, Gandhi was shot dead in Birla House, New Delhi, by Nathuram Godse. Godse was a Hindu radical with links to the extremist Hindu Mahasabha, who held Gandhi responsible for weakening India by insisting upon a payment to Pakistan. Godse and his co-conspirator Narayan Apte were later tried and convicted, and on 15 November 1949, were executed. Gandhi's memorial (or Samadhi) at Raj Ghat, New Delhi, bears the epigraph, which may be translated as "Oh God". These are widely believed to be Gandhi's last words after he was shot, though the veracity of this statement has been disputed by many. Jawaharlal Nehru addressed the nation through radio:

"Friends and comrades, the light has gone out of our lives, and there is darkness everywhere, and I do not quite know what to tell you or how to say it. Our beloved leader, Bapu as we called him, the father of the nation, is no more. Perhaps I am wrong to say that; nevertheless, we will not see him again, as we have seen him for these many years, we will not run to him for advice or seek solace from him, and that is a terrible blow, not only for me, but for millions and millions in this country."

According to his wish, the majority of Gandhi's ashes were immersed in all the major rivers of the world such as The Nile, Volga, Thames, etc. Also, a small portion was sent to Paramahansa Yogananda from Dr. V.M. Nawle, (a publisher and journalist from Poona, India) encased in a brass & silver coffer. The ashes were then enshrined at the Mahatma Gandhi World Peace Memorial in the Self-Realization Fellowship Lake Shrine within a thousand-year-old stone sarcophagus from China.

Gandhi's Principles

"Live as if you were to die tomorrow. Learn as if you were to live forever."

—Mahatma Gandhi

Truth: Gandhi dedicated his life to the wider purpose of discovering truth, or Satya. He tried to achieve this by learning from his own mistakes and conducting experiments on himself. He called his autobiography The Story of My Experiments with Truth.

Gandhi stated that the most important battle to fight was overcoming his own demons, fears, and insecurities. Gandhi summarized his beliefs first when he said "God is Truth." He would later change this statement to "Truth is God." Thus, Satya (Truth) in Gandhi's philosophy is "God".

Nonviolence: The concept of nonviolence (ahinsa) and nonresistance has a long history in Indian religious thought and has had many revivals in Hindu, Buddhist, Jain, Jewish and Christian contexts. Gandhi explains his philosophy and way of life in his autobiography The Story of My Experiments with Truth. He was quoted as saying:

"When I despair, I remember that all through history the way of truth and love has always won. There have been tyrants and murderers and for a time they seem invincible, but in the end, they always fall-think of it, always."

"What difference does it make to the dead, the orphans, and the homeless, whether the mad destruction is wrought under the name of totalitarianism or the holy name of liberty and democracy?"

"An eye for an eye makes the whole world blind."

"There are many causes that I am prepared to die for but no causes that I am prepared to kill for."

In applying these principles, Gandhi did not balk from taking them to their most logical extremes. In 1940, when invasion of the British Isles by Nazi Germany looked imminent, Gandhi offered the following advice to the British people (Non-Violence in Peace and War):

"I would like you to lay down the arms you have as being useless for saving you or humanity. You will invite Herr Hitler and Signor Mussolini to take what they want of the countries you call your possessions.... If these gentlemen choose to occupy your homes, you will vacate them. If they do not give you free passage out, you will allow yourselves, man, woman, and child, to be slaughtered, but you will refuse to owe allegiance to them."

However, Gandhi was aware that this level of nonviolence required incredible faith and courage, which he realized not everyone possessed. He therefore advised that everyone need not keep to nonviolence, especially if it was used as a cover for cowardice:

"Gandhi guarded against attracting to his satyagraha movement those who feared to take up arms or felt themselves incapable of resistance. 'I do believe,' he wrote, 'that where there is only a choice between cowardice and violence, I would advise violence.'"

"At every meeting I repeated the warning that unless they felt that in non-violence they had come into possession of a force infinitely superior to the one they had and in the use of which they were adept, they should have nothing to do with non-violence and resume the arms they possessed before. It must never be said of the Khudai Khidmatgars that once so brave, they had become or been made cowards under Badshah Khan's influence. Their bravery consisted not in being good marksmen but in defying death and being ever ready to bare their breasts to the bullets."

Vegetarianism: As a young child, Gandhi experimented in meat-eating. This was due partially to his inherent curiosity as well as his rather persuasive peer and friend Sheikh Mehtab. The idea of vegetarianism is deeply engrained in Hindu and Jain traditions in India, and, in his native land of Gujarat, many Hindus were vegetarian. The Gandhi family was no exception. Before leaving for his studies in London, Gandhi made a promise to his mother, Putlibai and his uncle, Becharji Swami that he would abstain from eating meat, taking alcohol, and engaging in promiscuity. He held fast to his promise and gained more than a diet, he gained a basis for his life-long philosophies. As Gandhi grew into adulthood, he became a strict vegetarian, though he was not against the consumption of eggs. He wrote articles on the subject, some of which were published in the London Vegetarian Society's publication: "The Vegetarian." Gandhi inspired many people around the world to become vegetarian. Gandhi, himself, became inspired by many great minds during this period and befriended a chairman of the London Vegetarian Society, Dr. Josiah Oldfield.

Having also read and admired the work of Henry Stephens Salt, the young Mohandas met and often corresponded with the vegetarian campaigner. Gandhi spent much time advocating vegetarianism during and after his time in London. To Gandhi, a vegetarian diet would not only satisfy the requirements of the body, it would also serve an economic purpose as meat was, and still is, generally more expensive than grains, vegetables, and fruits. Also, many Indians of the time struggled with low income, thus vegetarianism was seen not only as a spiritual practice but also a practical one. He abstained from eating for long periods, using fasting as a form of political protest. He refused to eat until his death or his demands were met. It was noted in his autobiography that vegetarianism was the beginning of his deep commitment to Brahmacharya; without total control of the palate his success in Bramacharya would have been likely to falter.

Brahmacharya: This decision was deeply influenced by the philosophy of Brahmacharya-spiritual and practical purity-largely associated with celibacy and asceticism. Gandhi saw brahmacharya as a means of going close to God and as a primary foundation for self realization. In his autobiography he tells of his battle against lustful urges and fits of jealousy with his childhood bride,

Kasturba. He felt it his personal obligation to remain celibate so that he could learn to love, rather than lust. For Gandhi brahmacharya meant control of the senses in thought, word and deed.

Simplicity: Gandhi earnestly believed that a person involved in social service should lead a simple life which he thought could lead to Brahmacharya. His simplicity began by renouncing the western lifestyle he was leading in South Africa. He called it "reducing himself to zero", which entailed giving up unnecessary expenditure, embracing a simple lifestyle and washing his own clothes. On one occasion he returned the gifts bestowed to him from the natals for his diligent service to the community.

Gandhi spent one day of each week in silence. He believed that abstaining from speaking brought him inner peace. This influence was drawn from the Hindu principles of mouna (silence) and shanti (peace). On such days he communicated with others by writing on paper. For three and a half years, from the age of 37, Gandhi refused to read newspapers, claiming that the tumultuous state of world affairs caused him more confusion than his own inner unrest. Returning to India from South Africa, where he had enjoyed a successful legal practice, he gave up wearing Western-style clothing, which he associated with wealth and success.

He dressed to be accepted by the poorest person in India, advocating the use of homespun cloth (khadi). Gandhi and his followers adopted the practice of weaving their own clothes from thread they themselves spun, and encouraged others to do so. While Indian workers were often idle due to unemployment, they had often bought their clothing from industrial manufacturers owned by British interests. It was Gandhi's view that if Indians made their own clothes, it would deal an economic blow to the British establishment in India. Consequently, the spinning wheel was later incorporated into the flag of the Indian National Congress. He would wear a dhoti all his life to show simplicity.

Faith: Gandhi was born a Hindu and practised Hinduism all his life, deriving most of his principles from Hinduism. As a common Hindu, he believed all religions to be equal, and rejected all efforts to convert him to a different faith. He was an avid theologian and read extensively about all major religions. He had the following to say about Hinduism:

"Hinduism as I know it entirely satisfies my soul, fills my whole being... When doubts haunt me, when disappointments stare me in the face, and when I see not one ray of light on the horizon, I turn to the Bhagavad Gita, and find a verse to comfort me; and I immediately begin to smile in the midst of overwhelming sorrow. My life has been full of tragedies and if they have not left any visible and indelible effect on me, I owe it to the teachings of the Bhagavad Gita."

Gandhi believed that at the core of every religion was Truth and Love (compassion, nonviolence and the Golden Rule). He also questioned hypocrisy, malpractices and dogma in all religions and was a tireless social reformer. Some of his comments on various religions are:

> *"Thus if I could not accept Christianity either as a perfect, or the greatest religion, neither was I then convinced of Hinduism being such. Hindu defects were pressingly visible to me. If untouchability could be a part of Hinduism, it could but be a rotten part or an excrescence. I could not understand the raison d'etre of a multitude of sects and castes. What was the meaning of saying that the Vedas were the inspired Word of God? If they were inspired, why not also the Bible and the Quran? As Christian friends were endeavouring to convert me, so were Muslim friends. Abdullah Sheth had kept on inducing me to study Islam, and of course he had always something to say regarding its beauty." (source: his autobiography)*
>
> *"As soon as we lose the moral basis, we cease to be religious. There is no such thing as religion over-riding morality. Man, for instance, cannot be untruthful, cruel or incontinent and claim to have God on his side."*
>
> *"The sayings of Muhammad are a treasure of wisdom, not only for Muslims but for all of mankind."*

Later in his life when he was asked whether he was a Hindu, he replied:

> *"Yes I am. I am also a Christian, a Muslim, a Buddhist and a Jew."*

In spite of their deep reverence to each other, Gandhi and Rabindranath Tagore got involved in protracted debates more than once. These debates exemplify the philosophical differences between the two most famous Indians at the time. On January 15, 1934, an earthquake hit Bihar and caused extensive damage and loss of life. Gandhi maintained this was because of the sin committed by upper caste Hindus by not letting untouchables in their temples (Gandhi was committed to the cause of improving the fate of untouchables, referring to them as Harijans, people of Krishna). Tagore vehemently opposed Gandhi's stance, maintaining that an earthquake can only be caused by natural forces, not moral reasons, however repugnant the practice of untouchability may be.

Legacy: Gandhi's birthday, 2 October is a national holiday, Gandhi Jayanti.

The word Mahatma, while often mistaken for Gandhi's given name in the West, is taken from the Sanskrit words maha meaning Great and atma meaning Soul. Most sources, such as Dutta and Robinson's Rabindranath Tagore: An Anthology, state that Rabindranath Tagore first accorded the title of Mahatma to Gandhi. Other sources state that Nautamlal Bhagavanji Mehta accorded him this title on January 21, 1915. In his autobiography, Gandhi nevertheless explains that he never felt worthy of the honour. According to the manpatra, the name Mahatma was given in response to Gandhi's admirable sacrifice in manifesting justice and truth.

Time Magazine named Gandhi the Man of the Year in 1930, the runner-up to Albert Einstein as "Person of the Century" at the end of 1999, and named The Dalai Lama, Lech Walesa, Dr. Martin Luther King, Jr., Cesar Chavez, Aung San Suu Kyi, Benigno Aquino Jr., Desmond Tutu, and Nelson Mandela as Children of Gandhi and his spiritual heirs to non-violence. The Government of India awards the annual Mahatma Gandhi Peace Prize to distinguished social workers, world leaders and citizens. Nelson Mandela, the leader of South Africa's struggle to eradicate racial discrimination and segregation, is a prominent non-Indian recipient. In 1996, the Government of India introduced the Mahatma Gandhi series of currency notes in rupees 5, 10, 20, 50, 100, 500 and 1000 denomination. Today, all the currency notes in circulation in India contain a portrait of Mahatma Gandhi. In 1969, the United Kingdom issued a series of stamps commemorating the centenary of Mahatma Gandhi.

In the United Kingdom, there are several prominent statues of Gandhi, most notably in Tavistock Square, London (near University College London), where he studied law. January 30 is commemorated in the United Kingdom as the "National Gandhi Remembrance Day." In the United States, there are statues of Gandhi outside the Union Square Park in New York City and the Martin Luther King, Jr. National Historic Site in Atlanta, and in Waikiki, Hawaii. The city of Pietermaritzburg, South Africa, where Gandhi was ejected in 1893 from a first-class train, now hosts a commemorative statue. There are wax statues of Gandhi at the Madame Tussaud's wax museums in New York and London, and other cities around the world.

Gandhi never received the Nobel Peace Prize, though he was nominated five times between 1937 and 1948. Decades later, the Nobel Committee publicly declared its regret for the omission, and admitted to deeply divided nationalistic opinion denying the award. Mahatma Gandhi was to receive the Prize in 1948, but his assassination prevented the award from coming to him. The war breaking out between the newly created states of India and Pakistan could have been a complicating factor for Mahatma Gandhi not being presented with the Prize in 1948. The Prize was not awarded in 1948, the year of Gandhi's death, on the grounds that "there was no suitable living candidate" that year, and when the Dalai Lama was awarded the Prize in 1989, the chairman of the committee said that this was "in part a tribute to the memory of Mahatma Gandhi". The Committee felt so terrible it had not conferred the prize on Mahatma Gandhi that it kept looking at "other Indians" over the years. Those considered over the years were Jawaharlal Nehru and Vinoba Bhave.

Gandhi in Film, Literature, Plays, and Popular Culture: Mahatma Gandhi has been portrayed in film, literature, and in the theatre. Ben Kingsley portrayed Gandhi in the 1982 award-winning film, Gandhi. Gandhi is also a central figure in the 2006 Bollywood film Lage Raho Munna Bhai. The philosophy of

Gandhism is an important thematic component of both the 2005 film, Water and the novel by author Bapsi Sidhwa based on the film, also called Water (Gandhi also appears as a character in both). The Making of the Mahatma documents Gandhi's 21 years in South Africa. The play Mahatma vs. Gandhi explores his troubled relationship with his eldest son Harilal Gandhi. A 2002 play Mohandas Karamchand Gandhi (play) gives the life story of Gandhi from the age of twelve until his death. The opera Satyagraha, composed by Philip Glass (in 1980), with a libretto by himself and Constance De Jong is based on the life of Gandhi. The tamil film 'Hey Ram' deals with the theme of Gandhi's assassination and its precursors.

Criticism: Dalit leader B. R. Ambedkar condemned Gandhi's terming the untouchable community as Harijans. This term meant "God's Children"; it was interpreted by some as saying that Dalits were socially immature, and that privileged caste Indians played a paternalistic role. Ambedkar and his allies also felt Gandhi was undermining Dalit political rights. Gandhi, although born into the vaishya caste, insisted that he was able to speak on behalf of Dalits, despite the availability of Dalit activists such as Ambedkar.

Muhammad Ali Jinnah and contemporary Pakistanis condemned Gandhi for undermining Muslim political rights. Vinayak Damodar Savarkar and his allies condemned Gandhi, accusing him of politically appeasing Muslims while turning a blind eye to their atrocities against Hindus, and for allowing the creation of Pakistan (despite having publically declared that "before partitioning India, my body will have to be cut into two pieces"). Savarkar himself was tried for conspiracy in the Gandhi Murder case, as he was the mentor of the assassin Nathuram Godse and an important Hindu Mahasabha leader.

However, he was acquitted following lack of any evidence of his involvement. In contemporary times, Marxist academicians like Ayesha Jalal blame Gandhi and the Congress for being unwilling to share power with Muslims and thus hastening partition. Hindu political activists like Pravin Togadia and Narendra Modi have been known to criticize Gandhi's leadership and actions. Gandhi also came under some political fire for his intolerance to those who attempted to achieve independence through more violent means. His refusal to protest against the hanging of Bhagat Singh, Sukhdev, Udham Singh and Rajguru were sources of condemnation throughout some parties within India. Economists, such as Jagdish Bhagwati, have criticized Gandhi's ideas of swadeshi.

As a rule, Gandhi was opposed to the concept of partition as it contradicted his vision of unity. On the topic of the partition of India to create Pakistan Gandhi wrote articles reprinted in Louis Fischer's The Essential Gandhi: An Anthology of His Writings on His Life, Work, and Ideas. The first was published in "Harijan" on 06 October 1946 and stated: "[The demand for Pakistan] as put forth by the Moslem League is un-Islamic and I have not hesitated to call it sinful. Islam stands for unity and the brotherhood of mankind, not for disrupting the oneness of the human family.

Therefore, those who want to divide India into possibly warring groups are enemies alike of India and Islam. They may cut me into pieces but they cannot make me subscribe to something which I consider to be wrong [...] we must not cease to aspire, in spite of [the] wild talk, to befriend all Moslems and hold them fast as prisoners of our love" In addition, Gandhi also stated to one of his disciples, "[If] India is divided she will be lost forever. Therefore...if India is to remain undivided, Hindus and Moslems must live together in brotherly love, not in hostile camps organized either for defensive action or retaliation." Gandhi also wrote letters and essays during the late 1930s in response to the topic of the partition of Palestine to create Israel.

He stated in "A Non-Violent Look at Conflict & Violence," "Several letters have been received by me asking me to declare my views about the Arab-Jew question in Palestine and persecution of the Jews in Germany. It is not without hesitation that I venture to offer my views on this very difficult question. My sympathies are all with the Jews. I have known them intimately in South Africa. Some of them became life-long companions. Through these friends I came to learn much of their age-long persecution.

They have been the untouchables of Christianity [...] But my sympathy does not blind me to the requirements of justice. The cry for the national home for the Jews does not make much appeal to me. The sanction for it is sought in the Bible and the tenacity with which the Jews have hankered after return to Palestine. Why should they not, like other peoples of the earth, make that country their home where they are born and where they earn their livelihood? Palestine belongs to the Arabs in the same sense that England belongs to the English or France to the French.

It is wrong and inhuman to impose the Jews on the Arabs. What is going on in Palestine today cannot be justified by any moral code of conduct." He continues this argument in a number of articles reprinted in Homer Jack's The Gandhi Reader: A Sourcebook of His Life and Writings. In the first, "Zionism and Anti-Semitism," he writes, "If I were a Jew and were born in Germany and earned my livelihood there, I would claim Germany as my home even as the tallest Gentile German might, and challenge him to shoot me or cast me in the dungeon; I would refuse to be expelled or to submit to discriminating treatment."

Gandhi was criticized for these statements and responded in the article "Questions on the Jews, "Friends have sent me two newspaper cuttings criticizing my appeal to the Jews. The two critics suggest that in presenting non-violence to the Jews as a remedy against the wrong done to them, I have suggested nothing new....what I have pleaded for is renunciation of violence of the heart and consequent active exercise of the force generated by the great renunciation." He discusses this issue further in "Reply to Jewish Friends" and "Jews and Palestine."

2

Bose: An Introduction

Subhash Chandra Bose, generally known as Netaji (lit. "Respected Leader"), was one of the most prominent and highly respected leaders of the Indian Independence Movement against the British Raj.

Bose was elected president of the Indian National Congress for two consecutive terms but resigned from the post following ideological conflicts with Mahatma Gandhi. Bose believed that Mahatma Gandhi's tactics of nonviolence would never be sufficient to secure India's independence, and advocated violent resistance. He established a separate political party, the All India Forward Bloc and continued to call for the full and immediate independence of India from British rule. He was imprisoned by the British authorities eleven times.

His stance did not change with the outbreak of the second world war, which he saw as an opportunity to take advantage of British weakness. At the outset of the war, he fled India and travelled to the Soviet Union, Germany and Japan seeking an alliance with the aim of attacking the British in India. With Japanese assistance he reorganised and later led the Indian National Army, formed from Indian prisoners-of-war and plantation workers from Malaya, Singapore and other parts of Southeast Asia, against British forces. With Japanese monetary, political, diplomatic and military assistance, he formed the Azad Hind Government in exile, regrouped and led the Indian National Army to battle against the allies in Imphal & Burma during the World War II.

His political views and the alliances he made with Nazi and other militarist regimes opposed to the British Empire have been the cause of arguments among historians and politicians, with some accusing him of Fascist sympathies and of Quislingist actions, while most others in India largely sympathetic towards his inculcation of realpolitik as a manifesto that guided his social and political choices. He is believed to have died on 18 August 1945 in a plane crash over Taiwan. However, contradictory evidence exists regarding his death in the accident.

EARLY LIFE

Subhash Chandra Bose was born in 1897 to an affluent Bengali family in Cuttack, Orissa in India. His father, Janakinath Bose, was a public prosecutor who believed in orthodox nationalism, and later became a member of the Bengal Legislative Council. Bose was educated at Ravenshaw Collegiate School, Cuttack, Scottish Church College, Calcutta and Fitzwilliam College at Cambridge University. In 1920, Bose took the Indian Civil Services entrance examination and was placed fourth with highest marks in English. However, he resigned from the prestigious Indian Civil Service in April 1921 despite his high ranking in the merit list, and went on to become an active member of India's independence movement. He joined the Indian National Congress, and was particularly active in its youth wing.

Still, Bose's ideals did not match those of Mahatma Gandhi's single belief in nonviolence. He therefore returned to Calcutta to work under Chittaranjan Das, the Bengali freedom fighter and co-founder (with Motilal Nehru) of the Swaraj Party.

In 1921, Bose organised a boycott of the celebrations to mark the visit of the Prince of Wales to India, which led to his imprisonment. In April 1924, Bose was elected to the post of Chief Executive Officer of the newly constituted Calcutta Corporation, In October that year, Bose was arrested on suspicion of terrorism. At first, he was kept in Alipore Jail and later he was exiled to Mandalay in Burma (where earlier Bal Gangadhar Tilak had spent 6 years in prison). On January 23, 1930, Bose was once again arrested for leading an "independence procession", protesting against British rule in India. After his release from jail on September 25, he was elected as the Mayor of the City of Calcutta. Over a span of 20 years, Bose was incarcerated eleven times by the British, either in India or in Rangoon. During the mid 1930s he was exiled by the British from India to Europe, where he championed India's cause and aspiration for self-rule before gatherings and conferences.

After his father's death, the British authorities allowed him to land at Calcutta's airport only for the religious rites, which would be followed by his swift departure. He travelled extensively in India and in Europe before stating his political opposition to Gandhi. During his stay in Europe from 1933 to 1936, he met several European leaders and thinkers. He came to believe that India could achieve political freedom only if it had political, military and diplomatic support from outside, and that an independent nation necessitated the creation of a national army to secure its sovereignty.

Subhash Chandra Bose married Emilie Schenkl, an Austrian born national, who was his secretary, in 1937. According to Schenkl, she and Bose were secretly married in Bad Gastein on 26 December 1937. They had one daughter, Anita, born in 1942. Bose wrote many letters to Schenkl during the period 1934–1942, of which many have been published in the book *Letters to Emilie Schenkl*, edited by Sisir Kumar Bose and Sugata Bose.

Bose became the president of the Haripura Indian National Congress in 1938, against Gandhi's wishes. Gandhi commented "Pattavi's defeat is my own defeat. Anyway, Subhash Bose is not an enemy of the country". Gandhi's continued opposition led to the latter's resignation from the Working Committee, and the possibility that the rest of the CWC would resign. In the face of this gesture of no-confidence, Bose himself resigned, and was left with no alternative but to form an independent party, the All India Forward Bloc. Bose also initiated the concept of the *National Planning Committee* in 1938.

ACTIONS DURING THE II WORLD WAR

Bose advocated the approach that the political instability of wartime Britain should be taken advantage of—rather than simply wait for the British to grant independence after the end of the war (which was the view of Gandhi, Nehru and a section of the Congress leadership at the time). In this, he was influenced by the examples of Italian statesmen Giuseppe Garibaldi and Giuseppe

Mazzini. His correspondence reveals that despite his clear dislike ...for British subjugation, he was deeply impressed by their methodical and systematic approach and their steadfastly disciplinarian outlook towards life. In England, he exchanged ideas on the future of India with British Labour Party leaders and political thinkers like Lord Halifax, George Lansbury, Clement Attlee, Arthur Greenwood, Harold Laski, J.B.S. Haldane, Ivor Jennings, G.D.H. Cole, Gilbert Murray and Sir Stafford Cripps.

He came to believe that a free India needed Socialist authoritarianism, on the lines of Turkey's Kemal Atatürk, for at least two decades. Bose was refused permission by the British authorities to meet Mr. Ataturk at Ankara for political reasons. It should be noted that during his sojourn in England, only the Labour Party and Liberal politicians agreed to meet with Bose when he tried to schedule appointments. Conservative Party officials refused to meet Bose or show him the slightest courtesy due to the fact that he was a politician coming from a colony, but it may also be recalled that in the 1930s leading figures in the Conservative Party had opposed even Dominion status for India. It may also be observed here that it was during the regime of the Labour Party (1945-1951), with Attlee as the Prime Minister, that India gained independence.

THE ESCAPE

On the outbreak of war, Bose advocated a campaign of mass civil disobedience to protest against Viceroy Lord Linlithgow's decision to declare war on India's behalf without consulting the Congress leadership. Having failed to persuade Gandhi of the necessity of this, Bose organised mass protests in Calcutta calling for the 'Holwell Monument' commemorating the Black Hole of Calcutta, which then stood at the corner of Dalhousie Square, to be removed. A reasonable measure of the contrast between Gandhi and Bose is captured in a saying attributable to him: "If people slap you once, slap them twice".

He was thrown in jail by the British, but was released following a seven-day hunger strike. Bose's house in Calcutta was kept under surveillance by the CBI, but their vigilance left a good deal to be desired. With two court cases pending, he felt the British would not let him leave the country before the end of the war. This set the scene for Bose's escape to Germany, via Afghanistan and the Soviet Union. Bose had never been to Afghanistan, and could not speak the local tribal language (Pashto).

Bose escaped from under British surveillance at his house in Calcutta. On January 19, 1941, accompanied by his nephew Sisir K. Bose, Bose gave his watchers the slip and journeyed to Peshawar. With the assistance of the Abwehr, he made his way to Peshawar where he was met at Peshawar Cantonment station by Akbar Shah, Mohammed Shah and Bhagat Ram Talwar. Bose was taken to the home of Abad Khan, a trusted friend of Akbar Shah's. On 26 January 1941, Bose began his journey to reach Russia through India's North West frontier with Afghanistan. For this reason, he enlisted the help of Mian Akbar Shah, then a Forward Bloc leader in the North West Frontier Province. Shah had been out of India *en route* to the Soviet Union, and suggested a novel disguise for Bose to assume. Since Bose could not speak one word of Pashto, it would make him an easy target of Pashto speakers working for the British. For this reason, Shah suggested that Bose act deaf and dumb, and let his beard grow to mimic those of the tribesmen.

Supporters of the Aga Khan helped him across the border into Afghanistan where he was met by an Abwehr unit posing as a party of road construction engineers from the Organization Todt who then aided his passage across Afghanistan via Kabul to the border with Soviet Russia. Once in Russia the NKVD transported Bose to Moscow where he hoped that Russia's traditional enmity to British rule in India would result in support for his plans for a popular rising in India. However, Bose found the Soviets' response disappointing and was rapidly passed over to the German Ambassador in Moscow, Count vonder Schulenburg. He had Bose flown on to Berlin in a special courier aircraft at the beginning of April where he was to receive a more favourable hearing from Joachim von Ribbentrop and the Foreign Ministry officials at the Wilhelmstrasse.

ATTEMPTS OF ASSASSINATION

In 1941, when the British learned that Bose had sought the support of the Axis Powers, they ordered their agents to intercept and assassinate Bose before he reached Germany. A recently declassified intelligence document refers to a top-secret instruction to the Special Operations Executive (SOE) of British intelligence to murder Bose. In fact, the plan to liquidate Bose has few parallels, and appears to be a last desperate measure against a man who had thrown the British Empire into a panic.

In Germany

Having escaped incarceration at home by assuming the guise of a Pashtun insurance agent ("Ziaudddin") to reach Afghanistan, Bose travelled to Moscow on the passport of an Italian nobleman "Count Orlando Mazzotta". From Moscow, he reached Rome, and from there he travelled to Germany, where he instituted the Special Bureau for India under Adam von Trott zu Solz, broadcasting on the German-sponsored Azad Hind Radio. He founded the *Free India Centre* in Berlin, and created the Indian Legion (consisting of some 4500 soldiers) out of Indian prisoners of war who had previously fought for the British in North Africa prior to their capture by Axis forces.

The Indian Legion was attached to the Wehrmacht, and later transferred to the Waffen SS; its members swore their allegiance to both Hitler and Bose to secure India's independence. He was also, however, prepared to envisage an invasion of India via the U.S.S.R. by Nazi troops, spearheaded by the Azad Hind Legion; many have questioned his judgment here, as it seems unlikely that the Germans could have been easily persuaded to leave after such an invasion, which might also have resulted in an Axis victory in the War.

The lack of interest shown by Hitler in the cause of Indian independence eventually caused Bose to become disillusioned with Hitler and he decided to leave Nazi Germany in 1943. Bose had been living together with his wife Schenkl in Berlin from 1941 until 1943, when he left for southeast Asia. He travelled by the German submarine *U-180* around the Cape of Good Hope to Imperial Japan (via Japanese submarine *I-29*). Thereafter the Japanese helped him raise his army in Singapore. This was the only civilian transfer across two submarines of two different navies in World War II.

SOUTH-EAST ASIA

Indian National Army

The Indian National Army (INA) was originally founded by Capt. Mohan Singh in Singapore in September 1942 with Japan's Indian POWs in the Far East. This was along the concept of-and with support of-what was then known as the Indian Independence League, headed by expatriate nationalist leader Rash Behari Bose. The first INA was however disbanded in December 1942 after disagreements between the Hikari Kikan and Mohan Singh, who came to believe that the Japanese High Command was using the INA as a mere pawn and Propaganda tool. Mohan Singh was taken into custody and the troops returned to the Prisoner-of-War camp. However, the idea of a liberation army was revived with the arrival of Subhash Chandra Bose in the Far East in 1943. In July, at a meeting in Singapore, Rash Behari Bose handed over control of the organisation to Subhash Chandra Bose. Bose was able to reorganise the fledging army and organise massive support among the expatriate Indian population in southeast Asia, who lent their support by both enlisting in the Indian National Army, as well as financially in response Bose's calls for sacrifice for the national cause. At its height it consisted of some 85,000 regular troops, including a separate women's unit, the Rani of Jhansi Regiment (named after Rani Lakshmi Bai), which is seen as a first of its kind in Asia.

Even when faced with military reverses, Bose was able to maintain support for the Azad Hind movement. Spoken as a part of a motivational speech for the Indian National Army at a rally of Indians in Burma on July 4, 1944, Bose's most famous quote was "Give me blood, and I shall give you freedom!". In this, he urged the people of India to join him in his fight against the British Raj. Spoken in Hindi, Bose's words are highly evocative. The troops of the INA were under the aegis of a provisional government, the Azad Hind Government, which came to produce its own currency, court and civil code, and was recognised by nine Axis states—Germany, Japan, Italy, the Independent State of Croatia, Wang Jingwei's Government in Nanjing, Thailand, a provisional government of Burma, Manchukuo and Japanese-controlled Philippines. Recent researches have shown that the USSR too had recognised the "Provisional Government of Free India". Of those countries, five were authorities established under Axis occupation. This government participated as a delegate or observer in the so-called Greater East Asia Co-Prosperity Sphere.

The INA's first commitment was in the Japanese thrust towards Eastern Indian frontiers of Manipur. INA's special forces, the Bahadur Group, were extensively involved in operations behind enemy lines both during the diversionary attacks in Arakan, as well as the Japanese thrust towards Imphal and Kohima, along with the Burmese National Army led by Ba Maw and Aung San. A year after the islands were taken by the Japanese, the Provisional Government and the INA were established in the Andaman and Nicobar Islands with Lt. Col. A.D Loganathan appointed its Governor General. The islands were renamed *Shaheed* (Martyr) and *Swaraj* (Self-rule). However, the Japanese Navy remained in essential control of the island's administration. During Bose's only visit to the islands in late in 1943, when he was carefully screened from the local population by the Japanese authorities, who at that time were torturing the leader of the Indian Independence League on the Islands, Dr. Diwan Singh (who later died of his injuries, in the Cellular Jail). The islanders made several attempts to alert Bose to their plight, but apparently without success. Enraged with the lack of administrative control, Lt. Col Loganathan later relinquished his authority to return to the Government's head quarters in Rangoon.

On the Indian mainland, an Indian Tricolour, modelled after that of the Indian National Congress, was raised for the first time in the town in Moirang, in Manipur, in northeastern India. The towns of Kohima and Imphal were placed under siege by divisions of the Japanese, Burmese and the *Gandhi* and *Nehru* Brigades of I.N.A. during the attempted invasion of India, also known as Operation U-GO. However, Commonwealth forces held both positions and then counter-attacked, in the process inflicting serious losses on the besieging forces, which were then forced to retreat back into Burma.

Bose had hoped that large numbers of soldiers would desert from the Indian Army when they would discover that INA soldiers were attacking British India from the outside. However, this did not materialise on a sufficient scale. Instead, as the war situation worsened for the Japanese, troops began to desert from the INA. At the same time Japanese funding for the army diminished, and Bose was forced to raise taxes on the Indian populations of Malaysia and Singapore, sometimes extracting money by force. When the Japanese were defeated at the battles of Kohima and Imphal, the Provisional Government's aim of establishing a base in mainland India was lost forever. The INA was forced to pull back, along with the retreating Japanese army, and fought in key battles against the British Indian Army in its Burma campaign, notable in Meiktilla, Mandalay, Pegu, Nyangyu and Mount Popa. However, with the fall of Rangoon, Bose's government ceased be an effective political entity. A large proportion of the INA troops surrendered under Lt. Col Loganathan when Rangoon fell. The remaining troops retreated with Bose towards Malaya or made for Thailand. Japan's surrender at the end of the war also led to the eventual surrender of the Indian National Army, when the troops of the British Indian Army were repatriated to India and some tried for treason...

His other famous quote was, "Delhi chalo", meaning "On to Delhi!". This was the call he used to give the INA armies to motivate them. "Jai Hind", or, "Glory to India!" was another slogan used by him and later adopted by the Government of India and the Indian Armed Forces.

Disappearance and Alleged Death

Officially, Bose died in a plane crash over Taiwan, while flying to Tokyo on 18 August 1945. However, his body was never recovered, and many theories have been put forward concerning his possible survival. One such claim is that Bose actually died in Siberia, while in Soviet captivity. Several committees have been set up by the Government of India to probe into this matter.

In May 1956, a four-man Indian team (known as the Shah Nawaz Committee) visited Japan to probe the circumstances of Bose's alleged death. The Indian government did not then request assistance from the government of Taiwan in the matter, citing their lack of diplomatic relations with Taiwan.

However, the Inquiry Commission under Justice Mukherjee, which investigated the Bose disappearance mystery in the period

1999-2005, did approach the Taiwanese government and obtained information from the Taiwan Government that no plane carrying Bose had ever crashed in Taipei. The Mukherjee Commission also received a report originating from the US State Department, supporting the claim of the Taiwan Government that no such air crash took place during that time frame. The Mukherjee Commission submitted its report to the Indian Government on November 8, 2005. The report was tabled in Parliament on May 17, 2006. The probe said in its report that Bose did not die in the plane crash and the ashes at Renkoji temple are not his. However, the Indian Government rejected the findings of the Commission.

Political Views

Bose's earlier correspondence (prior to 1939) also reflects his deep disapproval of the racist practices of, and annulment of democratic institutions in Nazi Germany. He also, however, expressed admiration for the authoritarian methods (though not the racial ideologies) which he saw in Italy and Germany during the 1930s, and thought they could be used in building an independent India.

Bose had clearly expressed his belief that democracy was the best option for India. The pro-Bose thinkers believe that his authoritarian control of the Azad Hind was based on political pragmatism and a post-colonial recovery doctrine rather than any anti-democratic belief.. However, during the war (and possibly as early as the 1930s) Bose seems to have decided that no democratic system could be adequate to overcome India's poverty and social inequalities, and he wrote that an authoritarian state, similar to that of Soviet Russia (which he had also seen and admired) would be needed for the process of national rebuilding. Accordingly some suggest that Bose's alliance with the Axis during the war was based on more than just pragmatism, and that Bose may have been a Fascist, though not a Nazi; alternatively, others consider he might have been using populist methods of mobilization common to many postcolonial leaders.

After the Independence of India, Subhash Chandra Bose did not get much importance, as the Gandhi-influenced Congress Party came to rule.

When one thinks of the Indian independence movement in the 1930s and early 1940s, two figures most readily come to mind: Mahatma Gandhi, the immensely popular and "saintly" frail pacifist, and his highly respected, Fabian Socialist acolyte, Jawaharlal Nehru.

Less familiar to Westerners is Subhash Chandra Bose, a man of comparable stature who admired Gandhi but despaired at his aims and methods, and who became a bitter rival of Nehru. Bose played a very active and prominent role in India's political life during most of the 1930s. For example, he was twice (1938 and 1939) elected President of the Indian National Congress, the country's most important political force for freedom from the *Raj*, or British rule.

While his memory is still held in high esteem in India, in the West Bose is much less revered, largely because of his wartime collaboration with the Axis powers. Both before and during the Second World War, Bose worked tirelessly to secure German and Japanese support in freeing his beloved homeland of foreign rule. During the final two years of the war, Bose—with considerable Japanese backing—led the forces of the Indian National Army into battle against the British.

IDEOLOGY OF FUSION

As early as 1930—in his inaugural speech as mayor of Calcutta—the fervent young Bose first expressed his support for a fusion of socialism and fascism:

> *"... I would say we have here in this policy and programme a synthesis of what modern Europe calls Socialism and Fascism. We have here the justice, the equality, the love, which is the basis of Socialism, and combined with that we have the efficiency and the discipline of Fascism as it stands in Europe today."*

In years that followed, the brilliant, eclectic Bengali would occasionally modify this radical doctrine, but would never abandon it entirely. For example, in late 1944—almost a decade-and-a-half later—in a speech to students at Tokyo University, he asserted that India must have a political system "of an authoritarian character... To repeat once again, our philosophy should be a synthesis between National Socialism and Communism."

In the wake of the crushing defeat in 1945 of Hitler and Mussolini, "fascism" has arguably been the most despised of all political ideologies. Postwar western society recognizes no fascist heroics, and even considers "fascist" traits—particularly the authoritarian, charismatic, personal style of leadership, and the positive evaluation of violence and the willingness to use it for political purposes—to be decidedly unpalatable. In India, though, Bose is regarded as a national hero, in spite of his repeated praise (as will be shown) for autocratic leadership and authoritarian government, and admiration for the European fascist regimes with which he allied himself.

Like the leaders he admired in Italy and Germany, Bose was (and still is) popularly known as *Netaji,* or "revered leader." "His name," explains Mihir Bose (no relation), one of Subhas' many biographers, "is given [in India] to parks, roads, buildings, sports stadiums, artificial lakes; his statues stand in place of those of discarded British heroes and his photograph adorns thousands of calendars and millions of *pan* (betel-nut) shops." It is always the same portrait, continues the writer: Bose in his Indian National Army uniform, "exhorting his countrymen forward to one last glorious struggle."

No less a figure than Gandhi paid tribute to Bose's remarkable courage and devotion. Six months after his death in an airplane crash on August 18, 1945, Gandhi declared: "The hypnotism of the Indian National Army has cast its spell upon us. Netaji's name is one to conjure with. His patriotism is second to none... His bravery shines through all his actions. He aimed high and failed. But who has not failed." On another occasion Gandhi eulogized: "Netaji will remain immortal for all time to come for his service to India."

Many of Bose's admirers have been inclined to downplay or even ignore the fascist elements in his ideology, and even to pretend they never existed. For example, the text of Bose's inaugural speech as mayor of Calcutta, cited above, was reprinted in a laudatory 1970 "Netaji Birthday Supplement" of the *Calcutta Municipal Gazette*, but with all references to fascism, including his support for a synthesis of fascism and socialism, carefully deleted. Several admiring biographers have found it easier to ignore the fascist elements in his ideology than to explain them. Their subjective accounts do not even inform the reader that Bose spoke positively about some features of fascism, or else, in an attempt to remove from their hero any possible taint, they qualify his remarks in ways that he himself did not. 'Fascist'?

During his lifetime, Bose was frequently denounced as a fascist or even a Nazi, particularly in the wake of the radical, revolutionary (as opposed to reformist) views he expressed in radio addresses broadcast to India from National Socialist Germany and, later, from quasi-fascist Japan. For example, *The Statesman*, a highly influential Calcutta periodical, charged in November 1941: "Mr. Bose's views are those of the Nazis, and he makes no secret of it," while the BBC, Britain's worldwide radio voice, frequently accused him of "Fascism" and "Nazism."

Additionally, historians and writers who do not admire Bose readily point up his "fascist" views. A.M. Nair, a historian who has written favourably of Indian revolutionary Rash Behari Bose (who had sought Japan's help during and after the First World War), found nothing to praise about Subhash Chandra Bose. After all, wrote Nair, he was clearly a fascist.

RECOGNIZED LEADERSHIP

Bose, a patriot of almost fanatical zeal, first joined the Indian national movement in 1921, working under C.R. Das, whom he idolized. He was jailed for six months in 1921-1922 because of his political activities. Immediately upon his release, the 25-year-old Bose organized (and presided over) the All-Bengal Young Men's Conference. As a result of his remarkable leadership abilities and ambition, he advanced quickly through nationalist ranks. He was soon elected General Secretary of the Bengal Provincial Congress Committee (BPCC). In 1924, at the age of 27, Bose was elected the Chief Executive Officer of the Calcutta Municipal Corporation, which effectively put him in charge of the second-largest city in the British empire. As a result of his close ties with nationalist terrorists, in late 1924 he was detained by British authorities and held, without trial, for three years in prison. In 1928, the 31-year-old Bose was elected president of the BPCC, and, at the Calcutta meeting of the Congress party held that December, he came to national prominence by pressing (unsuccessfully) for the adoption by his provincial committee of an independence resolution.

By 1930 Bose had formulated the broad strategy that he believed India must follow to throw off the yoke of British imperialism and assume its rightful place as a leader in Asia. During his years in Mandalay prison and another short term of imprisonment in Alipore jail in 1930, he read many works on political theory, including Francesco Nitti's *Bolshevism, Fascism and Democracy* and Ivanoe Bonomi's *From Socialism to Fascism*. It is clear that these works on fascism influenced him, and caused an immediate modification of his long-held socialist views: as noted above, in his inaugural speech as mayor of Calcutta, given a day after his release from Alipore jail, he revealed his support for a seemingly contradictory ideological synthesis of socialism and fascism.

Until his death 15 years later, Bose would continue publicly to praise certain aspects of fascism and express his hope for a synthesis of that ideology and socialism. His detailed comments on the matter in his book *The Indian Struggle: 1920-1934*, which was first published in 1935, accurately represent the views he held throughout most of his career. As such, the most important of them, along with Bose's own actions, will be analyzed here in some detail.

PROGRAM OUTLINED

Contending that the Indian National Congress was somewhat "out of date," and suffered from a lack of unity and strong leadership, Bose predicted in *The Indian Struggle* that out of a "Left-Wing revolt there will ultimately emerge a new full-fledged party with a clear ideology, programme and plan of action." The programme and plan of action of this new party would, wrote Bose, follow this basic outline:

1. The party will stand for the interests of the masses, that is, of the peasants, workers, etc., and not for the vested interests, that is, the landlords, capitalists and moneylending classes.
2. It will stand for the complete political and economic liberation of the Indian people.

3. It will stand for a Federal Government for India as the ultimate goal, but will believe in a strong Central Government with dictatorial powers for some years to come, in order to put India on her feet.
4. It will believe in a sound system of state-planning for the reorganization of the agricultural and industrial life of the country.
5. It will seek to build up a new social structure on the basis of the village communities of the past, that were ruled by the village "Panch" and will strive to break down the existing social barriers like caste.
6. It will seek to establish a new monetary and credit system in the light of the theories and the experiments that have been and are current in the modern world.
7. It will seek to abolish landlordism and introduce a uniform land-tenure system for the whole of India.
8. It will not stand for a democracy in the Mid-Victorian sense of the term, but will believe in government by a strong party bound together by military discipline, as the only means of holding India together and preventing a chaos, when Indians are free and are thrown entirely on their own resources.
9. It will not restrict itself to a campaign inside India but will resort to international propaganda also, in order to strengthen India's case for liberty, and will attempt to utilize the existing international organizations.
10. It will endeavour to unite all the radical organizations under a national executive so that whenever any action is taken, there will be simultaneous activity on many fronts.

Synthesis

Bose went on to note that Nehru had said in 1933: "I dislike Fascism intensely and indeed I do not think it is anything more than a crude and brutal effort of the present capitalist order to preserve itself at any cost." There is no middle road between Fascism and Communism, said Nehru, so one "had to choose between the two and I choose the Communist ideal."

To this Bose responded:

> *"The view expressed here is, according to the writer, fundamentally wrong... One is inclined to hold that the next phase in world-history will produce a synthesis between Communism and Fascism. And will it be a surprise if that synthesis in produced in India?... In spite of the antithesis between Communism and Fascism, there are certain traits in common. Both Communism and Fascism believe in the supremacy of the State over the individual. Both denounce parliamentary democracy. Both believe in party rule. Both believe in the dictatorship of the party and in the ruthless suppression of all dissenting minorities. Both believe in a planned industrial reorganization of the country. These common traits will form the basis of the new synthesis. That synthesis is called by the writer "Samyavada"—an Indian word, which means literally "the doctrine of synthesis or equality." It will be India's task to work out this synthesis."*

Before taking a closer look at these remarkable words, four points need to be made.

First, Bose's fascist model was almost certainly Mussolini's Italy, not Hitler's Germany. In 1934 Bose made the first of several visits to Fascist Italy and found both the regime and its leader very agreeable. On that occasion he had a cordial (first) meeting with Mussolini—"a man who really counts in the politics of modern Europe." After *The Indian Struggle* appeared in print in 1935, Bose made a special stop in Rome personally to present a copy to the *Duce*.

Second, the book was completed a full year before the commencement of the Italian invasion of Ethiopia (Abyssinia), in October 1935. While Bose would, by the time he completed his book, have known about such violent incidents as "The Night of the Long Knives"—the SS killing of dozens of SA men on June 30, 1934—he had no real reason to consider the European fascist regimes unusually violent, murderous or bellicose. "I should like to point out that when I was writing the book," he later explained,

> *"Fascism had not started on its imperialistic expedition, and it appeared to me merely an aggressive form of nationalism. .. What I really meant was that we in India wanted our national*

> *freedom, and having won it, we wanted to move in the direction of Socialism. This is what I meant when I referred to a "synthesis between Communism and Fascism." Perhaps the expression I used was not a happy one."*

Third, despite Bose's claim to represent the political left, and that a party supporting a fusion of fascism and socialism would be ushered in by a "Left-Wing revolt," the ideology he expounded might more appropriately be regarded as right wing. Bose's ideology was radical and contained socialist elements—such as the desire to abolish the traditional class structure and create a society of equal opportunity, and the claim to represent the peasants and workers. To that extent it can be considered left wing. It is worth noting that Hitler's "right wing" political movement—the National Socialist German Workers' Party—shared many of Bose's "socialist" goals. Nehru, a committed socialist, challenged Bose's characterization of himself and his followers as left wing: "It seems to me that many of the so-called Leftists are more Right than the so-called Rightists. Strong language and a capacity to attack the old Congress leadership is not a test of Leftism in politics."

Lastly, it should be noted that Bose was willing to tone down his more radical political beliefs on those occasions when he considered it advantageous or necessary to do so. For example, in his February 1938 inaugural speech as President of the Indian National Congress, Bose—probably in a sincere attempt to placate the Gandhian faction—made statements that appear to represent almost an about face from the political views he had expounded in *The Indian Struggle*. In a future independent India, he said,

> *"the party itself will have a democratic basis, unlike, for instance, the Nazi party which is based on the "leader principle." The existence of more than one party and the democratic basis of the Congress party will prevent the future Indian State becoming a totalitarian one. Further, the democratic basis of the party will ensure that leaders are not thrust upon the people from above, but are elected from below."*

It is possible that these statements reflect a temporary change of mind, but it is more likely that they reflect Bose's efforts during this period to gain further political respectability, to prove that he was more than just a radical and revolutionary Bengali. By doing so he apparently hoped to win wider acceptance of the policies he wanted to implement in his year as Congress President: policies which were not especially radical or revolutionary.

According to Nirad Chaudhuri, his former personal secretary, Bose tried very hard during this period to seek agreement with the Gandhian faction over the direction the Congress party should move, and even "showed something like tender filial piety towards Gandhi," of whom he had been very critical in *The Indian Struggle*. It is against this political background that Bose's statements to the Congress party meeting in February 1938 should be seen.

A year later he successfully recontested the presidential election, but two months afterwards was forced to resign because of his inability to resolve his differences with Gandhi and the Gandhian faction. Probably believing that his earlier suspicions of democracy had been proven correct, and feeling that there was now no use in trying to win the favour or approval of more conservative elements in the Congress party, Bose once again proclaimed his belief in the efficacy of authoritarian government and a synthesis of fascism and socialism. Many similar examples can be cited to show how Bose outwardly (but probably not inwardly) modified his views to suit changing political contexts.

A Life for India

Throughout his political career, India's liberation from British rule remained Bose's foremost political goal; indeed, it was a lifelong obsession. As he explained in his most important work, *The Indian Struggle*, the political party he envisioned "will stand for the complete political and economic liberation of the Indian people." Speaking of Bose a few days after his death in August 1945, Jawaharlal Nehru said:

> *"In the struggle for the cause of India's independence he has given his life and has escaped all those troubles which brave soldiers like him have to face in the end. He was not only brave but had deep love for freedom. He believed, rightly or wrongly, that whatever he did was for the independence of India... Although I personally did not agree with him in many respects, and he*

left us and formed the Forward Bloc, nobody can doubt his sincerity. He struggled throughout his life for the independence of India, in his own way."

Along with his abiding love for his country, Bose held an equally passionate hatred of the imperial power that ruled it: Great Britain. In a radio address broadcast from Berlin on March 1, 1943, he exclaimed that Britain's demise was near, and predicted that it would be " India's privilege to end that Satanic empire." The fundamental principle of his foreign policy, Bose declared in a May 1945 speech in Bangkok, is that " Britain's enemy is India's friend." Although these two speeches are from his final years, they express views he had held since before his April 1921 resignation from the Indian Civil Service. It was this principle of making friends with Britain's enemies in the hope that they would assist him in liberating India that brought him in 1941 to Germany and then, in 1943, to Japan.

Violence or Non-Violence?

Bose envisaged that "the complete political and economic liberation of the Indian people" would inevitably require the use of force. Just before resigning from the Indian Civil Service, he discussed with Dilip Kumar Roy, his closest friend, the subject of anti-British terrorism. "I admit is it regrettable," he said, "even ugly if you will, though it also has a terrible beauty of its own. But maybe that beauty does not unveil her face except for her devotees."

Violence was not new to Bose, even at that early stage of his career. In 1916 he had been expelled from Presidency College in Calcutta for his part in the violent assault on Professor Edward Oaten, who had allegedly insulted Indian students. Moreover, although he occasionally claimed to "detest" violence, and criticized isolated acts of terrorism (which he considered ineffective and counterproductive), he was never really committed to Gandhi's policy of nonviolence. He regarded the Gandhi-supported civil disobedience campaign as an effective means of paralyzing the administration, but regarded it as inadequate unless accompanied by a movement aimed at total revolution and prepared, if necessary, to use violence.

Militarism

Related to Bose's willingness to use violence to gain political objective was his belief—expressed in *The Indian Struggle*, for example—that a government by a strong party should be "bound together by military discipline." Indeed Bose was infatuated with military discipline, and later commented that his basic training in the University Unit of the India Defence Force (for which he volunteered in 1917, while a student at Scottish Church College in Calcutta) "gave me something which I needed or which I lacked. The feeling of strength and of self-confidence grew still further."

Bose was able to give much grander expression to his "militarism" when, in 1930, he volunteered to form a guard of honour during the ceremonial functions at the Calcutta session of the Congress party. Such guards of honour were not uncommon, but the one Bose formed and commanded was unlike anything previously seen.

More than 2,000 volunteers were given military training and organized into battalions. About half wore uniforms, with specially designed steel-chain epaulettes for the officers. Bose, in full dress uniform (peaked cap, standing collar, ornamental breast cords, and jodhpurs) even carried a Field Marshal's baton when he reviewed his "troops." Photographs taken at the conference show him looking entirely out of place in a sea of *khadi* (traditional Indian clothing). Gandhi and several other champions of Nonviolence (*Ahimsa*) were uncomfortable with this display.

INA

A high point in Bose's "military career" came in July 1943 in Singapore. At a mass meeting there on July 4, Rash Behari Bose (no relation) handed over to him the leadership of the Indian Independence League.

The next day, Subhash Bose reviewed for the first time the soldiers of the Indian National Army (INA), which then comprised 13,000 men. In his address to the troops, which is a good example of his speaking style, he cited George Washington and Giuseppi Garibaldi as examples of men who led armies that won independence for their respective countries.

Bose went on:

"Soldiers of India's army of liberation!...

"Every Indian must feel proud that this Army—his own Army—has been organized entirely under Indian leadership and that, when the historic moment arrives, under Indian leadership it will go to battle...

"Comrades! You have voluntarily accepted a mission that is the noblest that the human mind can conceive of. For the fulfilment of such a mission, no sacrifice is too great, not even the sacrifice of one's life...

"...Today is the proudest day of my life. For an enslaved people, there can be no greater pride, no higher honour, than to be the first soldier in the army of liberation. But this honour carries with it a corresponding responsibility, and I am deeply conscious of it. I assure you that I shall be with you in darkness and in sunshine, in sorrow and in joy, in suffering and in victory. For the present, I can offer you nothing except hunger, thirst, privation, forced marches and death. But if you follow me in life and in death, as I am confident you will, I shall lead you to victory and freedom. It does not matter who among us will live to see India free. It is enough that India shall be free, and that we shall give our all to make her free.

"May God now bless our Army and grant us victory in the coming fight!"

This "Free India Army" ("*Azad Hind Fauj*") would not only "emancipate India from the British yoke," he told the soldiers, but would, under his command, become the standing national army of the liberated nation.

Choreography for Impact

As his staging at the 1930 Calcutta session of the Congress party suggest, Bose understood early on the importance of political choreography and the aesthetics of mass meetings. After his visits to Fascist Italy and National Socialist Germany, he was even more mindful of the importance for any successful broad-based political movement of mass meetings, marches, visual symbols, and ceremonial or liturgical rituals. For example, at the 51st session of the Congress party at Haripura in 1938, Bose made sure that his entrance as the new Congress President would be spectacular. Escorted by 51 girls in saffron saris (the number corresponding with the number of the Congress session), he was seated in an ancient chariot drawn by 51 white bullocks, and taken on a two hour procession through 51 specially-constructed gates, accompanied by 51 brass bands.

Political choreography of this type—although not to this extreme degree—was very evident at all mass rallies (which sometimes attracted crowds numbering as many as 200,000) of the Forward Bloc party that Bose formed in 1939. Carefully chosen symbols slogans and songs, coupled with a flood of written propaganda, were used in an unsuccessful attempt to make the Forward Bloc into a mass party.

Even during the last years of the war, when he was in southeast Asia heading the Provisional Government of Free India and the INA, he continued to choreograph carefully all of his rallies, meetings and ceremonies, in order to maximize their impact. He also realized that his own role in this choreography was central. Even in the hottest tropical weather, for instance, he wore an imposing military uniform, including forage cap, khaki tunic and jodhpurs, and shiny, knee-length black boots.

Moreover, whenever he travelled "he demanded all the rights and privileges of a head of state. On his road travels in Malaya, for example, he insisted on a full ceremonial escort; Japanese military jeeps mounted with sub-machine guns, a fleet of cars, and motorcycle outriders."

Historian Mihir Bose argues persuasively that such carefully planned actions were manifestations not of megalomania, but rather of Subhash Bose's effort to create a sense of unity transcending class, caste and origin among the large and diverse populations of Indians in Southeast Asia, to increase their political awareness, to arouse and inspire both them and his INA troops, and to show the world that he regarded himself as a political leader of substance and importance.

This naturally raises the question of Bose's leadership style. In the passage from *The Indian Struggle* quoted above at length, he expressed his belief in what he called "the dictatorship of the party" (the party being the governing body of a free India), but he did not specify the precise nature of the party's leadership, or whether it, too, would be dictatorial. Most importantly, he did not state whether he saw himself as the party leader, or comment directly on what role he intended for himself in a free India. Nonetheless, clues about these details can be gleaned from other sections of *The Indian Struggle* and from the speeches and statements Bose made at various times throughout his career.

DETERMINED LEADERSHIP

Bose clearly admired strong, vigorous, military-type leaders, and in *The Indian Struggle* he listed several whom he particularly respected. These included Hitler, Mussolini, Stalin and even a former British governor of Bengal, Sir Stanley Jackson. Nowhere in this book is there any criticism of these individuals (three of them dictators) for having too much power, yet another man is chastised for this: Mahatma Gandhi. Bose admired Gandhi for many things, not least his ability to "exploit the mass psychology of the people, just as Lenin did the same thing in Russia, Mussolini in Italy and Hitler in Germany." But he accused Gandhi of accepting too much power and responsibility, of becoming a "Dictator for the whole country" who issued "decrees" to the Congress. According to Bose, Gandhi was a brilliant and gifted man, but, unlike Mussolini, Hitler and the others mentioned, a very ineffectual leader. Gandhi had failed to liberate India because of his frequent indecision and constant willingness to compromise with the Raj (something Bose said he would never do).

It is clear that Bose—who believed from his youth that he was destined for greatness —saw himself as a "strong" leader in the mold of those named above. "I ask those who have any doubts or suspicions in their minds to rely on me," he told the Indian Independence League Conference in Singapore on July 4, 1943. He continued:

> *"I shall always be loyal to India alone. I will never deceive my motherland. I will live and die for India. .. The British could not bring me to submission by inflicting hardships on me. British statesmen could neither induce me nor deceive me. There is no one who can divert me from the right path."*

Bose was decisive, aggressive and ambitious, and even as a university student, these features of his personality attracted many devoted followers. Dilip Kumar Roy, his companion during his days as a student at Cambridge, referred to him as "strength-inspiring," and the absolute leader of the Indian student population.

Bose's militarism, ambition and leadership traits do not necessarily indicate (contrary to popular opinion) that he was a leader in the fascist mold. If they did, one would have to consider all personalities with similar traits—Winston Churchill, for example—as "fascist." In this regard, it is worth noting that during his many years as head of various councils, committees and offices, and during 15-month tenure as President of the Indian National Congress (February 1938 to May 1939), Bose never acted in an undemocratic manner, nor did he claim powers or responsibilities to which he was not constitutionally or customarily entitled. Neither did he attempt in any way to foster a cult of his own personality (as, it could be argued, Gandhi did).

However, after he assumed control of the INA in July-August 1943, Bose's leadership style underwent a transformation. First, he allowed a cult of his personality to flourish among the two million or so Indians living in southeast Asia. Prayers were regularly said on his behalf, and his birthday celebrations were—like Gandhi's in India—major festivals. He was invincible, according to one Indian myth from this period, and could not be harmed by bombs or bullets. An image of Bose that stressed his strength of character, military prowess, and willingness to sacrifice for a free India was intentionally promoted in propaganda broadcasts and printed material. With his approval, the title *Netaji* ("Revered Leader") was added to his name in all articles about him appearing in the newspapers of the Indian Independence League; even his staff officers were permitted to address him with this title. By the end of the war, few Indians in south Asia still referred to him by name; he was always respectfully called *Netaji*.

AUTHORITARIAN RULE

Second, in contrast to his statement at the 1938 Haripura session of the Congress party (quoted above)—that leaders would be elected from below—Bose proclaimed, on October 21, 1943, the formation of the Provisional Government of Azad Hind ("Free India"). While retaining his post as Supreme Commander of the Indian National Army, he announced that he was naming himself Head of State, Prime Minister, and Minister for War and Foreign Affairs. (The most important of these positions—Head of State—he anticipated retaining in a free India.) These appointments involved no democratic process or voting of any kind. Further, the authority he exercised in these posts was dictatorial and often very harsh. He demanded total obedience and loyalty from the Indians in south Asia, and any who opposed him, his army or government faced imprisonment, torture, or even execution.

Additionally, if wealthy Indians did not contribute sufficient funds to Bose's efforts, they risked confiscation of their property. Bose's threats were taken very seriously, and had the desired effect: funds did pour in. His INA troops were obliged to swear an oath of loyalty to both the Provisional Government and to him personally. He ordered the summary execution of all INA deserters, and also prepared (but was never able to implement) law codes for the entire population of India. These laws, which stipulated the death penalty for a range of offences, were to come into force when the INA, together with the Japanese Army, entered India to fight against the British.

With regard to his leadership style during this 1943-1945 period, in fairness to Bose is should be pointed out that the entire world was then engulfed in a horrendous war, and political and military leaders everywhere, on all sides, adapted extraordinarily authoritarian and repressive measures. Some of the measures and policies adapted by the wartime government of the United States, for instance, were as oppressive and as severe as any planned or implemented by Bose.

A NEW INDIA

Bose clearly anticipated that the British would be driven out of India in an armed struggle (under his leadership), and that a social and political revolution would begin the moment the Indian people saw British rule under attack in India itself. This revolution, he believed, would bring an end to the old caste system and traditional social hierarchy, which would be replaced by an egalitarian, casteless and classless society based on socialist models. This process would require very careful guidance, with a firm hand, to prevent anarchy and chaos.

Bose had, in fact, held these beliefs since the early 1930s, as Mrs. Kitty Kurti, a close German friend of Bose, revealed in her anecdotal memoir. At a June 1933 meeting attended by Kurti, Bose explained that:

> *"Besides a plan of action which will lead up to the conquest of power, we shall require a programme for the new state when it comes into existence in India. Nothing can be left to chance. The group of men and women who will assume the leadership of the fight with Great Britain will also have to take up the task of controlling, guiding and developing the new state and, through the state, the entire Indian people. If our leaders are not trained for postwar leadership also there is every possibility that after the conquest of power a period of chaos will set in and incidents similar to those for the French Revolution of the 18th century may be repeated in India. ... The generals of the wartime period in India will have to carry through the whole programme of postwar reforms in order to justify to their countrymen the hopes and aspirations that they will have to rouse during the fight. The task of these leaders will not be over till a new generation of men and women are educated and trained after the establishment of the new state and this new generation are able to take complete charge of their country's affairs."*

This explains what Bose meant in *The Indian Struggle* when he wrote (as quoted above) of the need for a strong, single-party government, "bound together by military discipline" with "dictatorial powers for some years to come, in order to put India on her feet." Only an very strong government, strict discipline, and dictatorial rule would, according to Bose, prevent the anticipated revolution from falling into chaos and anarchy. That is why the government would not—"in the first years after liberation"—"stand for a democracy in the Mid-Victorian sense of the term." It would use whatever military force was necessary to maintain law and order, and would not relinquish authority or re-establish more regular forms of government until it felt confident that "the work of postwar social reconstruction" had been completed and "a new generation of men and women in India, fully trained and equipped for the battle of life" had emerged.

Bose clearly anticipated that authoritarian rule would not last beyond the period when social reconstruction was completed, and law and order were established—when India was "on its feet," as he often wrote. As he frequently stated, Bose aimed for nothing less than the formation of "a new India and a happy India on the basis of the eternal principles of liberty, democracy and socialism." He rejected Communism (at least as it was practiced in the Soviet Union) principally because of its internationalism, and because he believed that the theoretical ideal found in the writings of Marx could not be applied, without modification, to India. Still, he maintained socialist views throughout his adult life, and, on very many occasions, expressed his hope for an egalitarian (especially classless and casteless) industrialized society in which the state would control the basic means of production.

He was opposed to liberalism, believing that greater emphasis should be placed on social goals than on the needs or desires of individuals. Individual wishes, he reasoned, must be subordinated to the needs of the state, especially during the struggle for independence and the period of reconstruction immediately following liberation. Nonetheless, having himself been imprisoned eleven times and sent into exile three times, he was fully committed to upholding the rights of minority intellectual, religious, cultural and racial groups. He hoped for an "all-round freedom for the Indian people—that is, for social, economic and political freedom," and would, he said "wage a relentless war against bondage of every kind till the people can become really free."

It could be argued that he was not as committed to the principle of democracy as he was to socialism and freedom (as he defined it). While he extolled democracy on numerous occasions, at other times his words suggest a belief that other parties would have a place, in a free India, only as long as they were "working towards the same end, in whole or in part," as his governing party. Political pluralism did not appeal to him at all. He seems to have envisioned a free India that was more authoritarian than democratic. His own actions as head of the Provisional Government of Azad Hind illustrate a lack of regard for the democratic process.

Mass Mobilization

Bose was, nonetheless, a consistent advocate of total mobilization: the mustering of national resources on a scale normally associated with military-like action. Realizing that manpower was easily India's greatest resource (and arguably the only one available to the independence movement), he proclaimed that all Indians—male and female, urban and rural, rich and poor—should actively participate in the fight for freedom. From his earliest days in politics to his death in 1945, he sought to rouse the great Indian masses, and involve them directly in the political struggle. Their support for representatives at the provincial or national levels was not enough; they must themselves rise up and win independence.

During the 1930s, however, his political position was never strong enough to call for other resources than manpower, nor was India—under British control—able to offer other resources. Additionally, total mobilization during peacetime, without an impending war or revolution in the awareness of the masses, had never been achieved (not even by the Nazis) and, arguably, never could be achieved.

Bose, an astute man, no doubt realized this. With the formation of the Provisional Government of Azad Hind, he was at last in a position to appeal directly for total mobilization to the mass of Indians—at least in Southeast Asia, and, less directly to those in India itself. Along with his call for mass mobilization, he demanded that all available resources be provided for the cause of freedom. For example, he told a mass meeting in Singapore in July 9, 1943:

> *"Friends! You will now realize that the time has come for the three million Indians living in East Asia to mobilize all their available resources, including money and manpower. Half-hearted measures will not do. I want Total Mobilization and nothing less, for we have been told repeatedly, even by our enemies, that this is a total war... Out of this total mobilization I expect at least three hundred thousand soldiers and three crores of dollars [$30,000,000]. I want also a unit of brave women to form a death-defying regiment who will wield the sword which the brave Rani of Jhansi wielded..."*

Of course, Bose demanded not only the total mobilization of Indian resources in south Asia, but of Indian resources everywhere. He called for mass mobilization not only in support of his army, but also for his dynamic new government, the various branches of which required financing and manpower.

Women's Equality

As can be seen from the passage quoted above, Bose called on both men *and* women for total support. Unlike the German National Socialists and the Italian Fascists, who stressed the masculine in almost all spheres of social and political activity, Bose believed that women were the equals of men, and should therefore be likewise prepared to fight and sacrifice for India's liberation. Throughout the 1920s and 1930s he had campaigned in India to bring women more fully into the life of the nation. After his return to Asia in 1943, he called on women to serve as soldiers in the Indian National Army—at the time a most radical view. "When I express my confidence that you are today prepared to fight and suffer for the sake of your motherland," he told the women's section of the Independence League in July 1943,

"I do not mean only to cajole you with empty words. I know the capabilities of our womanhood well. I can, therefore, say with certainty that there is no task which our women cannot undertake and no sacrifice and suffering which our women cannot undergo... To those who say that it will not be proper for our women to carry guns, my only request is that they look into the pages of our history. What brave deeds the Rani of Jhansi performed during the First War of Independence in 1857... Indians—both common people and members of the British Indian army—who are on the border areas of India, will, on seeing you march with guns on your shoulders, voluntarily come forward to receive the guns from you and carry on the struggle started by you."

A women's regiment was formed in 1943, and came to number about 1,000 women. It was named, appropriately, the "Rani of Jhansi Regiment," after a heroine of the Indian rebellion of 1857-58 against British rule. While those less suited to combat duties were employed as nurses and in other support roles, the majority were trained as soldiers. When the INA attacked British forces from Burma in east India in mid-1944, the women of the Jhansi Regiment fought alongside the men, suffering equally heavy casualties. When the army was forced to withdraw, the women were given no privileges. Along with the men, they marched for more than a thousand kilometres.

Commitment to Youth

Lastly, Bose was also deeply committed to the youth movement, a devotion that featured prominently in his political ideology. Convinced that young people were by nature idealistic, restless and open to new ideas —such his own radical and militant outlook—Bose accordingly devoted a great deal of time and effort to the new Youth Leagues that were formed in a number of provinces during the 1920s.

Throughout his career he presided over far more youth conferences than any other all-India political figure, and his speeches to younger people he steadfastly urged a spirit of activism that contrasted sharply with the passivism preached by Gandhi and many of the older politicians. "One of the most hopeful signs of the time," he claimed at the 1928 Maharashtra Provincial Conference, "is the awakening among the youth of this country... Friends! I would implore you to assist in the awakening of youth and in the organization of the youth movement. Self-conscious youth will not only act, but will also dream; will not only destroy, but will also build. It will succeed where even you may fail; it will create for you a new India—and a free India—out of the failures, trials and experiences of the past."

India's liberation would be achieved not by Gandhi and the leading politicians of his generation, whose conservative, reformist policies bred passivity and inactivity. It would, Bose believed, be achieved only through the efforts and sacrifices of the militant, revolutionary and politically-conscious younger generation.

Economic Views

In contrast to the copious record of Bose's political ideology and actions, much less is available about other important elements of his outlook, such as his economic views and policies. For example, while he condemned capitalism and extolled socialism in the pages of *The Indian Struggle,* Bose was very vague about just what monetary or credit systems he foresaw in a free India. They would be set up, he simply wrote, "in the light of the theories and the experiments that have been and are current in the modern world." Throughout his career he never wrote or said anything more specific about such matters. He appears to have had no precise ideas about political economy, save that economics was not important in itself but must be subordinated to national political considerations. Any discussion here of what economic systems he favoured, and when and how he intended to implement them, would thus be merely speculative.

Unique Political Ideology

While Bose's political ideology can reasonably be described as essentially "fascistic," two qualifying points need to be made here.

First, his ideology and actions were not the result of any extreme neurotic or pathological psychosocial impulses. He was not a megalomaniac, nor did he display any of the pathological traits often attributed (rightly or wrongly) to fascist leaders, such as hostile aggression, obsessive hatred or delusions. Moreover, while he was an ardent patriot and nationalist, Bose's nationalism was cultural, not racialist.

Second, his radical political ideology was shaped by a consuming frustration with the unsuccessful efforts of others to gain independence for India. His "fascist" outlook did not come from a drive for personal power or social elevation. While he was ambitious, and clearly enjoyed the devotion of his followers, his obsession was not adulation or power, but rather freedom for his beloved Motherland—a goal for which he was willing to suffer and sacrifice, even at the cost of his life.

Bose was favourably impressed with the discipline and organizational strength of fascism as early as 1930, when he first expressed support for a synthesis of fascism and socialism. During his stays in Europe during the 1930s, he was deeply moved by the dynamism of the two major "fascist" powers, Italy and Germany. After observing these regimes first-hand, he developed a political ideology of his own that, he was convinced, could bring about the liberation of India and the total reconstruction of Indian society along vaguely authoritarian-socialist lines.

Bose's lack of success in his lifelong effort to liberate India from alien rule was certainly not due to any lack of effort. From 1921, when he became the first Indian to resign formally from the Indian Civil Service, until his death in 1945 as leader of an Indian government in exile, Subhash Chandra Bose struggled ceaselessly to achieve freedom and prosperity for his beloved homeland.

Tripuri Congress Redux

The purpose of this essay is not to belittle Mahatma Gandhi. The reader will notice that nowhere has Gandhi's campaign to oust Bose been termed as immoral or unethical. At the same time it is not possible to know the truth by imposing divinity on Gandhi.

The Tripuri Congress session of 1939 is a crucial event in the history of the Indian National Congress. The united resistance and non-cooperation of the conservative leadership cleared the way for the removal of the recently re-elected Congress president Subhash Chandra Bose.

Bose was compelled to resign very soon. It won't be an exaggeration to say that the Tripuri session was the theatre of the demise of Bose's political career. Mahatma Gandhi was not present in the Tripuri session, but later when Bose repeatedly sought his intervention to end the stalemate, his stubborn refusal only hastened Bose's resignation. Even today Tripuri remains in the collective memory of Bengalis as a gross injustice done by Gandhi to Bose and Bengal. The consequent loss of Gandhi's image continues till today. On re-evaluating the incident after almost 65 years, certain questions arise which have never been answered squarely. This essay raises those little-discussed issues.

Was Gandhi Afraid of Bose?

Gandhi himself proposed Bose's name as the President of Congress in the Haripura Session of 1938. But within a year he literally became desperate to remove Bose and did not hesitate to take recourse to any sort of tactics to serve the purpose. His only objective at that time was Bose's removal by any means. No opinion regarding whether Gandhi's move was ethical or not can be objective, but at the same time it is pertinent to ask if he was afraid of Bose. Blind followers of Gandhi will of course laugh away such a question. They will argue that at that the national level Gandhi's status and influence was supreme, whereas the sphere of Bose's influence was limited. In that case, the question that begs answer is why was Gandhi so worried? It was clear as daylight to the whole country that he did not want Bose to continue. Despite such explicit opposition from Gandhi how did Bose get re-elected? Certainly not by rigging the election! Perhaps Gandhi was not perturbed even by the British government to the extent as he was by Bose. If he was confident of himself, what was the reason for Gandhi not to confront Bose directly rather than reverting to political trickery?

It is important to be clear about one thing regarding this issue. Many intellectuals, despite having high regards for Bose, cannot consider the Bose-Gandhi feud objectively. It almost amounts to sin for them even to think that Gandhi can do something unethical. They meticulously desist from associating Gandhi with any sort of Machiavellian politics since they consider him as much above petty politics. Furthermore, they present the accounts of many contemporary revolutionaries who could not see any wrong in Gandhi's actions in spite of being Bose's followers. It is now time to show clearly how both schools of arguments do not hold ground.

Firstly, overwhelming evidence has come to light showing Gandhi directly involved in the conspiracy to remove Bose. Gandhi's statements, letters etc. of those days are now available with the publication of his complete works. However, it was not possible for the revolutionaries during the Tripuri session to understand Gandhi's intentions, which he did not share even with his closest associates. Thus, it was virtually impossible for those revolutionaries, who despite being followers of Bose respected Gandhi, to assess Gandhi's true character. Therefore, even as they were pained by the anti-Bose actions of Gandhi, they failed to realize the Machiavellian tactics adopted by him.

Secondly, the question of right or wrong is in once sense irrelevant here since Machiavellian strategies are to some extent required in realpolitik. If Gandhi was determined to get rid of Bose for the sake of his own power and influence then his actions can be regarded as the most unethical. On the other hand, if he was moved by the consideration that removing Bose was necessary for the good of the country then his actions cannot be labelled unethical, since the interest of the country is always larger than the individual. It is not easy to resolve this debate.

It can however be resolved easily if Gandhi is seen as a clever politician instead of placing him in the high pedestal as a divine personality, without going into the question of right or wrong. It is abundantly evident that Gandhi was bothered by the rise of Bose and that he took recourse to a confrontation by proxy rather than facing him in a direct way. It was almost a nonviolent guerilla war. From Gandhi's point of view he was right. It is foolish to expect that he would give up to his biggest political challenger. Rather it is expected that he would resist fiercely with his entire prowess.

Even if Gandhians are upset, it will have to be admitted that only when one is pushed to the wall one becomes as desperate to fight back as Gandhi was. From that perspective Bose emerged victorious at Tripuri. Gandhi's statement that Sitaramayya's defeat was an indirect defeat for him was true in essence. To wash off the bitter taste of defeat, Gandhi threw away his principle of means being more important than the goal. It was possible to see such an astonishing U-turn of Gandhism only due to Bose's victory.

Tripuri and the subsequent flow of events prove beyond any doubt that Gandhi jettisoned his cherished ideals and instead adopted a totally un-Gandhian approach. It can be said that changing strategies or positions in politics is not unethical. Therefore it will suffice to say, without raising the issue of ethics, that Gandhi became desperate and broke out of his own value system since he acutely felt an existential crisis. From that perspective, Tripuri saw the defeat of the conventional Gandhiism and the emergence of a new Machiavellian Gandhiism. The events of Tripuri provide the burning proof that Gandhiism is not based on eternal ideals and values.

Gandhi as an Avatar of Machiavelli

The name of the famous Italian intellectual Nicolo Machiavelli has been associated with all sorts of unethical means for achieving political goals. Machiavelli laid more importance on the goal than on the means and advocated the dissociation of religion from politics. In the second sense Gandhi was not Machiavellian since he advocated just the opposite, which is, associating religion with politics. In the first sense he did follow the Machiavellian way to remove Bose out of his way. Bose was ready to follow any path for the attainment of independence for India, but never adopted Machiavellian ways in case of internal politics of Congress. This is where he is different from Gandhi.

Although Bose understood perfectly the nature of the British Raj, he dangerously failed to understand Gandhi. It has been rightly said by Amalesh Tripathi that Bose did not realize that his real conflict was with Gandhi himself. In his letter to Jawaharlal Nehru on 28 August 1939 he complained, "If the old guard wanted to fight why did they not do so in a straightforward manner? Why did they bring Mahatma Gandhi between us?" On 4 April 1939 Sarat Chandra Bose, Bose's elder brother had written to Nehru along the same lines, "I believe I shall not be unjust if I say that the members of the Working Committee would have shown greater courage and straightforwardness if they had decided to act on their own and not used Mahatmaji as their cover. Their plain duty was to keep Mahatmaji above all controversy as he should be in our political life." Both put on the dock Gandhi's followers like Sardar Patel, Bhulabhai Desai etc.

Sarat Bose expressed his displeasure in a sharp letter written to Gandhi on 21 March 1939. He wrote, "Tripuri was an eye opener to me. The exhibition of truth and nonviolence of your chosen disciples stunk in my nostrils. The election of Subhash was not a defeat for yourself, but of the high command of which Sardar Patel is the shining light." In fact the conservative leadership comprising of Patel, Desai and others kicked up a vilification campaign against Bose at Tripuri after calling his illness a 'political fever.' Bose wrote about this painful experience in his essay "My strange Illness." Patel was the focus of his wrath in his letter of 28 March too. Bose wrote to Nehru, "Was there nothing wrong in Sardar Patel making full use of the name and authority of Mahatma Gandhi for electioneering purposes?" He failed to understand that his true opponent was Gandhi who was actually controlling the unfolding of events from behind the curtain. In that sense Patel and others did not take recourse to any trickery and confronted Bose openly. The allegations that Bose brought agains them should have been raised against Gandhi. Why was he fighting a proxy war instead of playing a frontal role?

Gandhi wrote to his secretary Mahadev Desai on 29 January 1939 that he might not attend the Tripuri session if Bose wins the election. On 3 February 1939 he wrote to Nehru that he will serve the country although he will not attend the Congress session. He left for Rajkot on 27 February and the infamous Pant resolution was proposed on 8 March 1939: a classic example of pure Machiavellian politics.

Gandhi knew well that the Pant resolution will be proposed in his absence, but then he will be able to deny any responsibility for the proposal. At a time when Bose was repeatedly asking for Gandhi's opinion and seeking his intervention, all he could say was that he did not want to impose his choice on Bose. He wrote on 10 April 1939 that the more he read the Pant proposal the worse he feels, but he can't explain. Today many intellectuals who have high regard for both Gandhi and Bose can't see any dishonesty in Gandhi's action.

They however cannot be blamed since Bose himself failed to see any dishonesty in Gandhi. He even rebuked Narendra Narayan Chakrabarty when he suggested so. The question that now arises is whether Gandhi would have felt it necessary to carry on with his programme of fast at Rajkot if Bose was defeated. Secondly, if Gandhi was unhappy with the Pant proposal why did he not ask for an amendment? Thirdly, while advising Bose to constitute his cabinet of similar thinking leaders, was Gandhi not aware of its impossibility at that point of time? It would be over simplification to say that Gandhi was revengeful, but the fact remains that such a crafty politician has rarely been seen in this country.

That was one area where Bose could not equal Gandhi as he was a staunch opponent of the trend of politicking in Congress. The British Raj however knew Gandhi as a clever Machiavellian politician. Although Bose opposed Gandhi's politics, he had high regards for him. Perhaps that is why he could not comprehend the true nature of Gandhi's politics. Now the question is, did

Gandhi play this game of war by proxy to maintain his image? If that was the case, it was a terrible miscalculation because the Tripuri events pained even many of his followers. In general his image suffered a blow. His true intentions were clear as daylight.

When he described Bose's victory as his own defeat, there was no deception. Rather such straight talk is laudable. Had be provided the leadership to the conservative politicians in opposing Bose then surely his image would have gained a new high and he would have been praised. But instead he chose a path which was murky. He gained a victory which was but temporary. It was impossible for Gandhi to suppress Bose. The evidence of that has been written in golden letters in future history.

Did Bose have a Weakness for Gandhi?

Bose started making efforts to bring an end to his conflict with Gandhi after the Tripuri session. Manabendra Nath Roy rightly advised him in a letter written on 1 February 1939 to accept Gandhi's challenge and constitute a cabinet of his liking. However Bose did not accept the advice. This was one reason of losing the support of the leftists. Revolutionary of the Juagantar group told the writer that Bose's seeking of Gandhi's support, who had meted him such undignified treatment, also led to anger in certain sections of the revolutionary groups. Late Manohar Mukhopadhyay, another revolutionary of the Jugantar group, also told the writer that Bose was hesitant act against Gandhi.

Perhaps there is some truth in such opinion, but if Bose showed any soft attitude in certain situations towards Gandhi it was due to strategic reasons, not due to any weakness. The former Prime Morarji Desai has made a laughable statement in his autobiography that Gandhi accepted Bose as the President in the Haripura Congress only after Bose promised that he will go by Gandhi's directions. Those familiar with Bose's character know well that he was not one to submit to Gandhi in such a way, but might have just restrained his extreme revolutionary identity for the time being.

Rajendra Prasad has written in his autobiography that if Bose had expressed his willingness to be re-elected to Gandhi perhaps the Tripuri conflict could have been avoided. How strange! Would

Bose beg Gandhi for his democratic rights? He did not compromise on this issue because with all his respect for Gandhi he was not prepared to take his words as the final. And if he had withdrawn himself from the contest in accordance with Gandhi's wishes, he could not have held his head high in future. This would have not only set a bad precedent, but would have stifled democracy in Congress.

Of course democracy was ultimately stifled in Congress due to Gandhi and his followers, but Bose was not involved with that. He did not sign the death warrant of democracy in Congress. It can of course be asked that why did Bose allow Pant resolution to be raised knowing that it was unconstitutional and undemocratic? He explained to Gandhi in a letter written on 25 March 1939 that he could have vetoed this proposal but did not do so because his democratic outlook had the priority over the issue of constitutional validity. He also wrote, "I felt it would be unmanly to take shelter behind the constitution at a time when I felt that there was the possibility of an adverse vote."

This is where Bose committed a blunder since it made easy for Gandhi to write on 30 March 1939, "Since you think that Pant's resolution was out of order and the clause relating to the Working Committee is clearly unconstitutional, and were ultra vires your course is absolutely clear. Your choice of the committee should be unfettered." Even if this might appear to be transparent, so certain questions are bound to arise. Firstly, why didn't Gandhi clearly comment on the Pant resolution? Gandhi asked Bose to form the cabinet of his choice only because Bose thought that the proposal was unconstitutional.

In other words, Gandhi himself did not think that the proposal was unconstitutional. He told Bose on 10 April 1939, "The framers meant well. But it does not answer the present difficulty. You should therefore give it your own interpretation." By talking about the good intention of the proposal Gandhi supported it indirectly, but never spelt it out clearly. It would have been manly if he had stated his opinion clearly, but instead he created a situation where there was no other way for Bose than to resign. It is true that Bose sought Gandhi's intervention repeatedly at that time, but that was not from his weakness for him.

He hoped against hope that Gandhi will resolve the internal conflict of Congress in the larger interest of the country. He wrote to Gandhi on 31 March 1939, "We are not vindictive and we do not nurse grievances. There is no doubt that today there is a wide gulf between the two main blocs or parties in the Congress. But the gulf can be bridged – that by you." In another letter he wrote, "I am temperamentally not a vindictive person and I do not nurse grievances. I have the mentality of a boxer that is to shake hands smilingly when the boxing bout is over and take the revolt in a sporting spirit."

Bose could never imagine that his sportsman spirit will have no impact on Gandhi's mind. Gandhi was so disturbed by him that he had already thought up his course of action. Usually action agenda in politics is determined according to time and expediency, but in this case it was determined much earlier in what can be called fait accompli. Gandhi can be asked if he had started considering himself as weak. His innovativeness shows through the methods he adopted to remove Bose from his position. It is unfortunate that instead of applying such political methods against the British Raj, he used it against a great son of India.

Bose was a staunch anti-imperialist, but due to irony of fate he became a victim to both imperialist oppression and subversive internal politics of Congress. He wanted a compromise with Gandhi in the interest of the larger interest of the country.

The British Raj always wanted to split India by its divide and rule policy. Bose wanted to rise above personal grievances realizing that the internal conflict will only strengthen the British policy of divide and rule. But Gandhi was immovable from his position and thus all efforts of Bose failed. It must be remembered that despite all this Bose kept the path of cooperation with Gandhi open. He also joined the special session of Congress on Gandhi's invitation at Wardha after being expelled from Congress. Bose-baiters might see an effort of appeasement in this but if Bose truly had any weakness for Gandhi he wouldn't have searched for an alternative to the Gandhian way.

Probably he had hoped that he would be able to convince Gandhi to accept the relevance and importance of his plan of action. When he realized that he was only chasing a mirage, he decided to leave the country. Whether the country gained or suffered a loss will be judged by history but the fact remains that Bose was the only leader who showed the courage of proposing an alternative to the Gandhian way. The main source of his conflict with Gandhi can be found in his unique nature.

Paradoxical Ethics

Many people have charged Gandhi for adopting unethical means to get rid of Bose. According to this writer, the whole issue needs to be judged from a different point of view. As Krishna advised the Pandavas to take recourse to action which apparently was Adharma to be able to ensure victory of truth, Gandhi wanted to achieve a larger ethical framework by going through apparently unethical means. This can be called paradox of morality. Concepts of right and wrong etc. are never absolute. These are relative and can vary according to the time, place, persons involved etc. Gandhi's stubborn attitude towards Bose actually proves the flexibility of his mental makeup because it clearly shows that he did not cling on to any particular idea about morality.

Many people have opined that the rigid attitude shown initially by Gandhi towards the issue of violence and nonviolence was much relaxed during his later years. According to this author, it was on the issue of morality that Gandhi showed the most flexibility. He surpassed even Machiavelli in political maneuvering. Yet many intellectuals are still skeptical about this. Actually they have accepted absolutely accepted whatever Gandhi said, that is, they think that whatever he propounded is equally applicable in all cases.

However, Gandhi himself changed his position on many occasions without being bound by the fetters of so-called traditional morality. Those who want to show Gandhi as an idealist by ignoring his practical nature, forget that he himself had said, "I am a practical idealist." The practical side of his character was exposed during his campaign to oust Bose. There is a need to remove the illusion of the learned scholars on this issue.

Let there be No Illusion

A few years back a learned argument through letters between two historians was published in the pages of Jayasree. Shri Sandip

Das and Shri Girish Chandra Maiti expressed their opposing views about the role of Gandhi in the Tripuri Congress. Girish Chandra provided the evidence that Gandhi was aware of the Pant proposal well beforehand and it is clear from his statement given on 5 May 1939 at the Gandhi Seva Sangh in Vrindavan that he was told about this proposal while he was fasting at Rajkot. Gandhi said that he himself would have gone beyond, that is, he would have introduced a no-confidence motion against Bose. He dared his followers in Wardha to introduce a no-confidence motion. Sandip Das, ignoring this vital piece of evidence, said that he learnt from many revolutionaries that Gandhi was not dishonest in his behaviour.

It has already been said in this essay that it was not possible for the revolutionaries to know the real intention of Gandhi at that time. Secondly, the above evidence emanates directly from Gandhi. Therefore it is pointless (unless the evidence is disproved) to say that Gandhi was not aware of the Pant proposal. If there is any doubt regarding the veracity of Gandhi's statement, that should be stated clearly. Historians have to depend on two kinds of sources – primary and secondary. Although oral history has gained currency at present, still rigorous research should place more importance on primary evidence rather than hearsay. Gandhi's statement is without doubt a primary evidence. It would be contrary to convention of historical research to reject that based on hearsay. If any documentary evidence to the contrary cannot be presented then the reliability of the above mentioned source is definitely established beyond doubt.

A critic definitely has the right to interpret and analyse events, but it is desirable to be rational rather than be driven by emotions. Thirdly, Shri Das has cited the following quote from Gandhi, "No doubt I like politics too. But it is a different kind. There is no place for scheming in it." There is no doubt about the veracity of the quote, it should be interpreted with an open mind. To say that there was no place of scheming in Gandhi's political activities or in his thoughts is to belittle him. Although the appeared as a saint actually he was a shrewd politician. Otherwise he couldn't have bothered the British Raj to that extent. The saintly prophetic image covered his true identity of a political leader of unlimited intelligence. Nothing is unmixed right or wrong in politics, but depends on the situation. What Gandhi meant by the above quote is that he cannot accept scheming for fulfilling petty ambitions of individuals. That does not mean he was indifferent to use of political maneuvering for achieving political goals. The tendency to paint Gandhi as a superhuman or a saint has stemmed from the traditional concepts of morality. Any assessment of Gandhi will be one-sided, nebulous and irrational if this illusion of traditionalism is not transcended.

The purpose of this essay is not to belittle Gandhi. The reader will notice that nowhere has Gandhi's campaign to oust Bose been termed as immoral or unethical. At the same time it is not possible to know the truth by imposing divinity on Gandhi. It is not possible to stay above conflicts after entering the world of politics. It is also a fact that once inside the political whirlpool, even great men show self-contradicting attributes. It is not desirable to ignore such attributes due to blind devotion. The centre space of politics is focused towards human beings and not divinities. Therefore any search for political values should be focused on human nature and not divine ones. The spiritual politics that Gandhi refers to is primarily morality-based politics but such morality is dynamic and ever changing. It is not bound by any ideological limits. It is the humble submission of this writer that many problems will be solved more easily if neither Gandhi nor Bose is treated as superhuman or divine beings, but as humans of flesh and blood.

3

VINAYAK DAMODAR SAVARKAR

Vinayak Damodar Savarkar ((May 28, 1883-February 26, 1966) was an Indian politician and an Indian Independence Movement activist, who is credited with developing the Hindu nationalist political ideology Hindutva. He is considered to be the central icon of modern Hindu nationalist political ·parties. Commonly addressed as Veer Savarkar, he is considered to be the central icon of modern Hindu nationalist political parties. His last years were clouded with accusations of involvement in Mahatma Gandhi's assassination.

Savarkar's revolutionary activities began when studying in India and England, where he founded student societies and publications, espousing the cause of complete Indian independence by revolutionary means. Savarkar would publish The Indian War of Independence about the Indian rebellion of 1857 that would be banned by British authorities and was arrested in 1910 for his connections with the revolutionary group India House. Following a failed attempt to escape while being transported from Marseilles, Savarkar was sentenced to 50-years imprisonment and moved to the Cellular Jail in the Andaman and Nicobar Islands.

While in jail, Savarkar would pen the work describing Hindutva, openly espousing Hindu nationalism. He would be released in 1921 under restrictions after signing a controversial plea for clemency in which he renounced revolutionary activities. Travelling widely, Savarkar became a forceful orator and writer, advocating Hindu political and social unity. Serving as the president of the Hindu Mahasabha, Savarkar endorsed the ideal of Hindus as a distinct nation and of India as a Hindu Rashtra and controversially opposed the Quit India struggle in 1942. He became a fierce critic of the Indian National Congress and its acceptance of India's partition, and was one of those accused in the assassination of Indian leader Mahatma Gandhi, though he was acquitted by the Court. He spent the last years of his life writing and expounding on Hindutva.

EARLY LIFE

Vinayak Damodar Savarkar was born in the village of Bhagur, near the city of Nasik, in what is now Maharashtra. He was one of four children-his brothers Ganesh (Babarao) and Narayan, and his sister Mainabai-born to Radhabai and Damodarpant Savarkar. His family was of Hindu and Marathi background, and belonged to the Chitpawan Brahmin community-his ancestral roots and heritage would be an important influence on Savarkar. Descending from a long line of jagirdars (landlords) and scholars of Sanskrit, the Savarkar family was well-respected and both parents encouraged and inculcated a love of learning in all their children. Savarkar's mother died when he was only nine years old, after suffering from an outbreak of cholera. For the next seven years, Savarkar was raised by his father until his father fell victim to plague in 1899.

Savarkar's elder brother Ganesh took the burdens of providing for the family, and would be a strong influence on the teenage Savarkar in this period of hardship. Despite financial difficulties, Babarao supported Savarkar's dreams for higher education. In this period, Savarkar had organised several local young men in a group called the Mitra Mela (Band of Friends), and soon began encouraging revolutionary and nationalist views and passions amongst the band. In 1901, Savarkar was married to Yamunbai, the daughter of Ramchandra Triambak Chiplunkar, who supported Savarkar's university education. After passing his matriculation examination, Savarkar enrolled in the Fergusson College in the provincial capital of Pune (then Poona) in 1902.

As a young man and student, Savarkar was enthralled by the rising Swadeshi (Home-made) campaign, and the political struggle against the partition of Bengal in 1905. His views and passions were guided by a new generation of radical political leaders such as Bal Gangadhar Tilak, Bipin Chandra Pal and Lala Lajpat Rai. Absorbed immediately into nationalist activities, he began organising college students across Pune in the promotion of Swadeshi goods, boycotting foreign-made alternatives and promoting Indian culture in condemnation of European influences. At the occasion of the Hindu festival of Dussehra in 1905, Savarkar and his friends set a large bonfire of foreign goods and clothes. Reorganising his friends and students into a political outfit called Abhinav Bharat, Savarkar committed himself to fighting for India's independence, envisioning a republic united by a common language.

Savarkar was expelled from college for his activities, yet permitted to take examinations to achieve his Bachelor of Arts degree. With the help of nationalist activist Shyam Krishnavarma, Savarkar embarked to study law in England on a scholarship. In the same year, India's main political organisation, the Indian National Congress split, with the followers of Tilak (collectively known as the Garam Dal (Hot Faction) rejecting the moderate Congress leadership, which advocated dialogue and reconciliation with the British Raj. A firebrand nationalist of Marathi background, Tilak advocated Swaraj (Self-Rule) for India and was imprisoned for his support of outright independence and revolutionary activities. His zeal was heightened following Tilak's arrest, and Savarkar took on the Indian leader as his mentor, imbibing the latter's ideas for India's political freedom as well as the revival of the ancient heritage of Indian civilisation. Although generally espousing atheism, Savarkar began studying Indian history, Hindu scripture and observing religious traditions.

Activities at India House

Savarkar enrolled at Gray's Inn, a law college in London and began living with fellow Indian students at the India House. Organised by expatriate social and political activist Pandit Shyamji, India House was a thriving centre for student political and intellectual activity, and with Savarkar's addition, it soon became a hot-bed of revolutionary thought and activities. Founding the Free India Society, Savarkar sought to organise fellow Indian students for the goal of independence through revolution:

> *"We must stop complaining about this British officer or that officer, this law or that law. There would be no end to that. Our movement must not be limited to being against any particular law, but it must be for acquiring the authority to make laws itself. In other words, we want absolute independence."*

Savarkar envisioned a guerrilla war for independence along the lines of the famous armed Independence Movement of 1857 (incorrectly taught as Sepoy Mutiny by some old fashioned outdated schools). Studying the history of the revolt from English as well as Indian sources, Savarkar wrote a major book, The History of the War of Indian Independence in which he analyzed the revolt and assailed British rule in India as unjust and oppressive. Savarkar became one of the first writers to allude to the revolt as the "First War for Independence." Karl Marx is also said to have written the Sepoy Mutiny of 1857 as the India's First War of Independence.

Banned from publication throughout the British Empire, Savarkar managed to smuggle his work to expatriate Indian revolutionary Madame Bhikaji Cama, who obtained its publication in the Netherlands, France and Germany. Widely smuggled and circulated, the book would attain great popularity and would influence rising young Indians and future revolutionaries, including Subhash Chandra Bose and Bhagat Singh. With a core group of fellow students, Savarkar began studying revolutionary methods and came into contact with a veteran of the Russian Revolution of 1905, who imparted the knowledge of bomb-making to Savarkar and his friends. Savarkar would print and circulate a manual amongst his friends, on bomb-making and other methods of guerrilla warfare.

In 1909, Madan Lal Dhingra, a keen follower and friend of Savarkar, assassinated British MP Sir Curzon Wylie in a public meeting. Dhingra's action provoked controversy across Britain and India, evoking enthusiastic admiration as well as condemnation. Savarkar published an article in which he all but endorsed the murder and worked to organise support, both political and for Dhingra's legal defence. At a meeting of Indians called for a condemnation of Dhingra's deed, Savarkar protested the intention of condemnation and was drawn into a hot debate and angry scuffle with other attendants. A secretive and restricted trial and a sentence awarding the death penalty to Dhingra provoked an outcry and protest across the Indian student and political community. Strongly protesting the verdict, Savarkar struggled with British authorities in laying claim to Dhingra's remains following his execution. Savarkar hailed Dhingra as a hero and martyr, and began encouraging revolution with greater intensity.

Cellular Jail

In India, Ganesh Savarkar had organised an armed revolt against the Morley-Minto reforms of 1909 for which he was arrested and sentenced to transportation for life, moved to the Cellular Jail in the Andaman and Nicobar Islands. The British police implicated Savarkar in the investigation for allegedly plotting the crime. Hoping to evade arrest, Savarkar moved to Madame Cama's home in Paris. He was nevertheless arrested by police on March 13, 1910. In the final days of freedom, Savarkar wrote letters to a close friend planning his escape. Knowing that he would most likely be shipped to India, Savarkar asked his friend to keep track of which ship and route he would be taken through. When the ship S.S. Morea reached the port of Marseilles on July 8, 1910, Savarkar escaped from his cell through a porthole and dived into the water, swimming a long distance to the shore in the hope that his friend would be there to receive him in a car.

But his friend was late in arriving, and the alarm having been raised, Savarkar was re-arrested. Arriving in Mumbai (then Bombay), he was taken to the Yeravda Central Jail (which was a high security prison then reserved for the most illustrious of Indian Freedom Fighters, even Mahatma Gandhi was later housed there). Following a trial, Savarkar was sentenced to 50-years imprisonment and transported on July 4, 1911 to the Cellular Jail in the Andaman and Nicobar Islands.

Infamously known as Kaalapani, his fellow captives included many political prisoners, and were forced to perform hard labour for many years. Reunited with his brother Ganesh, the Savarkars nevertheless struggled in the harsh environment. Forced to arise at 5 a.m., tasks including cutting trees and chopping wood, and working at the oil mill under regimental strictness, with talking amidst prisoners strictly prohibited during mealtime. Prisoners were subject to frequent mistreatment and torture. Contact with the outside world and home was restricted to the writing and mailing of one letter a year. In these years, Savarkar withdrew within himself and performed his routine tasks mechanically. Obtaining permission to start a rudimentary jail library, Savarkar would also teach some fellow convicts to read and write.

Savarkar appealed for clemency in 1911 and again during Sir Reginald Craddock's visit in 1913, citing poor health in the oppressive conditions. In 1920, even as the Indian National Congress and leaders such as Mahatma Gandhi, Vithalbhai Patel and Bal Gangadhar Tilak demanded his unconditional release, Savarkar controversially signed a statement endorsing the trial verdict and British law, and renouncing violence:

> *"I hereby acknowledge that I had a fair trial and just sentence. I heartily abhor methods of violence resorted to in days gone by and I feel myself duty bound to uphold law and constitution to the best of my powers and I am willing to make the [1919 Montague-Chelmsford Reforms] a success in so far as I may be allowed to do so in future." (from facsimile of Savarkar's letter to British authorities, Frontline, April 7, 1995. Pg. 94).*

In his appeal and a willingness to sign a statement renouncing revolutionary activities, Savarkar sparked intense criticism and controversy, which has continued till today. Critics allege that he bargained for his freedom at the expense of his ideals, while supporters assert that Savarkar was merely seeking to escape one way or another, and resume his activities.

On May 2, 1921, the Savarkar brothers were moved to a jail in Ratnagiri, and later to the Yeravda Central Jail. He was finally released on January 6, 1924 under stringent restrictions-he was not to leave Ratnagiri District and was to refrain from political activities for the next five years. However, police restrictions on his activities would not be dropped until the Congress came to power in 1937.

It is often alleged by Indian communists that Savarkar was employed by the British government in their 'Divide and rule' strategy to rule India. A more realistic view is that he was a patriot with strong Hindu revivalist feelings, who spent more than a decade in the Cellular Jail, which is something a lot of other 'freedom fighters' escaped.

Hindutva

During his incarceration, Savarkar's views began turning increasingly towards Hindu cultural and political nationalism, and the next phase of his life remained dedicated to this cause. In the brief period he spent at the Ratnagiri jail, Savarkar wrote his ideological treatise-Hindutva: Who is a Hindu?. Smuggled out of the prison, it was published by Savarkar's supporters under his alias "Mahratta." In this work, Savarkar promotes a radical new vision of Hindu social and political consciousness. Savarkar began describing a "Hindu" as a patriotic inhabitant of Bharatavarsha, venturing beyond a religious identity. While emphasising the need for patriotic and social unity of all Hindu communities, he described Hinduism, Jainism, Sikhism and Buddhism as one and same. He outlined his vision of a "Hindu Rashtra" (Hindu Nation) as "Akhand Bharat" (United India), purportedly stretching across the entire Indian subcontinent:

> *"the Aryans who settled in India at the dawn of history already formed a nation, now embodied in the Hindus.... Hindus are bound together not only by the tie of the love they bear to a common fatherland and by the common blood that courses through their veins and keeps our hearts throbbing and our affection warm but also by the tie of the common homage we pay to our great civilisation, our Hindu culture."(Page108)"*

Scholars, historians and Indian politicians have been divided in their interpretation of Savarkar's ideas. A self-described atheist, Savarkar regards being Hindu as a cultural and political identity. While often stressing social and community unity between Hindus, Sikhs, Buddhists and Jains, Savarkar's notions of loyalty to the fatherland are seen as an implicit criticism of Muslims and Christians, who regard Mecca, Medina and Jerusalem as their holiest places. Savarkar openly assailed what he saw as Muslim political separatism, arguing that the loyalty of many Muslims was conflicted. After his release, Savarkar founded the Ratnagiri Hindu Sabha on January 23, 1924, aiming to work for the social and cultural preservation of Hindu heritage and civilisation.

Becoming a frequent and forceful orator, Sarvakar agitated for the use of Hindi as a common national language and against caste discrimination and untouchability. Focusing his energies on writing, Savarkar authored the Hindu Padpadashashi-a book documenting and extolling the Maratha empire-and My Transportation for Life-an account of his early revolutionary days, arrest, trial and incarcertaion. He also wrote and published a collection of poems, plays and novels.

Leader of the Hindu Mahasabha

Although disavowing revolution and politics, Savarkar grew disenchanted with the Congress's emphasis of nonviolence and criticised Gandhi for suspending Non Cooperation Movement following the killing of 22 policemen in Chauri Chaura in 1922. He soon joined the Hindu Mahasabha, a political party founded in 1911 and avowed to Hindu political rights and empowerment. The party was disengaged from the Indian independence movement, allowing Savarkar to work without British interference. As his travel restrictions weakened, Savarkar began travelling extensively, delivering speeches exhorting Hindu political unity and criticising the Congress and Muslim politicians. Savarkar and the Mahasabha did not endorse the Salt Satyagraha launched by the Congress in 1930, and neither Savarkar nor any of his supporters participated in civil disobedience. Savarkar focused on expanding the party's membership, revamping its structure and delivering its message.

In the wake of the rising popularity of the Muslim League led by Muhammad Ali Jinnah, Savarkar and his party began gaining traction in the national political environment. Savarkar moved to Mumbai and was elected president of the Hindu Mahasabha in 1937, and would serve until 1943. The Congress swept the polls in 1937 but conflicts between the Congress and Jinnah would exacerbate Hindu-Muslim political divisions. Jinnah derided Congress rule as a "Hindu Raj," and hailed December 22, 1939 as a "Day of Deliverance" for Muslims when the Congress resigned en masse in protest of India's arbitrary inclusion into World War II. Savarkar's message of Hindu unity and empowerment gained increasing popularity amidst the worsening communal climate. Even as the League adopted the Lahore Resolution in 1940, calling for a separate Muslim state based on the Two-Nation Theory, Savarkar publicly stated that he did not disagree with Jinnah's contention that Hindus and Muslims were a separate nation. He was firmly opposed, however to the proposed partition of Indian territory, citing the existence of a Muslim homeland in the Middle East.

However, Savarkar and the Mahasabha joined several political parties including the League and the Communist Party of India in endorsing the war effort. Savarkar publicly encouraged Hindus to enlist in the military, which his supporters described as an effort for Hindus to obtain military training and experience potentially useful in a future confrontation with the British. When the Congress launched the Quit India rebellion in 1942, Savarkar criticised the rebellion and asked Hindus to stay active in the war effort and not disobey the government. Under his leadership, the Mahasabha won several seats in the central and provincial legislatures, but its overall popularity and influence remained small. Towards the end of the war, Savarkar and the Mahasabha became increasingly confrontational with the League and Muslim politicians. Hindu Mahasabha activists protested Gandhi's initiative to hold talks with Jinnah in 1944, which Savarkar denounced as "appeasement." He assailed the British proposals for transfer of power, attacking both the Congress and the British for making concessions to Muslim separatists. The Mahasabha's popularity was affected when the young and rising politician Syama Prasad Mookerjee left the party, believing it to be too radical and out-of-touch with most Hindus.

WORKS

Veer Savarkar wrote more than 10,000 pages in the Marathi language. His literary works in Marathi include "Kamala", "Mazi Janmathep" (My Life Sentence), and most famously "1857-The First war of Independence", about what the British referred to as the Sepoy Mutiny. Savarkar popularised the term 'First War of Independence'. Another noted book was "Kala Pani" (similar to Life Sentence, but on the island prison on the Andamans), which reflected the treatment of Indian freedom fighters by the British. In order to counter the then accepted view that India's history was a saga of continuous defeat, he wrote an inspirational historical work, "Saha Soneri Pane" (Six Golden Pages), recounting some of the Golden periods of Indian history. At the same time, religious divisions in India were beginning to fissure. He described what he saw as the atrocities of British and Muslims on Hindu residents in Kerala, in the book, "Mopalyanche Band" (Muslims' Strike) and also "Gandhi Gondhal" (Gandhi's Confusion), a political critique of Gandhi's politics. Savarkar, by now, had become a committed and persuasive critic of the Gandhian vision of India's future he was great poet & writer he wrote more than 10,000 pages in 'Marathi' & morethan 1,500 pages in 'English' languages.

He is also the author of poems like "Sagara pran talmalala", and "Jayostute" (written in praise of freedom), one of the most moving, inspiring and patriotic works in Marathi literature. When in the Cellular jail, Savarkar was denied pen and paper. He composed and wrote his poems on the prison walls with thorns and pebbles, memorised more than ten thousand lines of his poetry for years till other prisoners returning home brought them to India. Savarkar is credited with several popular neologisms in Hindi, like Digdarshak (leader, one who points in the right direction), Shatkar, Saptahik (Weekly) and Sansad (Parliament).

Partition and Gandhi's Murder

Savarkar had become one of the fiercest critics of Mahatma Gandhi, and attacked him and the Congress leadership for acquiescing to the partition of India. During the intense communal violence, Hindu Mahasabha activists were allegedly responsible for carrying out attacks on Muslim civilians. Savarkar blamed Gandhi for weakening Hindu society in face of Muslim separatism, and for agreeing to divide the Hindu homeland.

The anger of some Hindu refugees from Pakistan provoked fears of assassination attempts on Gandhi's life. Gandhi's fast-unto-death in January 1948, demanding immediate communal peace and the payment of outstanding shares of the treasury to Pakistan in spite of the Indo-Pakistani War of 1947 increased the consternation and anger of many Hindu Mahasabha activists, including Savarkar.

Following the murder of Mahatma Gandhi on January 30, 1948, police arrested the assassin Nathuram Godse and rounded up his companions. Police investigation revealed that Godse and his chief conspirator Narayan Apte had been a close political confidantes of Savarkar in the Hindu Mahasabha. Despite having publicly denounced Gandhi's murder, Savarkar was arrested on suspicion of having inspired and planned Gandhi's murder, and accordingly indicted. Witnesses during the trial testified that Savarkar had blessed Nathuram Godse before he shot Gandhi, with the words "Yashasvi howun yaa" (Marathi: Come back with success). Both Godse and Savarkar belonged to the Chitpawan Brahmin community. Even before the trial, However, Sardar Vallabhbhai Patel had, in a letter to Jawaharlal Nehru, clearly stated his doubts over allegations that Savarkar had masterminded the murder. In the court, approvers had testified to the intimate relationship between Savarkar and the Godse brothers, but there was no corroborative evidence to nail down Savarkar's assertion that he had merely formal relationships with them. Godse claimed full responsibility for planning and carrying out the attack, in absence of an independent corroboration of the prosecution witness Digambar Ramchandra Badge's evidence implicating Savarkar directly, the court exonerated him citing insufficient evidence.

Lingering doubts about this version of events led the government of India to appoint the Kapur Commission in the mid-1960s. The Kapur commission was fortunate in having access to testimonies of Savarkar's aides (including his bodyguard and his secretary) and important Hindu Mahasabha functionaries who were not available to the earlier court. The weight of this evidence led Justice Kapur to reverse the conclusions of the court trial and state unambiguously that "all these facts taken together were destructive of any theory other than the conspiracy to murder by Savarkar and his group".

Later Life

Despite his exoneration, Savarkar's role in the plot remains a source of intense controversy, but at the time the public held him answerable for instigating the murder. Public outrage over Gandhi's murder wrecked the fortunes of the Hindu Mahasabha, whose membership and activity dwindled into insignificance. Hindu nationalist organisations such as the RSS and the Bharatiya Jana Sangh disavowed any links with Savarkar and his ideology.

Savarkar's home in Mumbai was stoned by angry mobs, and his political influence and activism sharply curtailed by widespread public anger. His activities remained confined to occasional speeches and publishing his writings.

Although regarded with respect and admiration for his revolutionary activities and work on behalf of Hindus, most political parties refused to be associated with him. Yet Savarkar maintained a standing of a legendary freedom fighter, especially in Maharashtra. He attempted to organise a new political party based on Hindutva, but to no avail. Savarkar exercised Voluntary Euthanasia and passed away on February 27, 1966 and was mourned by large crowds that attended his cremation. His home, possessions and other personal relics have been preserved for public display. Corroboration of Badge's testimony came only after Savarkar's death when his secretary, Gajanan Vishnu Damle and bodyguard Appa Ramachandra Kasar deposed to Justice Kapur that Godse and accomplice Narayan Apte met Savarkar on January 23 or 24 on their return from Delhi well after they had met him on January 17.

Ideologue of Hindutva

Vinayak Damodar ("Veer") Savarkar can, with some justice, be described as the inspirational force behind the resurgence of militant Hinduism in contemporary India. His fame has been on the ascendancy since the Hindu right captured power in India less than a decade ago, and lately he has been lionized in the film "Veer Savarkar" by the filmmaker Sudhir Phadke, a fellow Maharashtrian.

In May 2002, L. K. Advani spoke glowingly of Savarkar and Hedgewar, the founder of the Rashtriya Swayamsevak Sangh [RSS], as men who had "kindled fierce nationalistic spirit that contributed to India's liberation." Savarkar's advocates view him as a luminous visionary, a supreme patriot who sacrificed much for the defense of Mother India, a great revolutionary and even social reformer; his opponents, who generally do not question his patriotism, nevertheless point to his political conservatism, his support of reactionary movements, and his advocacy of a communal-based politics verging on fascism.

Savarkar was born in Bhagur village in Nasik district of present-day Maharashtra on 28 May 1883 into a Chitpavan Brahmin family. His early exposure to the political activities of the Maharashtrian elite who were opposed to British rule may have come at the hands of his elder brother, Ganesh [Babarao], who is said to have been greatly inspired by the actions of Lokmanya Tilak, the Chapekar Brothers, and other revolutionaries. The Savarkar brothers were active in the Mitra Mela, a secret society formed with the aim of liberating, through the use of armed force, India from British rule. Veer Savarkar attended Fergusson College in Pune: his biographer, Dhananjay Keer, notes that Savarkar gathered around him a group of students who debated European political texts, discussed revolution, and championed swadeshi [self-reliance]. In 1906, Savarkar left for London to get credentialed in law; his passage was paid for by Shyam Krishnavarma, an Indian patriot settled in London who used his journal, The Indian Sociologist, to make a case for Indian independence.

The journal was advocating violent revolution by 1909; but before then, in 1907, Savarkar had published a Marathi translation of Mazzini's autobiography which did very well. By early 1909, according to the senior intelligence officer James Campbell Ker, author of Political Trouble in India 1907-1917 [1917, reprinted 1973 by Oriental Publishers, Delhi], Savarkar had taken charge of India House, the London headquarters of those Indians who claimed revolutionary credentials (p. 177). That year, on July 1, Madan Lal Dhingra assassinated Sir William Curzon-Wyllie at the Imperial Institute. This assassination, less than a month after Ganesh Savarkar was convicted on the charge of sedition and sentenced to transportation for life, is said to have been instigated by Savarkar's orders; yet Savarkar himself never wielded any arms. His critics, quite rightly, describe this cowardice as typical of Savarkar's conduct; and it is striking, of course, that nearly 40 years later Savarkar was again thought to have encouraged and instigated Nathuram Godse to murder Mahatma Gandhi, without himself having taken up arms. It is more than likely that Savarkar became a master at manipulating those who looked up to him, and sought to conduct his violent activities without explicitly implicating himself in gruesome deeds of murder.

A steady stream of publications emerged from Savarkar's pen over a course of five decades, and his first substantial work, the Indian War of Independence, appeared in 1908, or fifty years after the rebellion of 1857-58 had been crushed. Though in this work Savarkar argued that Hindus and Muslims had stood together in resistance to the British, in later works he showed himself much less enamoured of Hindu-Muslim unity, and for most of his adult life he would, in fact, become known for his advocacy of the rights of Hindus. Hindu Pad-Padashahi [1925], a treatise on Hindu Kingship, or more particularly on the glories of India under Maratha rule, showed as well the impact of political events on Savarkar's thinking: both the Khilafat movement, as well as the Moplah Rebellion, doubtless played a part in turning Savarkar against Muslims.

However, his signature piece, in this respect, was a "treatise" he penned in 1922, "Essentials of Hindutva", a more elaborate version of which appeared in 1928 as Hindutva: Who is a Hindu? (Nagpur, 1928). Savarkar vigorously set forth the idea that Hindus constituted a nation, bound together by common blood, and that Hindus were united "by the tie of a common heritage we pay to our great civilization — our Hindu culture". Savarkar eschewed the word "Hinduism"; to him, Hindutva represented the essence of the Hindu way of life. As he wrote, "If there be any word of alien growth it is this word Hinduism and so we should not allow our thoughts to get confused by this new fangled term." The Hindus' devotion to their motherland was supreme; indeed, whosoever was devoted to Hindustan, and considered it his or her holy land (punyabhoomi), was a Hindu.

The most elaborate legend, vigorously promoted by Savarkar's friends and admirers, has developed around his supposed bravery. In 1910, as Savarkar was being taken to India after a warrant had been issued for his arrest on charges of sedition and treason, he escaped as his ship docked at Marseilles. Upon being recaptured, Savarkar challenged the legality of his arrest in France, but the international court at Hague, though it took the view that an illegality had been committed when Savarkar was handed over to the British police, nonetheless ruled against Savarkar. Savarkar was, at his trial in Bombay, sentenced to imprisonment for life, and transported to the Andamans. In 1922, he was sent back to India, but confined to Ratnagiri District until 1937. Yet, to put it mildly, there are serious reasons to doubt whether Savarkar was deserving of the epithet of "Veer" [brave] that was bestowed on him. The indisputable fact remains that throughout his political life, Savarkar showed himself perfectly capable of not merely negotiating with the British, but serving as an active collaborator. When confined to jail in the Andamans, Savarkar negotiated with the British to have himself set free. Moreover, when Congress refused to form a government in the Central Provinces and Bengal, the Hindu Mahasabha under Savarkar's guidance opted to collaborate with the British. He thought it a God-given opportunity for the Mahasabha to flex its muscles while the Congress was in hibernation. Similarly, though the Congress declared itself opposed to offering the British any assistance during World War II, Savarkar was keen that Hindus should acquire experience in the use of firearms. Savarkar saw in World War II an opportunity for Hindus, who had been emasculated (in Savarkar's view) by centuries of oppression under Muslim and British rule, and rendered incapable of even elementary knowledge in the discharge of firearms by virtue of legislation that forbid ownership of guns among Indians to become versed in fighting strategies. Not only did the Hindu Mahasabha, whose presidency Savarkar assumed in 1937 upon the rescission of the order which confined him to Ratnagiri District, not oppose the British position in World War II, but the Mahasabha played no role in the Quit India movement and indeed even assisted the British in its suppression.

In the last analysis, Savarkar appears as an extraordinary embodiment of utter mediocrity. In the large corpus of his writings, there is barely anything to suggest a creative mind at work, and one searches in vain for any original idea. Savarkar imbibed the worst of Western political and social traditions, and his warped ideas about race superiority, the survival of the fittest, and the nation as a "blood entity", so to speak, were derived from the most objectionable strands of Western thinking.

In his avid desire to militarize the Hindus, he showed himself hostage to crude notions of realpolitik. He perfected the art of assassination and political intrigue by remote control, and his true disciple in this respect is Bal Thackeray. It is no surprise that he should appeal to the leadership of the present generation of Hindu extremists, who are similarly bereft of intellectual ideas, moral sentiments, and the barest standards of truth in public life, and whose idea of bravery entails murderous onslaught upon religious minorities. If Savarkar is at all to be remembered, let it not be forgotten that as Nathuram Godse plotted to take Mahatma Gandhi's life, Savarkar blessed him and wished him success in his God-given task.

Nathuram Godse, the RSS, and the Murder of Gandhi

On 30 January 1948, Mohandas Karamchand Gandhi, known around the world as Mahatma Gandhi, and to his countrymen and women as Bapu, the "Father of the Nation", was shot dead by Nathuram Vinayak Godse, a Chitpavan Brahmin from Pune. Much ink has been spilled on determining whether Godse was, at that time, a member of the RSS, or indeed of the Hindu Mahasabha, or perhaps of neither organization. Though Godse single-handedly carried out the execution of Gandhi, others were implicated in the assassination plot, and among those against whom the Indian government filed charges was Veer Savarkar. Godse, as investigations after Gandhi's murder were to reveal, appears to have been close to Savarkar, a prominent leader of the Hindu Mahasabha. Godse was certainly a frequent visitor to Savarkar's residence, and he did not, in the time that intervened between his arrest on January 30 and his execution upon conviction of the charge of murder nearly two years later, ever disown his association with the Mahasabha.

The general consensus appears to be that Nathuram, who saw himself as a passionate and ardent defender of the Hindu motherland against the depredations of Muslims, was at one point active in the RSS but resigned his membership in the early 1930s. This mere fact, if fact it be, has been pounced upon by the RSS in the five decades following Gandhi's assassination to argue that Godse had no association with the RSS, and curiously Nathuram's younger brother, Gopal Godse, who was convicted of partaking in the conspiracy to murder Gandhi and served a fifteen-year jail term and still speaks in the most bitter terms of Gandhi as the betrayer of India, has himself on more than one occasion had to issue a strong rejoinder to the RSS, with whose ideological outlook he is otherwise in complete sympathy, for attempting to disguise his brother's long-term association with the RSS. Thus, shortly after releasing Nathuram's book, Why I Assassinated Mahatma Gandhi, in December 1993, Gopal Godse in an interview with Frontline magazine stated: "All the [Godse] brothers were in the RSS. Nathuram, Dattatreya, myself and Govind. You can say we grew up in the RSS rather than in our home. It was like a family to us. Nathuram had become a baudhik karyavah [intellectual worker] in the RSS. He has said in his statement that he left the RSS. He said it because [Madhav Sadashiv] Golwalkar and the RSS were in a lot of trouble after the murder of Gandhi. But he did not leave the RSS." [See issue of 28 January 1994]

Whether Godse formally remained a member of the RSS is much less important than the fact that though the Hindu Mahasabha and the RSS had some ideological differences, both organizations were united in their extreme hostility to Gandhi as well as to Muslims. Golwalkar and Savarkar shared a platform in Pune in 1952, as Sitaram Yechury's What Is This Hindu Rashtra (Madras: Frontline Publications, 1993) has recently documented, and it is a little-known fact that at one point the RSS, eager to foment the impression that it did not stand by the virulently anti-Muslim sentiments expressed in Golwalkar's influential book, We or Our Nationhood Defined (1938), claimed that the author of the book was Babarao Savarkar, the brother of Veer Savarkar. Sardar Patel, the Deputy Prime Minister and Home Minister in Nehru's Cabinet, was himself inclined to view the Mahasabha and the RSS as organizations that had together created an atmosphere in which, as he wrote on 18 July 1848 to the Hindu Mahasabha leader, Shyam Prasad Mookerjee, "such a ghastly tragedy [Gandhi's assassination] became possible. There is no doubt in my mind that the extreme section of the Hindu Mahasabha was involved in this conspiracy." Yet, as Patel added, in terms that leave no room to doubt that from his standpoint the RSS also stood implicated in Gandhi's assassination, "The activities of the RSS constituted a clear threat to the existence of Government and the State. Our reports show that those activities, despite the ban, have not died down. Indeed, as time has marched on, the RSS circles are becoming more defiant and are indulging in their subversive activities in an increasing measure."

Two months later, on September 11th, Patel was again unequivocal in his denunciation of the role played by the RSS in Gandhi's assassination: addressing Golwalkar, Patel spoke about the "poison" spread by the RSS. Following Gandhi's murder, "Even an iota of the sympathy of the Government or of the people no more remained for the RSS. In fact opposition grew. Opposition turned more severe, when the RSS men expressed joy and distributed sweets after Gandhiji's death."

It scarcely matters, then, whether Nathuram Godse retained membership in the RSS when he shot Gandhi dead. Godse was involved in Hindu extremist organizations, including the RSS and the Hindu Mahasabha, his entire adult life, and the continuing attempts by RSS to evade responsibility for Gandhi's assassination are characteristic of that extreme pusillanimity and tendency to falsehood which have always been the signal trademarks of an organization that is determined to bring the idea of Hindu Rashtra to fruition.

4

Rabindranath Tagore

Rabindranath Tagore (7 May 1861 – 7 August 1941), also known by the sobriquet Gurudev, was a Bengali poet, Brahmo Samaj philosopher, visual artist, playwright, novelist, and composer whose works reshaped Bengali literature and music in the late 19th and early 20th centuries. He became Asia's first Nobel laureate when he won the 1913 Nobel Prize in Literature.

A Pirali Bengali Brahmin from Calcutta, Tagore first wrote poems at the age of eight. At the age of sixteen, he published his first substantial poetry under the pseudonym *Bhanushingho* ("Sun Lion") and wrote his first short stories and dramas in 1877. His home schooling, life in Shilaidaha, and travels made Tagore a nonconformist and pragmatist.

Tagore strongly protested against the British Raj and gave his support to the Indian Independence Movement and Mahatma Gandhi. Tagore's life was tragic—he lost virtually his entire family and was devastated to witness Bengal's decline—but his life's work endured, in the form of his poetry and the institution he founded, Visva-Bharati University.

Tagore wrote novels, short stories, songs, dance-dramas, and essays on political and personal topics. *Gitanjali* (*Song Offerings*), *Gora* (*Fair-Faced*), and *Ghare-Baire* (*The Home and the World*) are among his best-known works. His verse, short stories, and novels, which often exhibited rhythmic lyricism, colloquial language, meditative naturalism, and philosophical contemplation, received worldwide acclaim. Tagore was also a cultural reformer and polymath who modernised Bengali art by rejecting strictures binding it to classical Indian forms. Two songs from his *rabindrasangeet* canon are now the national anthems of Bangladesh and India: the *Amar Shonar Bangla* and the *Jana Gana Mana*.

EARLY LIFE

Tagore (nicknamed "Rabi") was born the youngest of thirteen surviving children in the Jorasanko mansion in Calcutta (now Kolkata, India) of parents Debendranath Tagore and Sarada Devi. After undergoing his *upanayan* (the *sacred thread* ceremony, a coming-of-age rite) at age eleven, Tagore and his father left Calcutta on 14 February 1873 to tour India for several months, visiting his father's Santiniketan estate and Amritsar before reaching the Himalayan hill station of Dalhousie. There, Tagore read biographies, studied history, astronomy, modern science, and Sanskrit, and examined the classical poetry of Klidsa. In 1877, he rose to notability when he composed several works, including a long poem set in the Maithili style pioneered by Vidyapati. As a joke, he maintained that these were the lost works of BhnusiCha, a newly discovered 17th-century VaicGava poet. He also wrote "Bhikharini" (1877; "The Beggar Woman"—the Bengali language's first short story) and *Sandhya Sangit* (1882) —including the famous poem "Nirjharer Swapnabhanga" ("The Rousing of the Waterfall").

Seeking to become a barrister, Tagore enrolled at a public school in Brighton, England in 1878. He studied law at University College London, but returned to Bengal in 1880 without a degree. On 9 December 1883 he married Mrinalini Devi (born Bhabatarini, 1873–1902); they had five children, two of whom later died before reaching adulthood. In 1890, Tagore began managing his family's estates in Shilaidaha, a region now in Bangladesh; he was joined by his wife and children in 1898. Known as "Zamindar Babu", Tagore traveled across the vast estate while living out of the family's luxurious barge, the *Padma*, to collect (mostly token) rents and bless villagers; in return, appreciative villagers held feasts in his honour. These years, which composed Tagore's *Sadhana* period (1891–1895; named for one of Tagore's magazines), were among his most fecund. More than half the stories of the three-volume and eighty-four-story *Galpaguchchha* written. With irony and emotional weight, they depicted a wide range of Bengali lifestyles, particularly village life.

SANTINIKETAN

In 1901, Tagore left Shilaidaha and moved to Santiniketan (West Bengal) to found an ashram, which would grow to include a marble-floored prayer hall ("The Mandir"), an experimental school, groves of trees, gardens, and a library. There, Tagore's wife and two of his children died. His father died on 19 January 1905, and he began receiving monthly payments as part of his inheritance. He received additional income from the Maharaja of Tripura, sales of his family's jewellery, his seaside bungalow in Puri, and mediocre royalties (Rs. 2,000) from his works. These works gained him a large following among Bengali and foreign readers alike, and he published such works as *Naivedya* (1901) and *Kheya* (1906) while translating his poems into free verse. On 14 November 1913, Tagore learned that he had won the 1913 Nobel Prize in Literature. According to the Swedish Academy, it was given due to the idealistic and—for Western readers—accessible nature of a small body of his translated material, including the 1912 *Gitanjali: Song Offerings*. In 1915, Tagore also accepted knighthood from the British Crown.

In 1921, Tagore and agricultural economist Leonard Elmhirst set up the Institute for Rural Reconstruction (which Tagore later renamed Shriniketan—"Abode of Peace") in Surul, a village near the ashram at Santiniketan. Through it, Tagore sought to provide an alternative to Gandhi's symbol- and protest-based *Swaraj* movement, which he denounced. He recruited scholars, donors, and officials from many countries to help the Institute use schooling to "free village[s] from the shackles of helplessness and ignorance" by "vitaliz[ing] knowledge". In the early 1930s, he also grew more concerned about India's "abnormal caste consciousness" and untouchability, lecturing on its evils, writing poems and dramas with untouchable protagonists, and appealing to authorities at the Guruvayoor Temple to admit Dalits.

TWILIGHT YEARS

In his last decade, Tagore remained in the public limelight, publicly upbraiding Gandhi for stating that a massive 15 January 1934 earthquake in Bihar constituted divine retribution for the subjugation of Dalits. He also mourned the incipient socioeconomic decline of Bengal and the endemic poverty of Calcutta; he detailed the latter in an unrhymed hundred-line poem whose technique of searing double-vision would foreshadow Satyajit Ray's film *Apur Sansar*. Tagore also compiled fifteen volumes of writings, including the prose-poems works *Punashcha* (1932), *Shes Saptak* (1935), and *Patraput* (1936). He continued his experimentations by developing prose-songs and dance-dramas, including *Chitrangada* (1914), *Shyama* (1939), and *Chandalika* (1938), and wrote the novels *Dui Bon* (1933), *Malancha* (1934), and *Char Adhyay* (1934). Tagore took an interest in science in his last years, writing *Visva-Parichay* (a collection of essays) in 1937. His exploration of biology, physics, and astronomy impacted his poetry, which often contained extensive naturalism that underscored his respect for scientific laws. He also wove the process of science (including narratives of scientists) into many stories contained in such volumes as *Se* (1937), *Tin Sangi* (1940), and *Galpasalpa* (1941).

Tagore's last four years were marked by chronic pain and two long periods of illness. These began when Tagore lost consciousness in late 1937; he remained comatose and near death for an extended period. This was followed three years later in late 1940 by a similar spell, from which he never recovered. The poetry Tagore wrote in these years is among his finest, and is distinctive for its preoccupation with death. After extended suffering, Tagore died on 7 August 1941 (22 Shravan 1348) in an upstairs room of the Jorasanko mansion in which he was raised; his death anniversary is still mourned in public functions held across the Bengali-speaking world.

TRAVELS

Owing to his notable wanderlust, between 1878 and 1932, Tagore visited more than thirty countries on five continents; many of these trips were crucial in familiarising non-Indian audiences to his works and spreading his political ideas. In 1912, he took a sheaf of his translated works to England, where they impressed missionary and Gandhi protégé Charles F. Andrews, Anglo-Irish poet William Butler Yeats, Ezra Pound, Robert Bridges, Ernest Rhys, Thomas Sturge Moore, and others. Indeed, Yeats wrote the preface to the English translation of Gitanjali, while Andrews joined Tagore at Santiniketan.

On 10 November 1912, Tagore toured the United States and the United Kingdom, staying in Butterton, Staffordshire with Andrews' clergymen friends. From 3 May 1916 until April 1917, Tagore went on lecturing circuits in Japan and the United States, during which he denounced nationalism—particularly that of the Japanese and Americans. He also wrote the essay "Nationalism in India", attracting both derision and praise (the latter from pacifists, including Romain Rolland). Shortly after returning to India, the 63-year-old Tagore visited Peru at the invitation of the Peruvian government, and took the opportunity to visit Mexico as well. Both governments pledged donations of $100,000 to the school at Shantiniketan (Visva-Bharati) in commemoration of his visits. A week after his November 6, 1924 arrival in Buenos Aires, Argentina, an ill Tagore moved into the Villa Miralrío at the behest of Victoria Ocampo. He left for India in January 1925. On 30 May 1926, Tagore reached Naples, Italy; he met fascist dictator Benito Mussolini in Rome the next day. Their initially warm rapport lasted until Tagore spoke out against Mussolini on 20 July 1926.

On 14 July 1927, Tagore and two companions began a four-month tour of Southeast Asia, visiting Bali, Java, Kuala Lumpur, Malacca, Penang, Siam, and Singapore. Tagore's travelogues from the tour were collected into the work "Jatri". In early 1930 he left Bengal for a nearly year-long tour of Europe and the United States. Once he returned to the UK, while his paintings were being exhibited in Paris and London, he stayed at a Friends settlement in Birmingham.

There, he wrote his Hibbert Lectures for the University of Oxford (which dealt with the "idea of the humanity of our God, or the divinity of Man the Eternal") and spoke at London's annual Quaker gathering. There (addressing relations between the British and Indians, a topic he would grapple with over the next two years), Tagore spoke of a "dark chasm of aloofness". He later visited Aga Khan III, stayed at Dartington Hall, then toured Denmark, Switzerland, and Germany from June to mid-September 1930, then the Soviet Union.

Lastly, in April 1932, Tagore—who was acquainted with the legends and works of the Persian mystic Hafez—was invited as a personal guest of Shah Reza Shah Pahlavi of Iran. Such extensive travels allowed Tagore to interact with many notable contemporaries, including Henri Bergson, Albert Einstein, Robert Frost, Thomas Mann, George Bernard Shaw, H.G. Wells and Romain Rolland. Tagore's last travels abroad, including visits to Persia and Iraq (in 1932) and Ceylon in 1933, only sharpened his opinions regarding human divisions and nationalism.

WORKS

Tagore's Bengali-language initials are worked into this "Ra-Tha" wooden seal, which bears close stylistic similarity to designs used in traditional Haida carvings. Tagore often embellished his manuscripts with such art. (Dyson 2001)

Tagore's literary reputation is disproportionately influenced by regard for his poetry; however, he also wrote novels, essays, short stories, travelogues, dramas, and thousands of songs. Of Tagore's prose, his short stories are perhaps most highly regarded; indeed, he is credited with originating the Bengali-language version of the genre. His works are frequently noted for their rhythmic, optimistic, and lyrical nature. Such stories mostly borrow from deceptively simple subject matter: the lives of ordinary people.

NOVELS AND NON-FICTION

Tagore wrote eight novels and four novellas, including *Chaturanga*, *Shesher Kobita*, *Char Odhay*, and *Noukadubi*. *Ghare Baire* (*The Home and the World*)—through the lens of the idealistic *zamindar* protagonist Nikhil—excoriates rising Indian nationalism, terrorism, and religious zeal in the *Swadeshi* movement; a frank expression of Tagore's conflicted sentiments, it emerged out of a 1914 bout of depression. Indeed, the novel bleakly ends with Hindu-Muslim sectarian violence and Nikhil's being (probably mortally) wounded. In some sense, *Gora* shares the same theme, raising controversial questions regarding the Indian identity. As with *Ghore Baire*, matters of self-identity (*jti*), personal freedom, and religion are developed in the context of a family story and love triangle. Another powerful story is *Yogayog* (*Nexus*), where the heroine Kumudini—bound by the ideals of *Shiva-Sati*, exemplified by Dkshyani—is torn between her pity for the sinking fortunes of her progressive and compassionate elder brother and his foil: her exploitative, rakish, and patriarchical husband. In it, Tagore demonstrates his feminist leanings, using *pathos* to depict the plight and ultimate demise of Bengali women trapped by pregnancy, duty, and family honour; simultaneously, he treats the decline of Bengal's landed oligarchy.

Other novels were more uplifting: *Shesher Kobita* (translated twice—*Last Poem* and *Farewell Song*) is his most lyrical novel, with poems and rhythmic passages written by the main character (a poet). It also contains elements of satire and postmodernism; stock characters gleefully attack the reputation of an old, outmoded, oppressively renowned poet who, incidentally, goes by the name of Rabindranath Tagore. Though his novels remain among the least-appreciated of his works, they have been given renewed attention via film adaptations by such directors as Satyajit Ray; these include *Chokher Bali* and *Ghare Baire;* many have soundtracks featuring selections from Tagore's own *rabindrasangit*. Tagore wrote many non-fiction books, writing on topics ranging from Indian history to linguistics. Aside from autobiographical works, his travelogues, essays, and lectures were compiled into several volumes, including *Iurop Jatrir Patro* (*Letters from Europe*) and *Manusher Dhormo* (*The Religion of Man*).

MUSIC AND ARTWORK

Tagore was a prolific musician and painter, writing around 2,230 songs. They compose *rabindrasangit* now an integral part of Bengali culture. Tagore's music is inseparable from his literature, most of which—poems or parts of novels, stories, or plays alike—became lyrics for his songs. Primarily influenced by the *thumri* style of Hindustani classical music, they ran the entire gamut of human emotion, ranging from his early dirge-like Brahmo devotional hymns to quasi-erotic compositions. They emulated the tonal colour of classical *ragas* to varying extents. Though at times his songs mimicked a given raga's melody and rhythm faithfully, he also blended elements of different ragas to create innovative works.

For Bengalis, their appeal, stemming from the combination of emotive strength and beauty described as surpassing even Tagore's poetry, was such that the *Modern Review* observed that "[t]here is in Bengal no cultured home where Rabindranath's songs are not sung or at least attempted to be sung ... Even illiterate villagers sing his songs". Music critic Arthur Strangways of *The Observer* first introduced non-Bengalis to *rabindrasangeet* with his book *The Music of Hindostan,* which described it as a "vehicle of a personality ... [that] go behind this or that system of music to that beauty of sound which all systems put out their hands to seize." Among them are Bangladesh's national anthem *Amar Shonar Bangla* and India's national anthem *Jana Gana Mana;* Tagore thus became the only person ever to have written the national anthems of two nations. In turn, *rabindrasangeet* influenced the styles of such musicians as siṭar maestro Vilayat Khan, and the *sarodiyas* Buddhadev Dasgupta and Amjad Ali Khan.

At age sixty, Tagore took up drawing and painting; successful exhibitions of his many works—which made a debut appearance in Paris upon encouragement by artists he met in the south of France—were held throughout Europe. Tagore—who likely exhibited protanopia ("colour blindness"), or partial lack of (red-green, in Tagore's case) colour discernment—painted in a style characterised by peculiarities in aesthetics and colouring schemes. Nevertheless, Tagore took to emulating numerous styles, including that of craftwork by the Malanggan people of northern New Ireland, Haida carvings from the west coast of Canada (British Columbia), and woodcuts by Max Pechstein. Tagore also had an artist's eye for his own handwriting, embellishing the scribbles, cross-outs, and word layouts in his manuscripts with simple artistic leitmotifs, including simple rhythmic designs.

THEATRICAL PIECES

Tagore's experience in theatre began at age sixteen, when he played the lead role in his brother Jyotirindranath's adaptation of Molière's *Le Bourgeois Gentilhomme*. At age twenty, he wrote his first drama-opera—*Valmiki Pratibha* (*The Genius of Valmiki*)—which describes how the bandit Valmiki reforms his ethos, is blessed by Saraswati, and composes the *Ramayana*. Through it, Tagore vigorously explores a wide range of dramatic styles and emotions, including usage of revamped *kirtans* and adaptation of traditional English and Irish folk melodies as drinking songs. Another notable play, *Dak Ghar* (*The Post Office*), describes how a child—striving to escape his stuffy confines—ultimately "fall[s] asleep" (which suggests his physical death). A story with worldwide appeal (it received rave reviews in Europe), *Dak Ghar* dealt with death as, in Tagore's words, "spiritual freedom" from "the world of hoarded wealth and certified creeds".

His other works—emphasizing fusion of lyrical flow and emotional rhythm tightly focused on a core idea—were unlike previous Bengali dramas. His works sought to articulate, in Tagore's words, "the play of feeling and not of action". In 1890 he wrote *Visarjan* (*Sacrifice*), regarded as his finest drama. The Bengali-language originals included intricate subplots and extended monologues. Later, his dramas probed more philosophical and allegorical themes; these included *Dak Ghar*. Another is Tagore's *Chandalika* (*Untouchable Girl*), which was modeled on an ancient Buddhist legend describing how Ananda—the Gautama Buddha's disciple—asks water of an *Adivasi* ("untouchable") girl. Lastly, among his most famous dramas is *Raktakaravi* (*Red Oleanders*), which tells of a kleptocratic king who enriches himself by forcing his subjects to mine. The heroine, Nandini, eventually rallies the common people to destroy these symbols of subjugation. Tagore's other plays include *Chitrangada*, *Raja*, and *Mayar Khela*. Dance dramas based on Tagore's plays are commonly referred to as *rabindra nritya natyas*.

SHORT STORIES

Tagore's "Sadhana" period, comprising the four years from 1891 to 1895, was named for one of Tagore's magazines. This period was among Tagore's most fecund, yielding more than half the stories contained in the three-volume *Galpaguchchha*, which itself is a collection of eighty-four stories. Such stories usually showcase Tagore's reflections upon his surroundings, on modern and fashionable ideas, and on interesting mind puzzles (which Tagore was fond of testing his intellect with). Tagore typically associated his earliest stories (such as those of the "*Sadhana*" period) with an exuberance of vitality and spontaneity; these characteristics were intimately connected with Tagore's life in the common villages of, among others, Patisar, Shajadpur, and Shilaida while managing the Tagore family's vast landholdings. There, he beheld the lives of India's poor and common people; Tagore thereby took to examining their lives with a penetrative depth and feeling that was singular in Indian literature up to that point.

In "The Fruitseller from Kabul", Tagore speaks in first person as town-dweller and novelist who chances upon the Afghani seller. He attempts to distil the sense of longing felt by those long trapped in the mundane and hardscrabble confines of Indian urban life, giving play to dreams of a different existence in the distant and wild mountains: "There were autumn mornings, the time of year when kings of old went forth to conquest; and I, never stirring from my little corner in Calcutta, would let my mind wander over the whole world. At the very name of another country, my heart would go out to it ... I would fall to weaving a network of dreams: the mountains, the glens, the forest .... ". Many of the other *Galpaguchchha* stories were written in Tagore's *Sabuj Patra* period (1914–1917; also named for one of Tagore's magazines).

Tagore's *Golpoguchchho* (*Bunch of Stories*) remains among Bengali literature's most popular fictional works, providing subject matter for many successful films and theatrical plays. Satyajit Ray's film *Charulata* was based upon Tagore's controversial novella, *Nastanirh* (*The Broken Nest*). In *Atithi* (also made into a film), the young Brahmin boy Tarapada shares a boat ride with a village zamindar. The boy reveals that he has run away from home, only to wander around ever since. Taking pity, the zamindar adopts him and ultimately arranges his marriage to the zamindar's own daughter. However, the night before the wedding, Tarapada runs off—again. *Strir Patra* (*The Letter from the Wife*) is among Bengali literature's earliest depictions of the bold emancipation of women. The heroine Mrinal, the wife of a typical patriarchical Bengali middle class man, writes a letter while she is traveling (which constitutes the whole story). It details the pettiness of her life and struggles; she finally declares that she will not return to her husband's home with the statement *Amio bachbo. Ei bachlum* ("And I shall live. Here, I live").

In *Haimanti*, Tagore takes on the institution of Hindu marriage, describing the dismal lifelessness of married Bengali women, hypocrisies plaguing the Indian middle classes, and how Haimanti, a sensitive young woman, must—due to her sensitiveness and free spirit—sacrifice her life. In the last passage, Tagore directly attacks the Hindu custom of glorifying Sita's attempted self-immolation as a means of appeasing her husband Rama's doubts. Tagore also examines Hindu-Muslim tensions in *Musalmani Didi*, which in many ways embodies the essence of Tagore's humanism. On the other hand, *Darpaharan* exhibits Tagore's self-consciousness, describing a young man harboring literary ambitions. Though he loves his wife, he wishes to stifle her own literary career, deeming it unfeminine. Tagore himself, in his youth, seems to have harboured similar ideas about women. *Darpaharan* depicts the final humbling of the man via his acceptance of his wife's talents. As many other Tagore stories, *Jibito o Mrito* provides the Bengalis with one of their more widely used epigrams: *Kadombini moriya proman korilo she more nai* ("Kadombini died, thereby proved that she hadn't").

POETRY

Tagore's poetry—which varied in style from classical formalism to the comic, visionary, and ecstatic—proceeds out a lineage established by 15th- and 16th-century VaicGava poets. Tagore was also influenced by the mysticism of the *rishi*-authors who—including Vyasa—wrote the Upanishads, the Bhakta-Sufi mystic Kabir, and Ramprasad. Yet Tagore's poetry became most innovative and mature after his exposure to rural Bengal's folk music, which included ballads sung by Bul folk singers—especially the bard Llan Zh. These—which were rediscovered and popularised by Tagore—resemble 19th-century Kartbhaj hymns that emphasize inward divinity and rebellion against religious and social orthodoxy. During his Shilaidaha years, his poems took on a lyrical quality, speaking via the *maner manus* (the Bauls' "man within the heart") or meditating upon the *jivan devata* ("living God within"). This figure thus sought connection with divinity through appeal to nature and the emotional interplay of human drama. Tagore used such techniques in his BhnusiCha poems (which chronicle the romanticism between Radha and Krishna), which he repeatedly revised over the course of seventy years.

Later, Tagore responded to the (mostly) crude emergence of modernism and realism in Bengali literature by writing experimental works in the 1930s. Examples works include *Africa* and *Camalia*, which are among the better known of his latter poems. He also occasionally wrote poems using *Shadhu Bhasha* (a Sanskritised dialect of Bengali); later, he began using *Cholti Bhasha* (a more popular dialect). Other notable works include *Manasi*, *Sonar Tori* (*Golden Boat*), *Balaka* (*Wild Geese*—the title being a metaphor for migrating souls), and *Purobi*. *Sonar Tori*'s most famous poem—dealing with the ephemeral nature of life and achievement—goes by the same name; it ends with the haunting phrase (*"Shunno nodir tire rohinu po°i / Jaha chhilo loe gêlo shonar tori"*—"all I had achieved was carried off on the golden boat—only I was left behind."). Internationally, *Gitanjali* is Tagore's best-known collection, winning him his Nobel Prize.

"My song has put off her adornments. She has no pride of dress and decoration. Ornaments would mar our union; they would come between thee and me; their jingling would drown thy whispers."

"My poet's vanity dies in shame before thy sight. O master poet, I have sat down at thy feet. Only let me make my life simple and straight, like a flute of reed for thee to fill with music."

"Klanti" the sixth poem in *Gitali*, reads:

Klanti amar khôma kôro, probhuPôthe jodi pichhie po°i kobhuEi je hia thôro thôro kãpe aji êmontôro,Ei bedona khôma kôro, khôma kôro probhu.Ei dinota khôma kôro, probhu,Pichhon-pane takai jodi kobhu.Diner tape roudrojalae shukae mala pujar thalae,Shei mlanota khôma kôro, khôma kôro, probhu.

Tagore's poetry has been set to music by various composers, among them classical composer Arthur Shepherd's triptych for soprano and string quartet.

POLITICAL VIEWS

Marked complexities characterise Tagore's political views. He criticised European imperialism and supported Indian nationalists and although he himself vehemently denied it at the time, the evidence produced during the Hindu-German Conspiracy trial, as well as some later accounts, he was aware of the conspiracy and even interviewed the then Japanese premier Count Terauchi and former premier Count Okuma on behalf of the conspirators to try and enlist Japanese support. However, he also lampooned the Swadeshi movement, denouncing it in "The Cult of the Charka", an acrid 1925 essay. Instead, he emphasized self-help and intellectual uplift of the masses, stating that British imperialism was not a primary evil, but instead a "political symptom of our social disease", urging Indians to accept that "there can be no question of blind revolution, but of steady and purposeful education". Such views inevitably enraged many, placing his life in danger: during his stay in a San Francisco hotel in late 1916, Tagore narrowly escaped assassination by Indian expatriates. The plot failed only because the would-be assassins fell into argument. Yet Tagore wrote songs lionizing the Indian independence movement and renounced his knighthood in protest against the 1919 Jallianwala Bagh Massacre. Two of Tagore's more politically charged compositions, "Chitto Jetha Bhayshunyo" ("Where the Mind is Without Fear") and "Ekla Chalo Re" ("If They Answer Not to Thy Call, Walk Alone"), gained mass appeal, with the latter favoured by Gandhi. Despite his tumultuous relations with Gandhi, Tagore was key in resolving a Gandhi-Ambedkar dispute involving separate electorates for untouchables, ending Gandhi's fast "unto death".

Tagore also criticised orthodox (rote-oriented) education, lampooning it in the short story "The Parrot's Training", where a bird—which ultimately dies—is caged by tutors and force-fed pages torn from books. These views led Tagore—while visiting Santa Barbara, California on 11 October 1917—to conceive of a new type of university, desiring to "make [his ashram at] Santiniketan the connecting thread between India and the world ... [and] a world center for the study of humanity ... somewhere beyond the limits of nation and geography." The school—which he named Visva-Bharati—had its foundation stone laid on 22 December 1918; it was later inaugurated on 22 December 1921. Here, Tagore implemented a *brahmacharya* pedagogical structure employing *gurus* to provide individualised guidance for pupils. Tagore worked hard to fundraise for and staff the school, even contributing all of his Nobel Prize monies. Tagore's duties as steward and mentor at Santiniketan kept him busy; he taught classes in mornings and wrote the students' textbooks in afternoons and evenings. Tagore also fundraised extensively for the school in Europe and the U.S. between 1919 and 1921.

IMPACT AND LEGACY

Tagore's post-death impact can be felt through the many festivals held worldwide in his honour—examples include the annual Bengali festival/celebration of *Kabipranam* (Tagore's birthday anniversary), the annual Tagore Festival held in Urbana, Illinois in the United States, the *Rabindra Path Parikrama* walking pilgrimages leading from Calcutta to Shantiniketan, and ceremonial recitals of Tagore's poetry held on important anniversaries. This legacy is most palpable in Bengali culture, ranging from language and arts to history and politics; indeed, Nobel laureate Amartya Sen noted that even for modern Bengalis, Tagore was a "towering figure", being a "deeply relevant and many-sided contemporary thinker". Tagore's collected Bengali-language writings—the 1939 *Rab+ndra Racanval+*—is also canonized as one of Bengal's greatest cultural treasures, while Tagore himself has been proclaimed "the greatest poet India has produced".

Tagore was famed throughout much of Europe, North America, and East Asia. He was key in founding Dartington Hall School, a progressive coeducational institution; in Japan, he influenced such figures as Nobel laureate Yasunari Kawabata. Tagore's works were widely translated into English, Dutch, German, Spanish, and other European languages by Czech indologist Vincent Slesny, French Nobel laureate André Gide, Russian poet Anna Akhmatova, and others. In the United States, Tagore's popular lecturing circuits (especially those between 1916–1917) were widely attended and acclaimed. Nevertheless, several controversies involving Tagore resulted in a decline in his popularity in Japan and North America after the late 1920s, contributing to his "near total eclipse" outside of Bengal.

Tagore, through Spanish translations of his works, also influenced leading figures of Spanish literature, including Chileans Pablo Neruda and Gabriela Mistral, Mexican writer Octavio Paz, and Spaniards José Ortega y Gasset, Zenobia Camprubí, and Juan Ramón Jiménez. Between 1914 and 1922, the Jiménez-Camprubí spouses translated no less than twenty-two of Tagore's books from English into Spanish. Jiménez, as part of this work, also extensively revised and adapted such works as Tagore's *The Crescent Moon*. Indeed, during this time, Jiménez developed the now-heralded innovation of "naked poetry" (Spanish: *«poesia desnuda»*). Ortega y Gasset wrote that "Tagore's wide appeal [may stem from the fact that] he speaks of longings for perfection that we all have ... Tagore awakens a dormant sense of childish wonder, and he saturates the air with all kinds of enchanting promises for the reader, who ... pays little attention to the deeper import of Oriental mysticism". Tagore's works were published in free editions around 1920 alongside works by Dante Alighieri, Miguel de Cervantes, Johann Wolfgang von Goethe, Plato, and Leo Tolstoy.

Tagore's talents came to be regarded as overrated by several westerners. Graham Greene doubted that "anyone but Mr. Yeats can still take his poems very seriously." Modern remnants of a once widespread Latin American reverence of Tagore were discovered, for example, by an astonished Salman Rushdie during a trip to Nicaragua.

LIFE OF RABINDRANATH TAGORE (1861–1901)

The life of Rabindranath Tagore (1861–1941) covers the first four decades of his life; these were formative of both his artistic and much of his political thinking. Rabindranath Tagore was a Bengali poet, Brahmo philosopher, and scholar.

FAMILY BACKGROUND

Tagore was born at No. 6 Dwarkanath Tagore Lane, Jorasanko — the address of his family mansion. In turn, Jorasanko was located in the Bengali section of north Kolkata, located near Chitpur Road. The area immediately around the Jorasanko Tagore mansion was rife with poverty and prostitution. He was the son of Debendranath Tagore and Sarada Devi. Debendranath Tagore had formulated the Brahmo faith propagated by his friend, the reformer Raja Ram Mohan Roy. Debendranath became the central figure in Brahmo society after Ray's death, who was addressed out of respect by followers as *maharishi*. He continued to lead the *Adi Brahmo Shomaj* until he died. Women who married into Tagore's clan were generally from the villages of East Bengal (now Bangladesh).

CHILDHOOD (1861–1878)

Tagore was born the youngest of fourteen children. As a child, Tagore lived amidst an atmosphere where literary magazines were published, musical recitals were held, and theatre performed. The Jorasanko Tagores were indeed at the center of a large and art-loving social group. Tagore's oldest brother, Dwijendranath, was a respected philosopher and poet. Another brother, Satyendranath, was the first ethnically Indian member appointed to the elite and formerly all-white Indian Civil Service. Yet another brother, Jyotirindranath Tagore, was a talented musician, composer, and playwright.

Among his sisters, Swarnakumari Devi earned fame as a novelist in her own right. Jyotirindranath's wife, Kadambari — who was slightly older than Tagore — was a dear friend and a powerful influence on Tagore. Her abrupt suicide in 1884 left him distraught for years, and left a profound mark on the emotional timbre of Tagore's literary life.

Tagore — nicknamed "Rabi" — was born the youngest of fourteen children. As part of the Jorasanko branch of the Tagore family, Tagore grew up exposed to the publication of literary magazines, in-home musical recitals, and theatrical performances. Tagore was also influenced by older brothers Dwijendranath (a philosopher), Satyendranath (the first Indian appointed to the elite Indian Civil Service), and Jyotirindranath (a musician, composer, and playwright). His female relatives included sister Swarna Kumari Devi (a novelist) and Kadambari (Jyotirindranath's wife, whose 1884 suicide burdened Tagore for years).

For the first decade or so of his life, Tagore remained distant from his father, who was frequently away touring northern India, England, and other places. Meanwhile, Tagore was mostly confined to the family compound — he was forbidden to leave it for any purpose other than traveling to school. He thereby grew increasingly restless for the outside world, open spaces, and nature. On the other hand, Tagore was intimidated by the mansion's perceived ghostly and enigmatic aura.

Further, Tagore was ordered about the house by servants in a period he would later designate as a "servocracy". Incidents included servants dunking the heads of Tagore and his siblings into drinking water held by giant clay cisterns — used as a means to quiet the children. In addition, Tagore often refused food to satisfy servants, was confined to a chalk circle by the second-in-command servant named Shyam in parody of an analogous forest trial that Sita underwent in the *Ramayana*, and was told horrific stories telling the bloody exploits of outlaw dacoits.

Tagore was also was tutored at home by Hemendranath, his brother. While being physically conditioned — for example, swimming in the Ganges River, taking long treks through hilly areas, and practicing judo and wrestling — he was also given Bengali-language lessons in anatomy, drawing, English language (Tagore's least favorite subject), geography, gymnastics, history, literature, mathematics, and Sanskrit imparted before and after school. Meanwhile, Tagore was developed an aversion towards formal learning and schooling, stating later that the role of teaching was not to explain things, but rather to

> *"knock at the doors of the mind. If any boy is asked to give an account of what is awakened in him by such knocking, he will probably say something silly. For what happens within is much bigger than what comes out in words. Those who pin their faith on university examinations as the test of education take no account of this."*

Tagore started writing poems around age eight, and he was urged by an older brother to recite these to people in the mansion — including to an impressed Brahmo nationalist, newspaper editor, and Hindu Mela organizer. At age eleven, Tagore underwent the *upanayan* coming-of-age rite: he and two relatives were shaved bald and sent into retreat, where they were to chant and meditate. Tagore instead rollicked, beating drums and pulling his brothers' ears, after which he received a sacred thread of investiture. Afterward, on February 14, 1873, Tagore experienced the first close contact with his father when they set out together from Calcutta on a months-long tour of India. They first made for Shantiniketan ("Abode of Peace"), a family estate acquired in 1863 by Debendranath composed of two rooms set amidst a mango grove, trees, and plants. Tagore later recalled his stay among the rice paddies:

> *"What I could not see did not take me long to get over — what I did see was quite enough. There was no servant rule, and the only ring which encircled me was the blue of the horizon, drawn around these [rural] solitudes by their presiding goddess. Within this I was free to move about as I chose."*

After several weeks, they traveled to Amritsar, staying near the Harmandir Sahib and worshipping at a Sikh gurudwara. They also read English- and Sanskrit-language books, exposing Tagore to astronomy, biographies of such figures as Benjamin Franklin, and Edward Gibbon's *The History of the Decline and Fall of the Roman Empire*.

Later, in mid-April, Tagore and his father set off for the remote and frigid Himalayan hill station of Dalhousie, India, near what is now Himachal Pradesh's border with Kashmir. There, at an elevation of some 2,300 meters (7,500 feet), they lived in a house high atop Bakrota hill. Tagore was taken aback by the region's deep gorges, alpine forests, and mossy streams and waterfalls. Yet Tagore was also made to study lessons — including such things as Sanskrit declensions — starting in the icy pre-dawn twilight. Tagore took a break from his readings for a noontime meal; thereafter, Tagore was to continue his studies, although Tagore was often allowed to fall asleep. Some two months later, Tagore left his father in Dalhousie and journeyed back to Calcutta.

SCHOOLING IN ENGLAND

In early October 1878, Tagore traveled to England with the intent of becoming a barrister. He first stayed for some months at a house that the Tagore family owned near Brighton and Hove, in Medina Villas; there, he attended a Brighton school (not, as has been claimed, Brighton College — his name does not appear in its admissions register). In 1877, his nephew and niece — Suren and Indira, the children of Tagore's brother Satyendranath — were sent together with their mother (Tagore's sister-in-law) to live with him. Later, after spending Christmas of 1878 with his family, Tagore was escorted by his elder brother's friend to London; there, Tagore's relatives hoped that he would focus more on his studies. He enrolled at University College London. However, he never did complete his degree, leaving England after just over a year's stay. This exposure to English culture and language would later percolate into his earlier acquaintance with Bengali musical tradition, allowing him to create new modes of music, poetry, and drama. Nevertheless, Tagore neither fully embraced English strictures nor his family's traditionally strict Hindu religious observances in either his life or in his art, choosing instead to pick the best from both realms of experience.

SHELAIDAHA

In 1890, Tagore began managing his family's estates in Shelaidaha, a region now in Bangladesh; he was joined by his wife and children in 1898. Tagore, known then as "Zamindar Babu", often traveled dozens of miles across the vast estate while living out of the *Padma*, the family's converted flat-bottomed keel-less barge (known as a "budgerow" or a *Daccai bajras*). His dealings with his tenants included the annual collection of (mostly token) rents and the blessing of villagers; in exchange for his generosity, villagers regularly held feasts in Tagore's honour — these featured such fare as dried rice and sour milk.

In this decade, Tagore authored many works and founded a new genre of Bengali writing: the short story. Tagore wrote some fifty-nine of them in 1891–1901; many had ironic elements or had emotional appeal while they dealt with a wide range of Bengali lifestyles. Examples include *Sonar Tari* (1894), *Chitra* (1896), and *Katha O Kahini* (1900); his essays, poems, and plays of the time also touched on village life.

LIFE OF RABINDRANATH TAGORE (1901–1932)

The life of Rabindranath Tagore (1901–1924) concerns his life in Santiniketan and extensive travels throughout Asia, Europe, and Japan. Rabindranath Tagore was a Bengali poet, Brahmo philosopher, and scholar.

SANTINIKETAN

In 1901, Tagore left Shelaidaha and moved to Shantiniketan, about one hundred miles to Calcutta's northwest in what is now

West Bengal. Shantiniketan, a spread of relatively arid and eroded red soil of seven acres bought in the 1860s by Debendranth, was made the home of Tagore's new ashram, a marble-floored prayer hall ("The Mandir"), experimental school, groves of trees, gardens, and a library. Unfortunately, his wife along with two of his children — Renuka (in 1903) and Samindranath (in 1907) — died in this period, leaving Tagore distraught. When Tagore's father — aged 87 — also died on January 19, 1905, Tagore began receiving 1,250–1,500 rupees (Rs.) monthly as an inheritance. This combined with income from the Maharaja of Tripura, sales of jewelry owned by him and his late wife, his bungalow at the seaside Puri, and mediocre royalties (Rs. 2,000) gleaned from the licensed publishing of thousands of copies of his works.

Thus, he gained a large following among Bengali readers. He published such works as *Naivedya* (1901) and *Kheya* (1906). Non-Bangla translations were also published, but these were frequently of mediocre quality. In response to requests by admirers (including painter William Rothenstein), Tagore began translating his poems into free verse. In 1912, he went to England while carrying a sheaf of his translated works. At readings there, these works impressed a number of Englishmen, including English missionary and Gandhi protégé Charles F. Andrews, Anglo-Irish poet William Butler Yeats, Ezra Pound, Robert Bridges, Ernest Rhys, and Thomas Sturge Moore. Indeed, Yeats later wrote the preface to the English translation of Gitanjali (published by the India Society), while Andrews joined Tagore in India to work with him.

On 10 November 1912, Tagore traveled to the United States, speaking at a Unitarian church in Urbana, Illinois. In that year, Tagore also toured the United Kingdom, meeting William Rothenstein and William Butler Yeats, who read his *Gitanjali*. Later, he stayed in Butterton, Staffordshire with C.F. Andrews' clergymen friends. On 14 November 1913, he received word that he had won the Nobel Prize in Literature; the award stemmed from the idealistic and accessible (for Western readers) nature of a small body of translated material, including the 1912 *Gitanjali: Song Offerings*.

Together with Mukul Dey, Charles F. Andrews and W. W. Pearson, Tagore again set off by boat on 3 May 1916, embarking on a lecturing circuit of Japan and the United States that was to last until April 1917. During a four-month layover in Japan, Tagore authored "On the Way to Japan" and "In Japan", which were later compiled into the book *Japanyatri* ("A Sojourn to Japan"), which detailed his admiration for the Japanese aesthetic. Yet Tagore also denounced nationalism, particularly that of the Japanese and Americans. He wrote the essay "Nationalism in India", attracting both derision and praise (the latter from pacifists and fellow internationalists like Romain Rolland).

Yet these views also endangered him: during his stay in a San Francisco hotel, Tagore narrowly escaped being assassinated by a pair of Indian expatriates— the plot failed only because the would-be assassins fell into argument concerning whether they should carry through with the murder. The following morning, Tagore left for Santa Barbara, near Los Angeles. There, Tagore meditated among orange groves and conceived of a new type of university, desiring to "make Shantiniketan the connecting thread between India and the world ... [and] a world center for the study of humanity ... somewhere beyond the limits of nation and geography."

The school — which he named Visva-Bharati — had its foundation stone ceremoniously laid on 22 December 1918; it was later inaugurated on 22 December 1921. Tagore's duties as steward and mentor at Santiniketan kept him busy; he taught classes in mornings and wrote textbooks for his students in afternoons and evenings. Of this routine, he wrote that "I long to discover some fairyland of holidays ... where all duties look delightfully undutiful, like clouds bearing rain appearing perfectly inconsequential". Tagore was also occupied with fundraising between 1919 and 1921, undertaking trips to Europe and the U.S.

LIFE OF RABINDRANATH TAGORE (1932–1941)

Last Works of 1932-1937

Tagore's international travels also sharpened his opinion that human divisions were shallow. During a May 1932 visit to a Bedouin encampment in the Iraqi desert, the tribal chief told him that "Our prophet has said that a true Muslim is he by whose words and deeds not the least of his brother-men may ever come to any harm ..." Tagore noted in his diary: "I was startled into recognizing in his words the voice of essential humanity."

In his last decade, Tagore compiled fifteen volumes of writings, including works of prose-poems such as *Punashcha* (1932), *Shes Saptak* (1935), and *Patraput* (1936). He also continued his experimentations by developing prose-songs and dance-dramas, including *Chitrangada* (1936), *Shyama* (1939), and *Chandalika* (1938). He also wrote the novels *Dui Bon* (1933), *Malancha* (1934), and *Char Adhyay* (1934). Tagore also took an interest in science in his last years, writing *Visva-Parichay* (a collection of essays) in 1937. He wrote on topics ranging from biology to physics, and astronomy; meanwhile, his poetry — containing extensive naturalism — underscored his respect for scientific laws. He also wove the process of science (including narratives of scientists) into many stories contained in such volumes as *Se* (1937), *Tin Sangi* (1940), and *Galpasalpa* (1941).

Illness of 1937-1941

Tagore's last four years (1937–1941) were marked by chronic pain and two long periods of illness. These began when Tagore lost consciousness in late 1937; he remained comatose and near death for an extended period. This was followed three years later in late 1940 by a similar spell, from which he never recovered. The poetry Tagore wrote in these twilight years are distinctive for their preoccupation with death; these more profound and mystical experimentations allowed Tagore to be branded a "modern poet". After extended suffering, Tagore died on August 7, 1941 (22 Shravan 1348) in an upstairs room of the Jorasanko mansion in which he was raised. This date is still mourned in public functions held across the Bangla-speaking world.

The last person to see Tagore alive was Amiya Kumar Sen (brother of Sukumar Sen, the first chief election commissioner); Tagore dictated his last poem to Sen, who wrote it down. Sen later donated the resulting draft to a museum in Kolkata.

Chokher Bali

Chokher Bali, literally *Sand of the Eye*, equivalent to *eye-sore*, is a Bengali novel written by Rabindranath Tagore in the early twentieth century, against the backdrop of the Indian Independence Movement.

Plot Summary

Binodini is a young widow left to her own devices when her sickly husband dies soon after they are married. She returns to her village and lives there for a couple of months until she accepts the invitation of Rajlakshmi to live with her and her son, Mahendra (who had rejected a former marriage proposal with Binodini). He is newly married to Ashalata, but eventually realises that he and Binodini are more compatible. The story details the relationships of these three and Mahendra's best friend Behari as they deal with issues like distrust, adultery, lies, and numerous fallings-out between them.

Critical Acclaim

Tagore elaborately records early 20th century Bengali society, through his central character, the rebellious widow, who wants to live a life of her own. In writing this novel he exposes the custom of perpetual mourning on the part of widows, who were not allowed to remarry and were condemned to a life of seclusion and loneliness. It is a melancholy, stirring tale of the deceit and sorrow that arise from dissatisfaction and sorrow. Tagore has said about the novel, "I have always regretted the ending".

ADAPTATIONS

Gitanjali

Gitanjali (Bangla *Gitanjoli*) is a collection of 103 English poems, largely translations, by the Bengali poet Rabindranath Tagore. This volume became very famous in the West, and was widely translated. Gitanjali is also the title of an earlier Bengali volume (1910) of mostly devotional songs. The word *gitanjoli* is a composed from "git", song, and "anjoli", offering, and thus means - "An offering of songs"; but the word for offering, *anjoli,* has a strong devotional connotation, so the title may also be interpreted as "prayer offering of song".

The English collection is not a translation of poems from the Bengali volume of the same name. While half the poems (52 out of 103) in the English text were selected from the Bengali volume, others were taken from these works (given with year and number of songs selected for the English text): *Gitimallo* (1914,17), *Noibeddo* (1901,15), *Khea* (1906,11) and a handful from other works. The translations were often radical, leaving out or altering large chunks of the poem and in one instance even fusing two separate poems (song 95, which unifies songs 89,90 of naivedya).

The translations were undertaken prior to a visit to England in 1912, where the poems were extremely well received. A slender volume was published in 1913, with an exhilarating preface by W. B. Yeats. In the same year, based on a corpus of three thin translations, Rabindranath became the first non-European to win the Nobel prize.

Poetry

The poems of Gitanjali express a largely metaphysical outlook, talking about a union with the "supreme"; but like much western poetry that explores similar themes, the language suggests the union of two earthly lovers. This type of anthropomorphic depiction of celestial love is quite common in the Vaishnava literature of India since the 12th c. (see Vidyapati or Jayadeva). Rabindranath encountered it also in his interactions with the Baul community in rural Bengal. For example, poem 7 in the English volume renders poem 125 from the Bengali gItanjali, *Amar e gan chhe°echhe tar shôkol ôlongkar* and talks of heavenly love in terms of the lover taking off her jewelry, which is getting in the way of the union. See also the poem 18, at the bottom of this page.

Some poems involve themes related to nature, but here, too, the spiritual is subtly present, as in this poem (no. 57), given here along with the Bangla text in Roman script:

Light, my light, the world-filling light, the eye-kissing light, heart-sweetening light!

Ah, the light dances, my darling, at the centre of my life; the light strikes, my darling, the chords of my love; the sky opens, the wind runs wild, laughter passes over the earth.

The butterflies spread their sails on the sea of light. Lilies and jasmines surge up on the crest of the waves of light.

The light is shattered into gold on every cloud, my darling, and it scatters gems in profusion.

Mirth spreads from leaf to leaf, my darling, and gladness without measure. The heaven's river has drowned its banks and the flood of joy is abroad.

Alo amar, alo ogo, alo bhubôn bhôraalo nôeon dhôoa amar, alo hridôe hara.Nache alo nache, o bhaï, amar praner kachhe — baje alo baje, o bhai, hridôe binar majhe —jage akash, chhoþe batash, hashe shôkol dhôra.Alor srote pal tulechhe hajar projapoti.Alor ðheue uþhlo mete mollika maloti.Meghe meghe shona, o bhai, jae na manik gona —patae patae hashi, o bhai, pulôk rashi rashi.Shuronodir kul bhorechhe shudha-nijhôr-jhôra. - Ôcholaeotôn

Legacy

In the English-speaking world, the writings of Tagore are no longer widely read. Nonetheless, for millions of Bangla speakers, the Bengali originals continue to resonate, as in this verse:

Alo amar, alo ogo, alo bhubon bhora

alo noeon dhooa amar, alo hridoe hara.

Nache alo nache, o bhai, amar praner kachhe --

baje alo baje, o bhai, hridoe binar majhe —

jage akash, chhoþe batash, hashe shokol dhora.

Alor srote pal tulechhe hajar projapoti.

Alor ðheue uþhlo mete mollika maloti.

Meghe meghe shona, o bhai, jae na manik gona —

patae patae hashi, o bhai, pulok rashi rashi.

Shuronodir kul bhorechhe shudha-nijhor-jhora. -Ocholaeoton

I stand mesmerized, wondering how you sing your notes hold the world spellbound - the light of your music lights up my universe.

(song 22 of Bengali Gitanjali, song 3 in the English.)

SATYAJIT RAY'S ADAPTATION OF TAGORE

As we think of the models of adaptation we are forced to work with formal definitions of literature or film. It is necessary to recognise the modes and limits of transaction, and that demands positing stable entities between which the transaction takes place. Nevertheless, we also know that it is not a medium but a practice that one has to think of as literary or film texts are produced, practice being itself always adaptive, always redefining the borders between what falls within the medium and what does not. To place adaptation in a historical context could mean considering practice itself as something that conditions the medium rather than the other way round. Besides social and historical contexts one has to also consider here the contexts of the media in question, their own levels of historical development. I would like to illustrate the point with the help of a modern classic from India, Satyajit Ray's *Charulata* (1964).

Soon after the release of *Charulata*, Ray became involved in an intense debate over the changes he made in the original text, 'Nastaneer' ('The Broken Nest'), a 1901 story written by Rabindranath Tagore (Ray 1982). An eminent critic called into question the very necessity of presenting the film as an adaptation of Tagore, whatever the merits of the film were, after such changes as those that Ray brought into 'both the theme and the plot' of the film (Rudra 1996). The story has the structure of a novelette; it is divided into twenty short chapters posing a challenge to a filmmaker who is looking for a tightly integrated narrative. The critic pointed out how Ray has virtually done away with the material of the last seven chapters and added several new elements, to mark a definite break with Tagore. Can departure itself be a mode of adaptation? Ray's reply came up with the most extensive analysis he ever wrote of his own films. He defended the deviations from the original in terms of the treatment of time, causality and character delineation, and in the process explained the primary imperatives of storytelling in cinema.

The story is set in the late nineteenth century Bengal. Bhupati, a well-meaning member of the nationalist gentry, spends most of his time on the political magazine he brings out in English. His young wife Charulata, following the custom, is confined to the inner quarters of the house, spends lonely hours reading novels and doing embroidery. She finds a companion in Bhupati's cousin Amal, a university student of her age. They exchange knowledge of novels, share enthusiasm for literary periodicals, they help each other grow into creative writers. All this happens with encouragement from Bhupati. For Amal, the realisation will come too late that the relationship has grown into love; and he will be in a position to break away from the bond, he will leave the house. For Charu, this organic aspect of growing up, of articulating herself into the world, will not be as easy to disown. She creates a new secret interior within the interior she inhabits as she learns to live with the new reality. Bhupati will come to know about all this after Charu has built that secret chamber, after she returns to him as a wife, so to speak. This discovery of the truth of the home also comes for Bhupati after his public enterprise, the magazine, fails, when he comes back to the inner quarters seeking his wife's company for the first time (see Tagore 1992).

In his essay, Ray explains the basic rules of screenwriting and direction in order to point out the specificity of his medium. The debate took place in the pages of one of the most prestigious literary periodicals of the time, *Parichay*, the readers and contributors of which might have been intellectually advanced in other ways but seemed to require a lesson in film language. The film society movement was still in its early phase, and it is Ray the film society activist speaking here, still engaged in some kind of awareness raising exercise, making audiences familiar with arguments about the autonomy of film. The struggle for autonomy is launched here against a 'literary' perception of cinema.

Ray was one of the founders of the Calcutta Film Society, the first of its kind in India, established in 1947. The critical discourse that he and his colleagues at the Film Society launched can be seen in many ways as a preamble to the realist break that Ray's debut film, *Pather Panchali*, brought about in 1955. But serious discussion of cinema began before this cineaste intervention, it goes back at least to the late 1920s. A spate of film magazines followed the arrival of sound in 1931. The new sound studios employed a large number of writers. Sound redefined Indian cinema in terms of regional practices, regions being linguistically divided in India.

A language - cinema- literature correspondence was established in critical discourse which also set into relief the categories of realism, authenticity and authorship. Writings on cinema from the 1930s and 40s, often by the writers and critics who had joined the industry, present a more or less consistent argument for a regionally grounded contemporary cinema that should mould itself into a novelistic discourse. The *Mythological* film, often thought to be characteristic of Indian popular cinema, became a minor genre in the sound cinema of the Studio Era (1931-55), giving way to the *Social* film as the dominant mode. The *Social* was the mainstream middle-class cinema negotiating the theme of social reform that has informed the novel in all Indian languages since the nineteenth century. The mutations set in motion in the *Social* in the 1940s will finally give rise to two formations, the realist art film launched with *Pather Panchali*, and the classic melodrama that came into being around the same time that *Pather Panchali* appeared.

The question of autonomy figured prominently in the new criticism that arrived in the wake of the Calcutta Film Society. Informed by an exposure to world cinema this criticism came to posit the idea of a national modern cinema, a cinema that would fashion a rational, democratic language free of the pre-modern, non-secular compulsions of the popular film. The arguments for textual autonomy and for rational form were of necessity interrelated.

The heteronomous address of Indian popular cinema, where blocks of spectacle are often combined through a logic of interruption, was the target of this critical discourse; but initially, there was also an older practice of the Studio- *Social* that had to be confronted. This was a kind of 'cinema du papa' - dominated by literary practitioners, where screenplays and films were often judged on the basis of the literary value of dialogue and characters. Major novelists such as Premendra Mitra and Sailajananda Mukhopadhyay were seen to have failed to break into a cinematic language because of their inability to conceive such language in its autonomy. Ray's defence of his adaptation is pitched against the lingering resistance to perceiving the film text in its own terms, the challenge being all the more serious here because of the Tagore factor.

Can we judge *Charulata* on the basis of its independence of literary procedures, of the generic protocols of the original story?

As we watch the film adaptation itself becomes an object of scrutiny. We relish the transformation that Tagore's rich prose has undergone in the wordless passages of *Charulata*, enjoy the method that translates spaces between the words into volume and movement. But there is a second level of contact between the two texts where the whole question of word and image transaction has to be re-considered. At this level, the film takes its distance in time from the original text as a material basis of adaptation; it begins to look at a past of which the literary text itself has become a constitutive element. Hence it was not only the camera penetrating the world captured in the story in order to transform it into another language, it was also a question of framing the story itself as part of a fabric of the past.

'Broken Nest' reads more like a compressed novel than a short story, it moves through extended passages and gaps in time, through episodes and broad developments in characters and situations. The long introductory sequence of *Charulata* is probably the best example of the masterly technique of compression and telescoping Ray uses to translate descriptive passages. Almost without any dialogue the sequence establishes a typical afternoon in Charu's life, her loneliness, her affinity to novels, the spatial limits of her movements. It brings to life an object-world that embodies time – the wallpaper, the furniture, the items of daily use, but also the street sounds and the street images. These images are glimpsed by Charu through an opera glass: as she opens one blind after another on the wall to peek at the comically graphic characters moving in the street, her socially restricted movement momentarily turns into a playful choreography. And then Charu frames the figure of her husband Bhupati with the opera glass - passing down the corridor not noticing her, lost in his book. Ray conjures up this interior with a dexterity that reminds us of the image of Charu's embroidery in the title sequence, A texture of words is dissolved into a weave of images effortlessly before our eyes.

But the world that is conjured up is also a world of texts in *Charulata*. And at this level, the cinematic moves are negotiated through literature rather than in terms of separation from it. The alphabet that Charu embroiders on the handkerchief signals the insistence of the letter in the film. The written word will take on a particular luminosity as the film progresses, and the world of writing that is invoked in the opening sequence will form the very basis of the re-created time and place. Charu hums the name of her favourite novelist, Bankim, as she browses idly through the bookshelf. Bankimchandra Chatterjee was a pioneer of the novel form in India and a crucial ideologue of nationalism. The film constantly refers to his novels; through a shared knowledge of these novels Charu and Amal come close to each other. Bhupati, and Charu's sister-in-law, Manda, fall outside this domain of exchange because of their lack of appreciation of Bankim. The name of Bankim will end up in a play of alliteration between Charu and Amal in their last extended conversation.

At a more discursive level, the whole film can be seen to be engaged in a dialogue with one of Bankim's essays, 'Women, Old and New', a major statement on what is known as the 'Women's Question' in the nineteenth century. All this is added to Tagore's original text which finds itself embedded in a tapestry of literary signs. Writers people the world - Taraknath Gangopadhyay, Rammohun Roy, Shakespeare, Byron, Addison, Steele, Emerson. The image of writing, the written word, forms a major visual motif – we closely watch Amal writing, Charu writing, Bhupati getting intoxicated with the printed word. The alphabet shining on the embroidery over the titles signals a process which will lead us to the very last image of the film: the hands of Charu and Bhupati freeze before they could meet, the title of Tagore's story appears on the screen in calligraphic design.

This would appear as merely explanatory and redundant (to say 'Broken Nest' here is to be literal) unless we follow the logic of appearance of the written word in the film. It is a final gesture of receding from the original story, of turning the work itself into an object of the film's gaze. The scene in which Bhupati comes to know about Charu's feelings for his cousin the camera makes a gesture very unusual for Ray: it climbs up the leg of a marble table slowly to reveal a letter lying on it while Charu and Bhupati are heard talking off-screen. The letter is from Amal and it will bring about an emotional outburst in Charu giving her feelings away. The very tendentious movement of the camera, drawing attention to the letter as the dramatic agent, would look odd in a work of concealed narration unless one remembers the role of the letter as such in the film.

Bankim's 'Women Old and New' was published in 1879 (Ray gives an exact time for the events, 1879, as we know from the dateline on the copy of the magazine that Bhupati shows Amal) where he argues for a new woman who would be modern in the traditional way. She would embody the resolution of the conflict between tradition and modernity by finding her place in a re-invented patriarchy. She would learn to be the new old woman. As the film launches a dialogue with this essay it maps Tagore's story onto a historical grid, the political drama is brought out into the open. The story tells us of the formation of the colonial subject, male and female, and of the inevitable irony and pain that attend the process.

Tagore begins his story by an ironic description of the domains his characters occupy. The idealistic, English educated Bhupati is worried about the expansion of British territories beyond the Afghan borders, but hasn't had the time to notice how his child bride has bloomed into womanhood; Charu's idleness is of a different kind, reminding one of a fruitless tree. As she develops an expressive selfhood, through her love and through her writing, the challenge of the demarcation of domains comes to face her, it demands a heavy price.

Tagore, writing more or less from within the social reality that he portrays, was not in a position to uncover the historical dynamics of this matrix. Ray casts a historical gaze at the story at this level too; he creates a design with characters and spaces and distributes the story along discursive lines of divide. The dichotomy of literature and politics suggested in the story is developed into a strong motif in the film. The first is associated with the woman, the second belongs to the man. Bhupati entrusts Amal with Charu's literary education admitting that he has no taste for such things, busy as he is with the 'real world' of politics. Ray also makes him say to Amal that this politics, critical though it is of the colonial government's policies, is not meant to be disloyal to the masters. And from Bhupati we also learn that how worried he and friends are about the outcome of the parliamentary elections in Britain;

one of his friends has vowed to sacrifice a goat at the Kali temple if the liberals win.

Bhupati writes politics in English, Amal and Charu write literature in Bengali. And then we come to a further division: Amal writes for public circulation, in an ornate register, Charu would like to write for a strictly private exchange, in an unadorned style through which she can evoke personal experiences. Towards the end, after Amal has left the house and Bhupati's magazine has failed, Charu and Bhupati go on a visit to the seaside and plan a poignantly illusory reconciliation between the poles of opposition– between the public and the private, home and the world, politics and culture. Why not bring out another magazine, they propose, which will have politics in English and literature in Bengali.

One can see Charu never believing in this. She is coming to a harder knowledge, she has had to grow up paying a dreadful price. The film brings out this irony of growing up in its most acute historical-political dimensions. It does away with a whole lot of events present in the original story not so much to bring out its essence but the political essence of the predicament that it deals with. Growing into modernity, into citizenship, into subjectivity of a nameable kind - all this, marked indelibly with the reality of living through colonialism, would not have been so strongly captured without the grand design of polarities that the film is grounded in. In devising his language Ray moves in and out of the field of literature, it would be difficult to recognise this aspect of his craft if we conceived of literature or film in their pure autonomy.

5

SARDAR VALLABHBHAI PATEL

Vallabhbhai Patel (31 October 1875 - 15 December 1950) was a political and social leader of India who played a major role in the country's struggle for independence and guided its integration into a united, independent nation. In India and across the world, he was often addressed as Sardar, which means Chief in many languages of India. He is hailed as the Iron Man of India.

Raised in the countryside of Gujarat and largely self-educated, Vallabhbhai Patel was employed in successful practice as a lawyer when he was first inspired by the work and philosophy of Mahatma Gandhi. Patel subsequently organised the peasants of Kheda, Borsad, and Bardoli in Gujarat in non-violent civil disobedience against oppressive policies imposed by the British Raj; in this role, he became one of the most influential leaders in Gujarat. He rose to the leadership of the Indian National Congress and was at the forefront of rebellions and political events, organising the party for elections in 1934 and 1937, and promoting the Quit India movement.

As the first Home Minister and Deputy Prime Minister of India, Patel organised relief for refugees in Punjab and Delhi, and led efforts to restore peace across the nation. Patel took charge of the task to forge a united India from the 565 semi-autonomous princely states and British-era colonial provinces. Using frank diplomacy backed with the option (and the use) of military action, Patel's leadership enabled the accession of almost every princely state. Hailed as the Iron Man of India, he is also remembered as the "Patron Saint" of India's civil servants for establishing modern all-India services. Patel was also one of the earliest proponents of property rights and free enterprise in India.

EARLY LIFE

Vallabhbhai Jhaverbhai Patel was born at his maternal uncle's house in Nadiad, Gujarat. His actual date of birth was never officially recorded - Patel entered 31 October as his date of birth on his matriculation examination papers. He was the fourth son of Jhaverbhai a Jain by religion and his wife Ladba Patel. They lived in the village of Karamsad, in the Kheda district where Jhaverbhai owned a homestead. Somabhai, Narsibhai and Vithalbhai Patel (also a future political leader) were his elder brothers. He had a younger brother, Kashibhai and a sister, Dahiba. As a young boy, Patel helped his father in the fields and bimonthly kept a day-long fast, abstaining from food and water - a Jain cultural observance that enabled him to develop physical toughness. When he was seventeen years old, Patel's marriage was arranged with Jhaverba, a young girl of twelve or thirteen years from a nearby village. As per custom, the young bride would continue to reside with her parents until her husband started earning and could establish their household.

Patel travelled to attend schools in Nadiad, Petlad and Borsad, living self-sufficiently with other boys. He reputedly cultivated a stoic character - a popular anecdote recounts how he lanced his own painful boil without hesitation, even as the barber supposed to do it trembled. Patel passed his matriculation at the late age of 22; at this point, he was generally regarded by his elders as an unambitious man destined for a commonplace job. But Patel himself harboured a plan - he would study to become a lawyer, work and save funds, travel to England and study to become a barrister. Patel spent years away from his family, studying on his own with books borrowed from other lawyers and passed examinations within two years. Fetching Jhaverba from her parents' home, Patel set up his household in Godhra and enrolled at the bar.

During the many years it took him to save money, Vallabhbhai-now a pleader - earned a reputation as a fierce and skilled lawyer. His wife bore him a daughter, Manibehn, in 1904 and later a son, Dahyabhai, in 1906. Patel also cared for a friend suffering from Bubonic plague when it swept across Gujarat. When Patel himself came down with the disease, he immediately sent his family to safety, left his home and moved into an isolated house in Nadiad (by other accounts, Patel spent this time in a dilapidated temple); there, he recovered slowly.

Patel practised law in Godhra, Borsad and Anand while taking on the financial burdens of his homestead in Karamsad. When he had saved enough for England and applied for a pass and a ticket, they arrived in the name of "V. J. Patel," at Vithalbhai's home, who bore the same initials. Having harboured his own plans to study in England, Vithalbhai remonstrated to his younger brother that it would be disreputable for an older brother to follow his younger brother. In keeping with concerns for his family's honour, Patel allowed Vithalbhai to go in his place. He also financed his brother's stay and began saving again for his own goals.

In 1909, Patel's wife Jhaverba was hospitalised in Mumbai (then Bombay) to undergo a major surgical operation for cancer. Her health suddenly worsened and despite successful emergency surgery, she died in the hospital. Patel was given a note informing him of his wife's demise as he was cross-examining a witness in court. As per others who witnessed, Patel read the note, pocketed it and continued to intensely cross-examine the witness and won the case. He broke the news to others only after the proceedings had ended.

Patel himself decided against marrying again. He raised his children with the help of his family and sent them to English-medium schools in Mumbai. At the age of 36, he journeyed to England and enrolled at the Middle Temple Inn in London. Finishing a 36-month course in 30 months, Patel topped his class despite having no previous college background. Returning to India, Patel settled in the city of Ahmedabad and became one of the city's most successful barristers.

Wearing European-style clothes and urbane mannerisms, he also became a skilled bridge player. Patel nurtured ambitions to expand his practise and accumulate great wealth and to provide his children with modern education. He had also made a pact with his brother Vithalbhai to support his entry into politics in the Bombay Presidency, while Patel himself would remain in Ahmedabad and provide for the family.

FIGHTING FOR INDEPENDENCE

At the urging of his friends, Patel won an election to become the sanitation commissioner of Ahmedabad in 1917. While often clashing with British officials on civic issues, he did not show any interest in politics. Upon hearing of Mohandas Gandhi, he joked to Mavlankar that Gandhi would "ask you if you know how to sift pebbles from wheat.

And that is supposed to bring independence." But Patel was deeply impressed when Gandhi defied the British in Champaran for the sake of the area's oppressed farmers. Against the grain of Indian politicians of the time, Gandhi wore Indian-style clothes and emphasised the use of one's mother tongue or any Indian language as opposed to English - the lingua franca of India's intellectuals.

Patel was particularly attracted to Gandhi's inclination to action - apart from a resolution condemning the arrest of political leader Annie Besant, Gandhi proposed that volunteers march peacefully demanding to meet her.

Patel gave a speech in Borsad in September 1917, encouraging Indians nationwide to sign Gandhi's petition demanding Swaraj - independence - from the British. Meeting Gandhi a month later at the Gujarat Political Conference in Godhra, Patel became the secretary of the Gujarat Sabha - a public body which would become the Gujarati arm of the Indian National Congress - at Gandhi's encouragement. Patel now energetically fought against veth - the forced servitude of Indians to Europeans - and organised relief efforts in wake of plague and famine in Kheda.

The Kheda peasants' plea for exemption from taxation had been turned down by British authorities. Gandhi endorsed waging a struggle there, but could not lead it himself due to his activities in Champaran.

When Gandhi asked for a Gujarati activist to devote himself completely to the assignment and Patel volunteered, much to Gandhi's personal delight. Though his decision was made on the spot, Patel later said that his desire and commitment came after intensive personal contemplation, as he realised he would have to abandon his career and material ambitions.

SATYAGRAHA IN GUJARAT

Supported by Congress volunteers Narhari Parikh, Mohanlal Pandya and Abbas Tyabji, Vallabhbhai Patel began a village-to-village tour in the Kheda district, documenting grievances and asking villagers for their support for a statewide revolt by refusing the payment of taxes. Patel emphasised potential hardships with the need for complete unity and non-violence despite any provocation. He received enthusiastic responses from virtually every village. When the revolt was launched and revenue refused, the government sent police and intimidation squads to seize property, including confiscating barn animals and whole farms. Patel organised a network of volunteers to work with individual villages - helping them hide valuables and protect themselves during raids. Thousands of activists and farmers were arrested, but Patel was not.

The revolt began evoking sympathy and admiration across India, including with pro-British Indian politicians. The government agreed to negotiate with Patel and decided to suspend the payment of revenue for the year, even scaling back the rate. Patel emerged as a hero to Gujaratis and admired across India. In 1920, he was elected president of the newly formed Gujarat Pradesh Congress Committee - he would serve as its president till 1945. Patel supported Gandhi's Non-cooperation movement and toured the state to recruit more than 300,000 members and raise over Rs. 1.5 million in funds. Helping organise bonfires of British goods in Ahmedabad, Patel threw in all his English-style clothes. With his daughter Mani and son Dahya, he switched completely to wearing khadi.

Patel also supported Gandhi's controversial suspension of resistance in wake of the Chauri Chaura incident. He worked extensively in the following years in Gujarat against alcoholism, untouchability and caste discrimination, as well as for the empowerment of women. In the Congress, he was a resolute supporter of Gandhi against his Swarajist critics. Patel was elected Ahmedabad's municipal president in 1922, 1924 and 1927 - during his terms, Ahmedabad was extended a major supply of electricity and the school system underwent major reforms. Drainage and sanitation systems were extended over all the city. He fought for the recognition and payment of teachers employed in schools established by nationalists (out of British control) and even took on sensitive Hindu-Muslim Issues. Sardar Patel personally led relief efforts in the aftermath of the intense torrential rainfall in 1927, which had caused major floods in the city and in the Kheda district and great destruction of life and property. He established refuge centres across the district, raised volunteers, arranged for supply of food, medicines and clothing, as well as emergency funds from the government and public.

When Gandhi was in prison, Sardar Patel was asked by Congressmen to lead the satyagraha in Nagpur in 1923 against a law banning the raising of the Indian flag. He organised thousands of volunteers from all over the country in processions hoisting the flag. Patel negotiated a settlement that obtained the release of all prisoners and allowed nationalists to hoist the flag in public. Later that year, Patel and his allies uncovered evidence suggesting that the police were in league with local dacoits in the Borsad taluka even as the government prepared to levy a major tax for fighting dacoits in the area. More than 6,000 villagers assembled to hear Patel speak and supported the proposed agitation against the tax, which was deemed immoral and unnecessary. He organised hundreds of Congressmen, sent instructions and received information from across the district. Every village in the taluka resisted payment of the tax, and through cohesion, also prevented the seizure of property and lands. After a protracted struggle, the government withdrew the tax. Historians believe that one of Patel's key achievements was the building of cohesion and trust amongst the different castes and communities, which were divided on socio-economic lines.

In April 1928, Sardar Patel returned to the freedom struggle from his municipal duties in Ahmedabad when Bardoli suffered from a serious predicament of a famine and steep tax hike. The revenue hike was steeper than it had been in Kheda even though the famine covered a large portion of Gujarat. After cross-examining and talking to village representatives, emphasizing the potential hardship and need for non-violence and cohesion, Patel initiated the struggle - complete denial of taxes. Sardar Patel organised volunteers, camps and an information network across affected areas. The revenue refusal was stronger than in Kheda and many sympathy satyagrahas were undertaken across Gujarat. Despite arrests, seizures of property and lands, the struggle intensified. The situation reached a head in August, when through sympathetic intermediaries, he negotiated a settlement repealing the tax hike, reinstating village officials who had resigned in protest and the return of seized property and lands. It was during the struggle and after the victory in Bardoli that Patel was increasingly addressed by his colleagues and followers as Sardar.

LEADING THE CONGRESS

As Gandhi embarked on the Dandi Salt March, Patel was arrested in the village of Ras and tried without witnesses, with no lawyer or pressman allowed to attend. Patel's arrest and Gandhi's subsequent arrest caused the Salt Satyagraha to greatly intensify in Gujarat - districts across Gujarat launched an anti-tax rebellion until and unless Patel and Gandhi were released. Once released, Patel served as interim Congress president, but was re-arrested while leading a procession in Mumbai. After the signing of the Gandhi-Irwin Pact, Patel was elected Congress president for its 1931 session in Karachi - here the Congress ratified the pact, committed itself to the defence of fundamental rights and human freedoms, and a vision of a secular nation, minimum wage and the abolition of untouchability and serfdom.

Patel used his position as Congress president in organising the return of confiscated lands to farmers in Gujarat. Upon the failure of the Round Table Conference in London, Gandhi and Patel were arrested in January 1932 when the struggle re-opened, and imprisoned in the Yeravda Central Jail. During this term of imprisonment, Patel and Gandhi grew close to each other, and the two developed a close bond of affection, trust, and frankness. Their mutual relationship could be described as that of an elder brother - Gandhi - and his younger brother - Patel. Despite having arguments with Gandhi, Patel respected his instincts and leadership. During imprisonment, the two would discuss national and social issues, read Hindu epics and crack jokes. Gandhi also taught Patel Sanskrit language. Gandhi's secretary Mahadev Desai kept detailed records of conversations between Gandhi and Patel. When Gandhi embarked on a fast-unto-death protesting the separate electorates allocated for untouchables, Patel looked after Gandhi closely and himself refrained from partaking of food. Patel was later moved to a jail in Nașik, and refused a British offer for a brief release to attend the cremation of his brother Vithalbhai, who had died in 1934. He was finally released in July of the same year.

Patel headed Congress's all-India election campaign in 1934 and 1937 - he would collect funds, select candidates, determine the Congress stance on issues and opponents. Not contesting a seat for himself, Patel nevertheless guided Congressmen elected in the provinces and at the national level. In 1935, Patel underwent surgery for hemorrhoids, yet guided efforts against plague in Bardoli and again when a drought struck Gujarat in 1939. Patel would guide the Congress ministries that had won power across India with the aim of preserving party discipline - Patel feared that the British would use opportunities to create conflicts among elected Congressmen, and he did not want the party to be distracted from the goal of complete independence. But Patel would clash with Nehru, opposing declarations of the adoption of socialism at the 1936 Congress session, which he believed was a diversion from the main goal of achieving independence. In 1938, Patel organized rank and file opposition to the attempts of then-Congress president Subhash Bose to move away from Gandhi's principles of non-violent resistance. Patel considered Bose to be authoritarian and desirous of more power over the party. He led senior Congress leaders in a protest, which resulted in Bose's resignation. But criticism arose from Bose's supporters, socialists and other Congressmen that Patel himself was acting in an authoritarian manner in his defense of Gandhi's authority.

QUIT INDIA

When World War II broke out, Patel supported Nehru's decision to withdraw the Congress from central and provincial legislatures, contrary to Gandhi's advice, as well as an initiative by senior leader Chakravarthi Rajagopalachari to offer Congress's full support to Britain if it promised Indian independence at the end of the war and install a democratic government right away. Gandhi had refused to support Britain on the grounds of his moral opposition to war, while Subhash Bose was in militant opposition to the British. The British rejected Rajagopalachari's initiative, and Patel embraced Gandhi's leadership again. He participated in Gandhi's call for individual disobedience, and was arrested in 1940 and imprisoned for nine months. He also opposed the proposals of the Cripps' mission in 1942. Patel lost more than twenty pounds during his period in jail. While Nehru, Rajagopalachari and Maulana Azad initially criticized Gandhi's proposal for an all-out campaign of civil disobedience to force the British to Quit India, Patel was its most fervent supporter.

Arguing that the British would retreat from India as they had from Singapore and Burma, Patel stressed that the campaign start without any delay. Though feeling that the British would not quit immediately, Patel favored an all-out rebellion which would galvanize Indian people, who had been divided in their response to the war, In Patel's view, an all-out rebellion would force the British to concede that continuation of colonial rule had no support in India, and thus speed power transfer to Indians. Believing strongly in the need for revolt, Patel stated his intention to resign from the Congress if the revolt was not approved.

Gandhi strongly pressured the All India Congress Committee to approve of an all-out campaign of civil disobedience, and the AICC approved the campaign on 7 August 1942. Though Patel's health had suffered during his stint in jail, Patel gave emotional speeches to large crowds across India, asking people to refuse paying taxes and participate in civil disobedience, mass protests and a shutdown of all civil services. He raised funds and prepared a second-tier of command as a precaution against the arrest of national leaders. Patel made a climactic speech to more than 100,000 people gathered at Gowalia Tank in Bombay (Mumbai) on August 7:

> *"The Governor of Burma boasts in London that they left Burma only after reducing everything to dust. So you promise the same thing to India?... You refer in your radio broadcasts and newspapers to the government established in Burma by Japan as a puppet government? What sort of government do you have in Delhi now?...When France fell before the Nazi onslaught, in the midst of total war, Mr. Churchill offered union with England to the French. That was indeed a stroke of inspired statesman-*

ship. But when it comes to India? Oh no! Constitutional changes in the midst of a war? Absolutely unthinkable...The object this time is to free India before the Japanese can come and be ready to fight them if they come. They will round up the leaders, round up all. Then it will be the duty of every Indian to put forth his utmost effort - within non-violence. No source is to be left untapped; no weapon untried. This is going to be the opportunity of a lifetime."

Historians believe that Patel's speech was instrumental in electrifying nationalists, who had been skeptical of the proposed rebellion. Patel's organising work in this period is credited by historians for ensuring the success of the rebellion across India. Patel was arrested on 9 August and was imprisoned with the entire Congress Working Committee from 1942 to 1945 at the fort in Ahmednagar. Here he spun cloth, played bridge, read a large number of books, took long walks, practised gardening. He also provided emotional support to his colleagues while awaiting news and developments of the outside.

Patel was deeply pained at the news of the deaths of Mahadev Desai and Kasturba Gandhi later in the year. But Patel wrote in a letter to his daughter that he and his colleagues were experiencing "fullest peace" for having done "their duty." Even though other political parties had opposed the struggle and the British had employed ruthless means of suppression, the Quit India movement was "by far the most serious rebellion since that of 1857," as the viceroy cabled to Winston Churchill.

More than one hundred thousand people were arrested and thousands killed in police firings. Strikes, protests and other revolutionary activities had broken out across India. When Patel was released on 15 June 1945 he realised that the British were preparing proposals to transfer power to Indian hands.

INDEPENDENCE, INTEGRATION AND ROLE OF GANDHI

In the 1946 election for the Congress presidency, Patel stepped down in favor of Nehru at the request of Gandhi. The election's importance stemmed from the fact that the elected President would lead free India's first Government. Gandhi asked all 16 states representatives and Congress to elect the right person and Sardar

Patel's name was proposed by 13 states representatives out of 16, but Patel respected Gandhi's request to not be the first prime minister. As a Home Minister, Patel merged all parts of India under federal control but Jammu and Kashmir was left out because of Nehru. After the election of Nehru as the party's president, Patel began directing the Congress campaign for the general elections of the Constituent Assembly of India.

In the elections, the Congress won a large majority of the elected seats, dominating the Hindu electorate. But the Muslim League led by Muhammad Ali Jinnah won a large majority of Muslim electorate seats. The League had resolved in 1940 to demand Pakistan - an independent state for Muslims - and was a fierce critic of the Congress. The Congress formed governments in all provinces save Sindh, Punjab and Bengal, where it entered into coalitions with other parties.

CABINET MISSION AND PARTITION

When the British mission proposed two plans for transfer of power, there was considerable opposition within the Congress to both. The plan of 16 May 1946 proposed a loose federation with extensive provincial autonomy, and the "grouping" of provinces based on religious-majority. The plan of 16 June 1946 proposed the partition of India on religious lines, with over 600 princely states free to choose between independence or accession to either dominion. The League approved both plans, while the Congress flatly rejected the June 16 proposal. Gandhi criticised the May 16 proposal as being inherently divisive, but Patel, realizing that rejecting the proposal would mean that only the League would be invited to form a government, lobbied the Congress Working Committee hard to give its assent to the 16 May proposal. Patel engaged the British envoys Sir Stafford Cripps and Lord Pethick-Lawrence and obtained an assurance that the "grouping" clause would not be given practical force, Patel converted Nehru, Rajendra Prasad and Rajagopalachari to accept the plan. When the League retracted its approval of the 16 May plan, the viceroy Lord Wavell invited the Congress to form the government. Under Nehru, who was styled the "Vice President of the Viceroy's Executive Council," Patel took charge of the departments of home affairs and information and broadcasting. He moved into a government house on 1, Aurangzeb Road in Delhi - this would be his residence till his death in 1950.

Vallabhbhai Patel was one of the first Congress leaders to accept the partition of India as a solution to the rising Muslim separatist movement led by Muhammad Ali Jinnah. He had been outraged by Jinnah's Direct Action campaign, which had provoked communal violence across India and by the viceroy's vetoes of his home department's plans to stop the violence on the grounds of constitutionality. Patel severely criticised the viceroy's induction of League ministers into the government, and the revalidation of the grouping scheme by the British without Congress approval. Although further outraged at the League's boycott of the assembly and non-acceptance of the plan of 16 May despite entering government, he was also aware that Jinnah did enjoy popular support amongst Muslims, and that an open conflict between him and the nationalists could degenerate into a Hindu-Muslim civil war of disastrous consequences. The continuation of a divided and weak central government would in Patel's mind, result in the wider fragmentation of India by encouraging more than 600 princely states towards independence. Between the months of December 1946 and January 1947, Patel worked with civil servant V. P. Menon on the latter's suggestion for a separate dominion of Pakistan created out of Muslim-majority provinces. Communal violence in Bengal and Punjab in January and March of 1947 further convinced Patel of the soundness of partition. Patel, a fierce critic of Jinnah's demand that the Hindu-majority areas of Punjab and Bengal be included in a Muslim state, obtained the partition of those provinces, thus blocking any possibility of their inclusion in Pakistan. Patel's decisiveness on the partition of Punjab and Bengal had won him many supporters and admirers amongst the Indian public, which had tired of the League's tactics, but he was criticised by Gandhi, Nehru, secular Muslims and socialists for a perceived eagerness to do so. When Lord Louis Mountbatten formally proposed the plan on 3 June 1947, Patel gave his approval and lobbied Nehru and other Congress leaders to accept the proposal. Knowing Gandhi's deep anguish regarding proposals of partition, Patel engaged him in frank discussion in private meetings over the perceived practical unworkability of any

Congress-League coalition, the rising violence and the threat of civil war. At the All India Congress Committee meeting called to vote on the proposal, Patel said:

"I fully appreciate the fears of our brothers from [the Muslim-majority areas]. Nobody likes the division of India and my heart is heavy. But the choice is between one division and many divisions. We must face facts. We cannot give way to emotionalism and sentimentality. The Working Committee has not acted out of fear. But I am afraid of one thing, that all our toil and hard work of these many years might go waste or prove unfruitful. My nine months in office has completely disillusioned me regarding the supposed merits of the Cabinet Mission Plan. Except for a few honourable exceptions, Muslim officials from the top down to the chaprasis (peons or servants) are working for the League. The communal veto given to the League in the Mission Plan would have blocked India's progress at every stage. Whether we like it or not, de facto Pakistan already exists in the Punjab and Bengal. Under the circumstances I would prefer a de jure Pakistan, which may make the League more responsible. Freedom is coming. We have 75 to 80 percent of India, which we can make strong with our own genius. The League can develop the rest of the country."

Following Gandhi's and Congress' approval of the plan, Patel represented India on the Partition Council, where he oversaw the division of public assets, and selected the Indian council of ministers with Nehru. However, neither he nor any other Indian leader had foreseen the intense violence and population transfer that would take place with partition. Patel would take the lead in organising relief and emergency supplies, establishing refugee camps and visiting the border areas with Pakistani leaders to encourage peace. Despite these efforts, estimates on the death toll vary from around two hundred thousand, to over a million people. The estimated number of refugees in both countries exceeds 15 million. Understanding that Delhi and Punjab policemen, accused of organising attacks on Muslims, were personally affected by the tragedies of partition, Patel called out the Indian Army with South Indian regiments to restore order, imposing strict curfews and shoot-at-sight orders. Visiting the Nizamuddin Auliya Dargah area in Delhi, where thousands of Delhi Muslims feared attacks, he prayed at the shrine, visited the people and reinforced the presence of police.

He suppressed from the press reports of atrocities in Pakistan against Hindus and Sikhs to prevent retaliatory violence. Establishing the Delhi Emergency Committee to restore order and organising relief efforts for refugees in the capital, Patel publicly warned officials against partiality and neglect. When reports reached Patel that large groups of Sikhs were preparing to attack Muslim convoys heading for Pakistan, Patel hurried to Amritsar and met Sikh and Hindu leaders. Arguing that attacking helpless people was cowardly and dishonourable, Patel emphasised that Sikh actions would result in further attacks against Hindus and Sikhs in Pakistan. He assured the community leaders that if they worked to establish peace and order and guarantee the safety of Muslims, the Indian government would react forcefully to any failures of Pakistan to do the same. Additionally, Patel addressed a massive crowd of an estimated 200,000 refugees who had surrounded his car after the meetings:

> *"Here, in this same city, the blood of Hindus, Sikhs and Muslims mingled in the bloodbath of Jallianwala Bagh. I am grieved to think that things have come to such a pass that no Muslim can go about in Amritsar and no Hindu or Sikh can even think of living in Lahore. The butchery of innocent and defenceless men, women and children does not behove brave men... I am quite certain that India's interest lies in getting all her men and women across the border and sending out all Muslims from East Punjab. I have come to you with a specific appeal. Pledge the safety of Muslim refugees crossing the city. Any obstacles or hindrances will only worsen the plight of our refugees who are already performing prodigious feats of endurance. If we have to fight, we must fight clean. Such a fight must await an appropriate time and conditions and you must be watchful in choosing your ground. To fight against the refugees is no fight at all. No laws of humanity or war among honourable men permit the murder of people who have sought shelter and protection. Let there be truce for three months in which both sides can exchange their refugees. This sort of truce is permitted even by laws of war. Let us take the initiative in breaking this vicious*

circle of attacks and counter-attacks. Hold your hands for a week and see what happens. Make way for the refugees with your own force of volunteers and let them deliver the refugees safely at our frontier."

Following his dialogue with community leaders and his speech, no further attacks occurred against Muslim refugees, and a wider peace and order was re-established soon over the entire area. However, Patel was criticised by Nehru, secular Muslims and taxed by Gandhi over his alleged wish to see Muslims from other parts of India depart. While Patel vehemently denied such allegations, the acrimony with Maulana Azad and other secular Muslim leaders increased when Patel refused to dismiss Delhi's Sikh police commissioner, who was accused of discrimination. Hindu and Sikh leaders also accused Patel and other leaders of not taking Pakistan sufficiently to task over the attacks on their communities there, and Muslim leaders further criticised him for allegedly neglecting the needs of Muslims leaving for Pakistan, and concentrating resources for incoming Hindu and Sikh refugees. Patel clashed with Nehru and Azad over the allocation of houses in Delhi vacated by Muslims leaving for Pakistan - Nehru and Azad desired to allocate them for displaced Muslims, while Patel argued that no government professing secularism must make such exclusions. However, Patel was publicly defended by Gandhi and received widespread admiration and support for speaking frankly on communal issues and acting decisively and resourcefully to quell disorder and violence.

POLITICAL INTEGRATION OF INDIA

Under the June 3 plan, more than 600 princely states were given the option of joining either India or Pakistan, or choosing independence. Indian nationalists and large segments of the public feared that if these states did not accede, a vast majority of the people and territory would be fragmented. The Congress as well as senior British officials considered Patel the best man for the task of achieving unification of the princely states with the Indian dominion. Gandhi had said to Patel "the problem of the States is so difficult that you alone can solve it". He was considered a statesman of integrity with the practical acumen and resolve to accomplish a monumental task. Patel asked V. P. Menon, a senior civil servant with whom he had worked over the partition of India, to become his right-hand as chief secretary of the States Ministry. On 6 May 1947, Patel began lobbying the princes, attempting to make them receptive towards dialogue with the future Government and trying to forestall potential conflicts.

Patel used social meetings and unofficial surroundings to engage most monarchs, inviting them to lunch and tea at his home in Delhi. At these meetings, Patel stated that there was no inherent conflict between the Congress and the princely order. Nonetheless, he stressed that the princes would need to accede to India in good faith by 15 August 1947. Patel invoked the patriotism of India's monarchs, asking them to join in the freedom of their nation and act as responsible rulers who cared about the future of their people. He persuaded the princes of 565 states of the impossibility of independence from the Indian republic, especially in the presence of growing opposition from their subjects. He proposed favourable terms for the merger, including creation of privy purses for the descendants of the rulers. While encouraging the rulers to act with patriotism, Patel did not rule out force, setting a deadline of 15 August 1947 for them to sign the instrument of accession document. All but three of the states willingly merged into the Indian union - only Jammu and Kashmir, Junagadh, and Hyderabad did not fall into his basket.

Junagadh was especially important to Patel, since it was in his home state of Gujarat. The Nawab had under pressure from Sir Shah Nawaz Bhutto acceded to Pakistan. It was however, quite far from Pakistan and 80% of its population was Hindu. Patel combined diplomacy with force, demanding that Pakistan annul the accession, and that the Nawab accede to India. He sent the Army to occupy three principalities of Junagadh to show his resolve. Following widespread protests and the formation of a civil government, or Aarzi Hukumat, both Bhutto and the Nawab fled to Karachi, and under Patel's orders, Indian Army and police units marched into the state. A plebiscite later organised produced a 99.5% vote for merger with India. In a speech at the Bahauddin College in Junagadh following the latter's take-over, Patel emphasised his feeling of urgency on Hyderabad, which he felt was more vital to India than Kashmir:

"If Hyderabad does not see the writing on the wall, it goes the way Junagadh has gone. Pakistan attempted to set off Kashmir against Junagadh. When we raised the question of settlement in a democratic way, they (Pakistan) at once told us that they would consider it if we applied that policy to Kashmir. Our reply was that we would agree to Kashmir if they agreed to Hyderabad."

Hyderabad was the largest of the princely states, and included parts of present-day Andhra Pradesh, Karnataka, and Maharashtra states. Its ruler, the Nizam Osman Ali Khan was a Muslim, although over 80% of its people were Hindu. The Nizam sought independence or accession with Pakistan. Muslim forces loyal to Nizam, called the Razakars, under Qasim Razvi pressed the Nizam to hold out against India, while organising attacks with militant Communists on people on Indian soil. Even though a Standstill Agreement was signed due to the desperate efforts of Lord Mountbatten to avoid a war, the Nizam rejected deals and changed his positions. In September 1948, Patel emphasised in Cabinet meetings that India should take no more, and reconciled Nehru and the Governor-General, Chakravarti Rajgopalachari to military action. Following preparations, Patel ordered the Indian Army to integrate Hyderabad (in his capacity as Acting Prime Minister) when Nehru was touring Europe. The action was termed Operation Polo, in which thousands of Razakar forces had been killed, but Hyderabad was comfortably secured into the Indian Union. The main aim of Mountbatten and Nehru in avoiding a forced annexation was to prevent an outbreak of Hindu-Muslim violence. Patel insisted that if Hyderabad was allowed to continue with its antics, the prestige of the Government would fall and then neither Hindus nor Muslims would feel secure in its realm. After defeating Nizam, Patel retained him as the ceremonial chief of state, and held talks with him.

LEADING INDIA

Governor General Chakravarti Rajagopalachari, Nehru and Patel formed the triumvirate which ruled India from 1948 to 1950. Prime Minister Nehru was intensely popular with the masses, but Patel enjoyed the loyalty and faith of rank and file Congressmen, state leaders and India's civil services. Patel was a senior leader in the Constituent Assembly of India and was responsible in a large measure for shaping India's constitution. Patel was a key force behind the appointment of Dr. Bhimrao Ramji Ambedkar as the chairman of the drafting committee, and the inclusion of leaders from a diverse political spectrum in the process of writing the constitution.

Patel was the chairman of the committees responsible for minorities, tribal and excluded areas, fundamental rights and provincial constitutions. Patel piloted a model constitution for the provinces in the Assembly, which contained limited powers for the state governor, who would defer to the President - he clarified it was not the intention to let the governor exercise power which could impede an elected government. He worked closely with Muslim leaders to end separate electorates and the more potent demand for reservation of seats for minorities. Patel would hold personal dialogues with leaders of other minorities on the question, and was responsible for the measure that allows the President to appoint Anglo-Indians to Parliament. His intervention was key to the passage of two articles that protected civil servants from political involvement and guaranteed their terms and privileges. He was also instrumental in the founding the Indian Administrative Service and the Indian Police Service, and for his defence of Indian civil servants from political attack, he is known as the "patron saint" of India's services.

When a delegation of Gujarati farmers came to him citing their inability to send their milk production to the markets without being fleeced by middlemen, Patel exhorted them to organise the processing and sale of milk by themselves, and guided them to create the Kaira District Co-operative Milk Producers' Union Limited, which preceded the Amul milk products brand. Patel also pledged the reconstruction of the ancient but dilapidated Somnath Temple in Saurashtra - he oversaw the creation of a public trust and restoration work, and pledged to dedicate the temple upon the completion of work (the work was completed after Patel's death, and the temple was inaugurated by the first President of India, Dr. Rajendra Prasad).

When the Pakistani invasion of Kashmir began in September 1947, Patel immediately wanted to send troops into Kashmir. But agreeing with Nehru and Mountbatten, he waited till Kashmir's monarch had acceded to India. Patel then oversaw India's military operations to secure Srinagar, the Baramulla Pass and the forces retrieved a lot of territory from the invaders. Patel, along with Defence Minister Baldev Singh administered the entire military effort, arranging for troops from different parts of India to be rushed to Kashmir and for a major military road connecting Srinagar to Pathankot be built in 6 months. Patel strongly advised Nehru against going for arbitration to the United Nations, insisting that Pakistan had been wrong to support the invasion and the accession to India was valid. He did not want foreign interference in a bilateral affair. Patel opposed the release of Rs. 55 crores to the Government of Pakistan, convinced that the money would go to finance the war against India in Kashmir. The Cabinet had approved his point but it was reversed when Gandhi, who feared an intensifying rivalry and further communal violence, went on a fast-unto-death to obtain the release. Patel, though not estranged from Gandhi, was deeply hurt at the rejection of his counsel and a Cabinet decision.

In 1949, a crisis arose when the number of Hindu refugees entering West Bengal, Assam and Tripura from East Pakistan climbed over 800,000. The refugees in many cases were being forcibly evicted by Pakistani authorities, and were victims of intimidation and violence. Nehru invited Liaquat Ali Khan, Prime Minister of Pakistan to find a peaceful solution. Despite his aversion, Patel reluctantly met Khan and discussed the matters. Patel strongly criticised, however, Nehru's intention to sign a pact that would create minority commissions in both countries and pledge both India and Pakistan to a commitment to protect each other's minorities. Syama Prasad Mookerjee and K.C. Neogy, two Bengali ministers resigned and Nehru was intensely criticised in West Bengal for allegedly appeasing Pakistan. The pact was immediately in jeopardy. Patel however, publicly came out to Nehru's aid. He gave emotional speeches to members of Parliament, and the people of West Bengal, and spoke with scores of delegations of Congressmen, Hindus, Muslims and other public interest groups, persuading them to give peace a final effort. The pact was approved and within a year, most of the Hindu refugees had returned to East Pakistan.

GANDHI'S DEATH AND RELATIONS WITH NEHRU

Patel was intensely loyal to Gandhi and both he and Nehru looked to him to arbitrate disputes. However, Nehru and Patel sparred over national issues. When Nehru asserted control over Kashmir policy, Patel objected to Nehru's sidelining his home ministry's officials. Nehru was offended by Patel's decision-making regarding the states' integration, having neither consulted him nor the cabinet. Patel asked Gandhi to relieve him of his obligation to serve, knowing that he lacked Nehru's youth and popularity. He believed that an open political battle would hurt India. After much personal deliberation and contrary to Patel's prediction, Gandhi on 30 January 1948 told Patel not to leave the government. A free India, according to Gandhi, needed both Patel and Nehru. Patel was the last man to privately talk with Gandhi, who was assassinated just minutes after Patel's departure. At Gandhi's wake, Nehru and Patel embraced each other and addressed the nation together. Patel gave solace to many associates and friends and immediately moved to forestall any possible violence. Within two months of Gandhi's death, Patel suffered a major heart attack; the timely action of his daughter, his secretary and nurse saved Patel's life. Speaking later, Patel attributed the attack to the "grief bottled up" due to Gandhi's death.

Criticism arose from the media and other politicians that Patel's home ministry had failed to protect Gandhi. Emotionally exhausted, Patel tendered a letter of resignation, offering to leave the government. Patel's secretary convinced him to withhold the letter, seeing it as fodder for Patel's political enemies and political conflict in India. However, Nehru sent Patel a letter dismissing any question of personal differences and his desire for Patel's ouster. He reminded Patel of their 30-year partnership in the freedom struggle and asserted that after Gandhi's death, it was especially wrong for them to quarrel. Nehru, Rajagopalachari and other Congressmen publicly defended Patel. Moved, Patel publicly endorsed Nehru's leadership and refuted any suggestion of discord. Patel publicly dispelled any notion that he sought to be prime minister. Though the two committed themselves to joint leadership and non-interference in Congress party affairs, they would criticise each other in matters of policy, clashing on the issues of

Hyderabad's integration and UN mediation in Kashmir. Nehru declined Patel's counsel on sending assistance to Tibet after its 1950 invasion by the People's Republic of China and ejecting the Portuguese from Goa by military force.

When Nehru pressured Dr. Rajendra Prasad to decline a nomination to become the first President of India in 1950 in favour of Rajagopalachari, he thus angered the party, which felt Nehru was attempting to impose his will. Nehru sought Patel's help in winning the party over, but Patel declined and Prasad was duly elected. Nehru opposed the 1950 Congress presidential candidate Purushottam Das Tandon, a conservative Hindu leader, endorsing Jivatram Kripalani instead and threatening to resign if Tandon was elected. Patel rejected Nehru's views and endorsed Tandon in Gujarat, where Kripalani received not one vote despite hailing from that state himself. Patel believed Nehru had to understand that his will was not law with the Congress, but he personally discouraged Nehru from resigning after the latter felt that the party had no confidence in him.

Death

On 29 March 1949, authorities lost radio contact with a plane carrying Patel, his daughter Manibehn and the Maharaja of Patiala. Engine failure caused the pilot to make an emergency landing in a desert area in Rajasthan. With all passengers safe, Patel and others tracked down a nearby village and local officials. When Patel returned to Delhi, thousands of Congressmen gave him a resounding welcome. In Parliament, MPs gave a long, standing ovation to Patel, stopping proceedings for half an hour. In his twilight years, Patel was honoured by members of Parliament and awarded honorary doctorates of law by the Punjab University and Osmania University.

Patel's health declined rapidly through the summer of 1950. He later began coughing blood, whereupon Manibehn began limiting his meetings and working hours and arranged for a personalised medical staff to begin attending to Patel. The Chief Minister of West Bengal and doctor Bidhan Roy heard Patel make jokes about his impending end, and in a private meeting Patel frankly admitted to his ministerial colleague N. V. Gadgil that he was not going to live much longer. Patel's health worsened after

2 November, when he began losing consciousness frequently and was confined to his bed. He was flown to Mumbai on 12 December to recuperate at his son Dahyabhai's flat - his condition deemed critical, Nehru and Rajagopalachari came to the airport to see him off. After suffering a massive heart attack (his second), he died on 15 December 1950. In an unprecedented and unrepeated gesture, on the day after his death more than 1,500 officers of India's civil and police services congregated to mourn at Patel's residence in Delhi and pledged "complete loyalty and unremitting zeal" in India's service. His cremation in Sonapur, Mumbai, was attended by large crowds, Nehru, Rajagopalachari, President Prasad, and many Congressmen and freedom fighters.

CRITICISM AND LEGACY

During his lifetime, Vallabhbhai Patel received criticism of an alleged bias against Muslims during the time of partition. He was criticised by nationalist Muslims such as Maulana Azad as well as Hindu nationalists for readily plumping for partition. Patel was criticised by supporters of Subhash Bose for acting coercively to put down politicians not supportive of Gandhi. Socialist politicians such as Jaya Prakash Narayan and Asoka Mehta criticised him for his personal proximity to Indian industrialists such as the Birla and Sarabhai families. Some historians have criticised Patel's actions on the integration of princely states as undermining the right of self-determination for those states.

However, Patel is credited for being almost single-handedly responsible for unifying India on the eve of independence. He won the admiration of many Indians for speaking frankly on the issues of Hindu-Muslim relations and not shying from using military force to integrate India. His skills of leadership and practical judgement were hailed by British statesmen - his opponents in the freedom struggle - such as Lord Wavell, Cripps, Pethick-Lawrence and Mountbatten. Some historians and admirers of Patel such as Rajendra Prasad and industrialist J.R.D. Tata have expressed opinions that Patel would have made a better prime minister for India than Nehru. Nehru's critics and Patel's admirers cite Nehru's belated embrace of Patel's advice regarding the UN and Kashmir and the integration of Goa by military action. Proponents of free enterprise cite the failings of Nehru's socialist policies as opposed to Patel's defence of property rights and his mentorship of the Amul co-operative project.

Among Patel's surviving family, Manibehn Patel lived in a flat in Mumbai for the rest of her life following her father's death; she often led the work of the Sardar Patel Memorial Trust - which organises the prestigious annual Sardar Patel Memorial Lectures- and other charitable organisations. Dahyabhai Patel was a businessman who eventually was elected to serve in the Lok Sabha (the lower house of the Indian Parliament) as an MP in the 1960s. For many decades after his death, there was a perceived lack of effort from the Government of India, the national media and the Congress party regarding the commemoration of Patel's life and work. However, Patel is lionised as a hero in Gujarat and his family home in Karamsad is still preserved in his memory. Patel was officially awarded the Bharat Ratna, India's highest civilian honour posthumously in 1991.

Patel's birthday, 31 October, is celebrated nationally in India as Sardar Jayanti. The Sardar Patel National Memorial was established in 1980 at the Moti Shahi Mahal in Ahmedabad. It composes of a museum, a gallery of portraits and historical pictures and a library, which stores important documents and books associated with Patel and his life. Amongst the exhibits are many of Patel's personal effects and relics from various periods of his personal and political life. Patel is the namesake of many public institutions in India. A major initiative to build dams, canals and hydroelectric power plants on the Narmada river valley to provide a tri-state area with drinking water, electricity and increase agricultural production was christened the Sardar Sarovar. Patel is also the namesake of the Sardar Vallabhbhai National Institute of Technology, the Sardar Patel University and the Sardar Patel Vidyalaya, which are among the nation's premier institutions. In Richard Attenborough's Gandhi (1982), actor Saeed Jaffrey portrayed Patel. In 1993, the biopic Sardar was produced and directed by Ketan Mehta and featured noted Indian actor Paresh Rawal as Patel; it focused on Patel's leadership in the years leading up to independence, the partition of India, India's political integration and Patel's relationship with Gandhi and Nehru.

6

Dr. B.R. Ambedkar

Dr. B.R. Ambedkar is viewed as messiah of dalits and downtrodden in India. He was the chairman of the drafting committee that was constituted by the Constituent Assembly in 1947 to draft a constitution for the independent India. He played a seminal role in the framing of the constitution. Bhimrao Ambedkar was also the first Law Minister of India. For his yeoman service to the nation, B.R. Ambedkar was bestowed with Bharat Ratna in 1990.

Dr. Bhimrao Ambedkar was born on April 14, 1891 in Mhow (presently in Madhya Pradesh). He was the fourteenth child of Ramji and Bhimabai Sakpal Ambedkar. B.R. Ambedkar belonged to the "untouchable" Mahar Caste. His father and grandfather served in the British Army. In those days, the government ensured that all the army personnel and their children were educated and ran special schools for this purpose. This ensured good education for Bhimrao Ambedkar, which would have otherwise been denied to him by the virtue of his caste.

Bhimrao Ambedkar experienced caste discrimination right from the childhood. After his retirement, Bhimrao's father settled in Satara Maharashtra. Bhimrao was enrolled in the local school. Here, he had to sit on the floor in one corner in the classroom and teachers would not touch his notebooks. In spite of these hardships, Bhimrao continued his studies and passed his Matriculation examination from Bombay University with flying colours in 1908. Bhimrao Ambedkar joined the Elphinstone College for further education. In 1912, he graduated in Political Science and Economics from Bombay University and got a job in Baroda.

In 1913, Bhimrao Ambedkar lost his father. In the same year Maharaja of Baroda awarded scholarship to Bhimrao Ambedkar and sent him to America for further studies. Bhimrao reached New York in July 1913. For the first time in his life, Bhimrao was not demeaned for being a Mahar. He immersed himself in the studies and attained a degree in Master of Arts and a Doctorate in Philosophy from Columbia University in 1916 for his thesis "National Dividend for India: A Historical and Analytical Study." From America, Dr. Ambedkar proceeded to London to study economics and political science. But the Baroda government terminated his scholarship and recalled him back.

The Maharaja of Baroda appointed Dr. Ambedkar as his political secretary. But no one would take orders from him because he was a Mahar. Bhimrao Ambedkar returned to Bombay in November 1917. With the help of Shahu Maharaj of Kolhapur, a sympathiser of the cause for the upliftment of the depressed classes, he started a fortnightly newspaper, the "Mooknayak" (Dumb Hero) on January 31, 1920. The Maharaja also convened many meetings and conferences of the "untouchables" which Bhimrao addressed. In September 1920, after accumulating sufficient funds, Ambedkar went back to London to complete his studies. He became a barrister and got a Doctorate in science.

After completing his studies in London, Ambedkar returned to India. In July 1924, he founded the Bahishkrit Hitkarini Sabha (Outcastes Welfare Association). The aim of the Sabha was to uplift the downtrodden socially and politically and bring them to the level of the others in the Indian society. In 1927, he led the Mahad March at the Chowdar Tank at Colaba, near Bombay, to give the untouchables the right to draw water from the public tank where he burnt copies of the 'Manusmriti' publicly.

In 1929, Ambedkar made the controversial decision to cooperate with the all-British Simon Commission which was to look into setting up a responsible Indian Government in India. The Congress decided to boycott the Commission and drafted its own version of a constitution for free India. The Congress version had no provisions for the depressed classes. Ambedkar became more skeptical of the Congress's commitment to safeguard the rights of the depressed classes.

When a separate electorate was announced for the depressed classes under Ramsay McDonald 'Communal Award', Gandhiji went on a fast unto death against this decision. Leaders rushed to Dr. Ambedkar to drop his demand. On September 24, 1932, Dr. Ambedkar and Gandhiji reached an understanding, which became the famous Poona Pact. According to the pact the separate electorate demand was replaced with special concessions like reserved seats in the regional legislative assemblies and Central Council of States.

Dr. Ambedkar attended all the three Round Table Conferences in London and forcefully argued for the welfare of the "untouchables". Meanwhile, British Government decided to hold provincial elections in 1937. Dr. B.R. Ambedkar set up the "Independent Labour Party" in August 1936 to contest the elections in the Bombay province. He and many candidates of his party were elected to the Bombay Legislative Assembly.

In 1937, Dr. Ambedkar introduced a Bill to abolish the "khoti" system of land tenure in the Konkan region, the serfdom of agricultural tenants and the Mahar "watan" system of working for the Government as slaves. A clause of an agrarian bill referred to the depressed classes as "Harijans," or people of God. Bhimrao was strongly opposed to this title for the untouchables. He argued that if the "untouchables" were people of God then all others would be people of monsters. He was against any such reference. But the Indian National Congress succeeded in introducing the term Harijan. Ambedkar felt bitter that they could not have any say in what they were called.

In 1947, when India became independent, the first Prime Minister Pt. Jawaharlal Nehru, invited Dr. Bhimrao Ambedkar, who had been elected as a Member of the Constituent Assembly from Bengal, to join his Cabinet as a Law Minister. The Constituent Assembly entrusted the job of drafting the Constitution to a committee and Dr. Ambedkar was elected as Chairman of this Drafting Committee. In February 1948, Dr. Ambedkar presented the Draft Constitution before the people of India; it was adopted on November 26, 1949.

In October 1948, Dr. Ambedkar submitted the Hindu Code Bill to the Constituent Assembly in an attempt to codify the Hindu law. The Bill caused great divisions even in the Congress party.

Consideration for the bill was postponed to September 1951. When the Bill was taken up it was truncated. A dejected Ambedkar relinquished his position as Law Minister. On May 24, 1956, on the occasion of Buddha Jayanti, he declared in Bombay, that he would adopt Buddhism in October. On October 14, 1956 he embraced Buddhism along with many of his followers. On December 6, 1956, Baba Saheb Dr. B.R. Ambedkar died peacefully in his sleep.

Overcoming numerous social and financial obstacles, Ambedkar became one of the first untouchables to obtain college education in India. He went on to pursue higher studies in the United States and England, where he earned law degrees and multiple doctorates for his studies and works in law, economics and political science. A famous scholar, Ambedkar practised law for a few years before he began publishing journals advocating political rights and social freedom for India's untouchables. Leading numerous public agitations, he would become a fierce critic of Mahatma Gandhi and the Indian National Congress.

Ambedkar organised untouchable political parties and social organisations, and served in the legislative councils of British India. He would intensify his criticism of orthodox Hindu society and would oppose nationalist rebellions. Despite this, his reputation as a scholar led to his appointment as free India's first law minister, and chairman of the committee responsible to draft a constitution. Ambedkar's work would guarantee political, economic and social freedoms for untouchables and other ethnic, social and religious communities of India. His polemical condemnation of Hinduism and attacks on Islam would make him unpopular and controversial, although his conversion to Buddhism sparked a revival in interest of Buddhist philosophy in India.

Bhimrao Ramji Ambedkar was born in the British-founded town and military cantonment of Mhow in the Central Provinces (now in Madhya Pradesh). He was the 14th and last child of Ramji Maloji Sakpal and Bhimabai Murbadkar. His family was of Marathi background from the town of Ambavade in the Ratnagiri district of modern-day Maharashtra. They belonged to the Hindu Mahar caste, who were treated as untouchables and subjected to intense socioeconomic discrimination. Ambedkar's ancestors had for long been in the employ of the army of the British East India Company, and his father served in the Indian Army at the Mhow cantonment, rising to the rank of Subedar. He had received a degree of formal education in Marathi and English, and encouraged his children to learn and work hard at school.

Belonging to Kabir Panth, Ramji Sakpal encouraged his children to read the Hindu classics, especially the Mahabharata and the Ramayana. He used his position in the army to lobby for his children to study at the government school, as they faced resistance owing to their caste. Although able to attend school, Ambedkar and other Untouchable children were segregated and given no attention or assistance from the teachers. Ramji Sakpal retired in 1894 and the family moved to Satara two years later. Shortly after their move, Ambedkar's mother died. The children were cared for by their paternal aunt, and lived in difficult circumstances. Only three sons—Balaram, Anandrao and Bhimrao—and two daughters—Manjula and Tulasa—of the Ambedkars would go on to survive them. Of his brothers and sisters, only Ambedkar succeeded in passing his examinations and graduate to a bigger school. His native village name was "Ambavade" in Ratnagiri District so he changed his name from "Sakpal" to "Ambedkar" with the recommendation and faith of a Brahmin teacher that believed in Bhimrao.

Ramji Sakpal remarried in 1898, and the family moved to Mumbai (then Bombay), where Ambedkar became the first untouchable student at the Government High School near Elphinstone Road. Although excelling in his studies, Ambedkar was increasingly disturbed by his segregation and discrimination. In 1907, he passed his matriculation examination and entered the University of Mumbai, becoming one of the first persons of untouchable origin to enter college in India. This success provoked celebrations amongst his community, and after a public ceremony, he was given a biography of the Buddha by his teacher Krishnaji Arjun Keluskar also known as Dada Keluskar a Maratha caste scholar. Ambedkar's marriage had been arranged the previous year as per Hindu custom, to Ramabai, a nine-year old girl from Dapoli. In 1908, he entered the Elphinstone College and obtained a scholarship of Rs. 25 a month from the Gaikwad ruler of Baroda, Sahyaji Rao III for higher studies in USA. By 1912, he obtained his degree in economics and political science, and prepared to take up employment with the Baroda state government. His wife gave birth to his first son, Yashwant in the same year. Ambedkar had just moved his young family and started work, when he dashed back to Mumbai to see his ailing father, who died on February 2, 1913.

A few months later, Ambedkar was selected by the Gaikwad ruler to travel to the United States and enrol at Columbia University, with a scholarship of $11.5 pounds per month. Arriving in New York City, Ambedkar was admitted for graduate studies at the political science department. After a brief stay at the dormitory, he moved to a housing club run by Indian students and took up rooms with a Parsi friend, Naval Bhathena. In 1916, he was awarded a Ph.D. for a thesis which he eventually published in book form as The Evolution of Provincial Finance in British India. His first published work, however, was a paper on Castes in India: Their Mechanism, Genesis and Development. Winning his degree and doctorate, he travelled to London and enrolled at Gray's Inn and the London School of Economics, studying law and preparing a doctoral thesis in economics. The expiration of his scholarship the following year forced him to temporarily abandon his studies and return to India amidst World War I.

Ambedkar wrote very learned and theories obtained his M.A and Ph.D. degrees. He returned to India on the 21st of August 1917. There is one thing to note in the years of Ambedkar's education. He studied English and Persian languages in India. In America he studied Political Science, Ethics, Anthropology, Social Science and Economics. In this way he studied many subjects. He obtained his doctorate. Even at that time Ambedkar had a revolutionary mind. He had made an unshakable resolution to wipe out the injustice done to the people of the low cast; in this way he wanted to bring about a revolution in the Hindu Society. But–and this is important before becoming a revolutionary he increased his knowledge. Because of this his thoughts were not mere froth. They had a solid foundation of information. This enabled him to pay a very effective part in framing the Constitution of India. Returning to work as military secretary for Baroda state, Ambedkar was distressed by the sudden reappearance of discrimination in his life, and left his job to work as a private tutor and accountant, even starting his own consultancy business that failed owing to his social status. With the help of an English acquaintance, the former Bombay Governor Lord Syndenham, he won a post as professor of political economy at the Syndenham College of Commerce and Economics in Mumbai. He was able to return to England in 1920 with the support of the Maharaja of Kolhapur, his Parsi friend and his own savings. By 1923 he completed a thesis on The Problem of the Rupee. He was awarded a D.Sc. by the University of London, and finishing his law studies, he was simultaneously admitted to British Bar as a barrister. On his way back to India, Ambedkar spent three months in Germany, where he conducted further studies in economics at the University of Bonn. He would be formally awarded a Ph.D. by the Columbia University on June 8, 1927.

In 1926, he became a nominated member of the Bombay Legislative Council, and led a satyagraha — nonviolent protest and civil disobedience as pioneered by Mahatma Gandhi — Mahad to fight for the right of the untouchable community to draw water from the main water tank of the town. On January 1, 1927 Ambedkar organised a ceremony at the Koregaon Victory Memorial near Pune, which commemorated the Indian soldiers who died during World War I. Here he inscripted the names of the soldiers from his Mahar community on a marble tablet. In a Depressed Classes Conference on December 24, he condemned the ancient Hindu classical text, the Manusmriti (Laws of Manu). Condemning it for justifying the system of caste discrimination and untouchability, Ambedkar and his supporters burned copies of the texts. In 1927, he would begin his second journal, the Bahiskrit Bharat (Excluded India), later rechristened as Janata (The People). He would be appointed to the Bombay Presidency Committee to work with the all-European Simon Commission in 1928. This commission had sparked great protests across India, and while its report was ignored by most Indians, Ambedkar himself wrote a separate set of recommendations for future constitutional reforms. He was injured in an accident that occurred during a visit to Chalisgaon on October 23, 1929. Hoping to help the untouchable community, which was facing a social boycott from orthodox Hindus, he was confined in bed there till the end of the year.

In this speech, Ambedkar criticized the Salt Satyagraha launched by Gandhi and the Congress. Ambedkar's criticisms and political work had made him very unpopular with orthodox Hindus, as well as many Congress politicians who had condemned untouchability and worked against discrimination across India. His prominence and popular support amongst the untouchable community had increased, and he was invited to attend the Second Round Table Conference in London in 1931. Here he sparred verbally with Gandhi on the question of awarding separate electorates to untouchables. A fierce opponent of separate electorates on religious and sectarian lines, Gandhi feared that separate electorates for untouchables would divide Hindu society for future generations.

When the British agreed with Ambedkar and announced the awarding of separate electorates, Gandhi began a fast-unto-death while imprisoned in the Yeravada Central Jail of Pune in 1932. Exhorting orthodox Hindu society to eliminate discrimination and untouchability, Gandhi asked for the political and social unity of Hindus. Gandhi's fast provoked great public support across India, and orthodox Hindu leaders, Congress politicians and activists such as Madan Mohan Malaviya and Pawlankar Baloo organized joint meetings with Ambedkar and his supporters at Yeravada. Fearing a communal reprisal and killings of untouchables, had Gandhi died, Ambedkar agreed to drop the demand for separate electorates, under massive coercion from the supporters of Gandhi, and settled for a reservation of seats. Ambedkar was to criticise the fast of Gandhi as a gimmick to deny political rights to the untouchables and the coercion he faced to give up the demand of separate electorates, in all his writings later.

His Birth and Greatness Foretold : On April 14th, 1891 a son was born to Bhimabai and Ramji Ambedkar. His father Ramji was an army officer stationed at Mhow in Madhya Pradesh—he had risen to the highest rank an Indian was allowed to hold at that time under British rule. His mother decided to call her son Bhim. Before the birth, Ramji's uncle, who was a man living the religious life of a sanyasi, foretold that this son would achieve worldwide fame. His parents already had many children. Despite that, they resolved to make every effort to give him a good education.

Early Life and First School: Two years later, Ramji retired from the army, and the family moved to Dapoli in the Ratnagiri district of Maharashtra, from where they came originally. Bhim was enrolled at school when he was five years old. The whole family had to struggle to live on the small army pension Ramji received.

Even from his boyhood Ambedkar had a mind of steel. Once it was raining very heavily. The boy Ambedkar said the would go to school. His friends said, "These are empty words, how can you go in this heavy rain?" In the downpour, the boy did go to school and that, too, without an umbrella! When some friends found Ramji a job at Satara, things seemed to be looking up for the family, and they moved again. Soon after, however, tragedy struck. Bhimabhai, who had been ill, died. Bhim's aunt Mira, though she herself was not in good health, took over the care of the children. Ramji read stories from the epics Mahabharata and Ramayana to his children, and sang devotional songs to them. In this way, home life was still happy for Bhim, his brothers and sisters. He never forgot the influence of his father. It taught him about the rich cultural tradition shared by all Indians.

The Shock of Prejudice—Casteism: Bhim began to notice that he and his family were treated differently. At high school he had to sit in the corner of the room on a rough mat, away from the desks of the other pupils. At break-time, he was not allowed to drink water using the cups his fellow school children used. He had to hold his cupped hands out to have water poured into them by the school caretaker. Bhim did not know why he should be treated differently—what was wrong with him? Once, he and his elder brother had to travel to Goregaon, where their father worked as a cashier, to spend their summer holidays. They got off the train and waited for a long time at the station, but Ramji did not arrive to meet them. The station master seemed kind, and asked them who they were and where they were going. The boys were very well-dressed, clean, and polite. Bhim, without thinking, told him they were Mahars (a group classed as 'untouchables'). The station master was stunned—his face changed its kindly expression and he went away.

Bhim decided to hire a bullock-cart to take them to their father—this was before motor cars were used as taxis—but the cart-men had heard that the boys were 'untouchables', and wanted nothing to do with them. Finally, they had to agree to pay double the usual cost of the journey, plus they had to drive the cart themselves, while the driver walked beside it. He was afraid of being polluted by the boys, because they were 'untouchables'. However, the extra money persuaded him that he could have his cart 'purified' later! Throughout the journey, Bhim thought constantly about what had happened—yet he could not understand the reason for it. He and his brother were clean and neatly dressed. Yet they were supposed to pollute and make unclean everything they touched and all that touched them. How could that be possible?

Bhim never forgot this incident. As he grew up, such senseless insults made him realise that what Hindu society called 'untouchability' was stupid, cruel, and unreasonable. His sister had to cut his hair at home because the village barbers were afraid of being polluted by an 'untouchable'. If he asked her why they were 'untouchables', she could only answer—that is the way it has always been." Bhim could not be satisfied with this answer. He knew that—it has always been that way" does not mean that there is a just reason for it—or that it had to stay that way forever. It could be changed.

An Outstanding Scholar: While in school, Bhim's teacher Ambedkar, entered his last name into the school records as Ambedkar. Teacher Ambedkar and Pendse, were the only ones in the entire school who were kind and affectionate to young him. They made the few fond memories Dr. B.R. Ambedkar had of his school days. At this time in his young life, with his mother dead, and father working away from the village where Bhim went to school, he had some good fortune. His teacher, though from a 'high' caste, liked him a lot. He praised Bhim's good work and encouraged him, seeing what a bright pupil he was. He even invited Bhim to eat lunch with him—something that would have horrified most high caste Hindus. The teacher also changed Bhim's last name to Ambedkar—his own name.

When his father decided to remarry, Bhim was very upset—he still missed his mother so much. Wanting to run away to Bombay, he tried to steal his aunt's purse. When at last he managed to get hold of it, he found only one very small coin. Bhim felt so ashamed. He put the coin back and made a vow to himself to study very hard and to become independent.

Soon he was winning the highest praise and admiration from all his teachers. They urged Ramji to get the best education for his son Bhim. So Ramji moved with his family to Bombay. They all had to live in just one room, in an area where the poorest of the poor lived, but Bhim was able to go to Elphinstone High School—one of the best schools in all of India. In their one room everyone and everything was crowed together and the streets outside were very noisy. Bhim went to sleep when he got home from school. Then his father would wake him up at two o'clock in the morning! Everything was quiet then—so he could do his homework and study in peace. In the big city, where life was more modern than in the villages, Bhim found that he was still called an 'untouchable' and treated as if something made him different and bad—even at his famous school.

One day, the teacher called him up to the blackboard to do a sum. All the other boys jumped up and made a big fuss. Their lunch boxes were stacked behind the blackboard—they believed that Bhim would pollute the food! When he wanted to learn Sanskrit, the language of the Hindu holy scriptures, he was told that it was forbidden for 'untouchables' to do so. He had to study Persian instead—but he taught himself Sanskrit later in life.

Matriculation and Marriage: In due course, Bhim passed his Matriculation Exam. He had already come to the attention of some people interested in improving society. So when he passed the exam, a meeting was arranged to congratulate him—he was the first 'untouchable' from his community to pass it.

Bhim was then 17 years old. Early marriage was common in those days, so he was married to Ramabai the same year. He continued to study hard and passed the next Intermediate examination with distinction. However, Ramji found himself unable to keep paying the school fees. Through someone interested in his progress, Bhim was recommended to the Maharaja Gaikwad of Baroda. The Maharaja granted him a monthly scholarship. With the help of this, Bhimrao ('rao' is added to names in Maharashtra as a sign of respect) passed his B.A. in 1912. Then he was given a job in the civil service—but only two weeks after starting, he had to rush home to Bombay. Ramji was very ill, and died soon afterwards. He had done all he could for his son, laying the foundations for Bhimrao's later achievements.

Studies in the USA and the UK: The Maharaja of Baroda had a scheme to send a few outstanding scholars abroad for further studies. Of course, Bhimrao was selected—but he had to sign an agreement to serve Baroda state for ten years on finishing his studies. In 1913, he went to the USA where he studied at the world-famous Columbia University, New York. The freedom and equality he experienced in America made a very strong impression on Bhimrao. It was so refreshing for him to be able to live a normal life, free from the caste prejudice of India. He could do anything he pleased—but devoted his time to studying. He studied eighteen hours a day. Visits to bookshops were his favourite entertainment!

His main subjects were Economics and Sociology. In just two years he had been awarded an M.A.—the following year he completed his Ph.D. thesis. Then he left Columbia and went to England, where he joined the London School of Economics. However, he had to leave London before completing his course because the scholarship granted by the State of Baroda expired. Bhimrao had to wait three years before he could return to London to complete his studies.

The British Museum in London has a very good library. It used to open at eight in the morning, and every day Ambedkar would be there by eight. He read till five o'clock. In London he came to know a student called Asnodkar. He belonged to a rich family. He was not interested in study. Ambedkar said to him, "Your people may have made plenty of money. But think, you have born a man, what are you going to achieve? The Goddess of Learning will not come to you whenever you want. We must get her blessings when she comes." In 1922 Ambedkar became a barrister and the nest year he came back to India.

Return to India—Nightmare in Baroda: So he was called back to India to take up a post in Baroda as agreed. He was given an excellent job in the Baroda Civil Service. Bhimrao now held a doctorate, and was being trained for a top job. Yet, he again ran into the worst features of the Hindu caste system. This was all the more painful, because for the past four years he had been abroad, living free from the label of 'untouchable.'

No one at the office where he worked would hand over files and papers to him—the servant threw them onto his desk. Nor would they give him water to drink. No respect was given to him, merely because of his caste. He had to go from hotel to hotel looking for a room, but none of them would take him in. At last he had found a place to live in a Parsi guest house, but only because he had finally decided to keep his caste secret. He lived there in very uncomfortable conditions, in a small bedroom with a tiny cold-water bathroom attached. He was totally alone there with no one to talk to. There were no electric lights or even oil lamps—so the place was completely dark at night. Bhimrao was hoping to find somewhere else to live through his civil service job, but before he could, one morning as he was leaving for work a gang of angry men carrying sticks arrived outside his room. They accused him of polluting the hotel and told him to get out by evening—or else! What could he do? He could not stay with either of the two acquaintances he had in Baroda for the same reason—his low caste. Bhimrao felt totally miserable and rejected.

Bombay—Beginning Social Activity: He had no choice. After only eleven days in his new job, he had to return to Bombay. He tried to start a small business there, advising people about investments—but it too failed once customers learned of his caste. In 1918, he became a lecturer at Sydenham College in Bombay. There, his students recognised him as a brilliant teacher and scholar. At this time he also helped to found a Marathi newspaper 'Mook Nayak' (Leader of the Dumb) to champion the cause of the 'untouchables'. He also began to organise and attend conferences, knowing that he had to begin to proclaim and publicise the humiliations suffered by the Dalits—'the oppressed'—and fight for equal rights. His own life had taught him the necessity of the struggle for emancipation.

Completion of Education—Leader of India's Untouchables: In 1920, with the help of friends, he was able to return to London to complete his studies in Economics at LSE. He also enrolled to study as a Barrister at Gray's Inn. In 1923, Bhimrao returned to India with a Doctorate in Economics from the LSE—he was perhaps the first Indian to have a Doctorate from this world-famous institution. He had also qualified as a Barrister-at-Law.

Back in India, he knew that nothing had changed. His qualifications meant nothing as far as the practice of Untouchability was concerned—it was still an obstacle to his career. However, he had received the best education anyone in the world could get, and was well equipped to be a leader of the Dalit community. He could argue with and persuade the best minds of his time on equal terms. He was an expert on the law, and could give convincing evidence before British commissions as an eloquent and gifted speaker. Bhimrao dedicated the rest of his life to his task.

He became known by his increasing number of followers—those 'untouchables' he urged to awake—as Baba Saheb. Knowing the great value and importance of education, in 1924 he founded an association called Bahiskrit Hitakarini Sabha. This set up hostels, schools, and free libraries. To improve the lives of Dalits, education had to reach everyone. Opportunities had to be provided at grass roots level—because knowledge is power.

Leading Peaceful Agitation: In 1927 Baba Saheb presided over a conference at Mahad in Kolaba District. There he said:—It is time we rooted out of our minds the ideas of high and low. We can attain self-elevation only if we learn self-help and regain our self-respect."

Because of his experience of the humiliation and injustice of untouchability, he knew that justice would not be granted by others. Those who suffer injustice must secure justice for themselves. The Bombay Legislature had already passed a Bill allowing everyone to use public water tanks and wells. (We have seen how Bhim was denied water at school, in his office, and at other places. Public water facilities were always denied to 'untouchables' because of the superstitious fear of 'pollution.') Mahad Municipality had thrown open the local water tank four years earlier, but so far not one 'untouchable' had dared to drink or draw water from it. Baba Saheb led a procession from the Conference on a peaceful demonstration to the Chowdar Tank. He knelt and drank water from it. After he set this example, thousands of others felt courageous enough to follow him. They drank water from the tank and made history. For many hundreds of years, 'untouchables' had been forbidden to drink public water.

When some caste Hindus saw them drinking water, they believed the tank had been polluted and violently attacked the Conference, but Baba Saheb insisted violence would not help—he had given his word that they would agitate peacefully. Baba Saheb started a Marathi journal Bahishkrit Bharat ('The Excluded of India').

In it, he urged his people to hold a satyagraha (nonviolent agitation) to secure the right of entry to the Kala Ram Temple at Nasik, 'untouchables' had always been forbidden to enter Hindu temples. The demonstration lasted for a month. Then they were told they would be able to take part in the annual temple festival. However, at the festival they had stones thrown at them—and were not allowed to take part. Courageously, they resumed their peaceful agitation. The temple had to remain closed for about a year, as they blocked its entrance.

Round Table Conferences—Gandhi: Meanwhile, the Indian Freedom Movement had gained momentum under the leadership of Mahatma Gandhi. In 1930, a Round Table Conference was held by the British Government in London to decide the future of India. Baba Saheb represented the 'untouchables'. He said there:—The Depressed Classes of India also join in the demand for replacing the British Government by a Government of the people and by the people... Our wrongs have remained as open sores and have not been righted although 150 years of British rule have rolled away. Of what good is such a Government to anybody?"

The British had done nothing to alleviate the status of the depressed classes. He declared that India must have a minimum of Dominion Status. He pressed for a separate electorate for the depressed classes.

Soon a second conference was held, which Mahatma Gandhi attended representing the Congress Party. Baba Saheb met Gandhi in Bombay before they went to London. Gandhi told him that he had read what Baba Saheb said at the first conference. Gandhi told Baba Saheb he knew him to be a real Indian patriot.

At the Second Conference, Baba Saheb asked for a separate electorate for the Depressed Classes—Hinduism, "he said—has given us only insults, misery, and humiliation." A separate electorate would mean that the 'untouchables' would vote for their own candidates and be allotted their votes separate from the Hindu majority.

Baba Saheb was made a hero by thousands of his followers on his return from Bombay—even though he always said that people should not idolise him. News came that separate electorates had been granted. Gandhi felt that separate electorates would separate the Harijans from the Hindus. The thought that the Hindus would be divided pained him grievously. He started a fast, saying that he would fast unto death.

The Mahatma's Fast: Gandhiji felt that separate electrorates would only separate the Harijans from the Hindus. The very thought that the Hindu would be divided pained him much. He started a fast against separate electorates. He said he would fast unto death in necessary. There was anxiety in the country because of Gandhiji's fast.

Many Congress leaders went to Ambedkar to save Gandhiji. "Muslims, Christians and Sikhs have obtained the right of separate electorates. Gandhiji did not fast to oppose them. Why should Gandhiji fast to oppose Harijans getting separate electorates?" questioned Ambedkar. "If you are unwilling to give the 'untouchables' separate electorates, what other solution is there? It is essential to save Gandhiji. But just to save him I am not prepared to give up the interests of the backward classes," he declared. He said, reserve a larger number of seats for the untouchables' than the British have given; then I will give up the claim for separate electorates."

Only Baba Saheb could save Gandhi's life—by withdrawing the demand for separate electorates. At first he refused, saying it was his duty to do the best he could for his people—no matter what. Later he visited Gandhi, who was at that time in Yeravda jail. Gandhi persuaded Baba Saheb that Hinduism would change and leave its bad practices behind. Finally Baba Saheb agreed to sign the Poona Pact with Gandhi in 1932. Instead of separate electorates, more representation was to be given to the Depressed Classes. However, it later became obvious that this did not amount to anything concrete.

In the Prime of His Life: Baba Saheb had by this time collected a library of over 50,000 books, and had a house named Rajgriha built at Dadar in north Bombay to hold it. In 1935 his beloved wife Ramabai died. The same year he was made Principal of the Government Law College, Bombay.

Also in 1935 a conference of Dalits was held at Yeola. Baba Saheb told the conference:—We have not been able to secure the barest of human rights... I am born a Hindu. I couldn't help it, but I solemnly assure you that I will not die a Hindu." This was the first time that Baba Saheb stressed the importance of conversion from Hinduism for his people—for they were only known as 'untouchables' within the fold of Hinduism.

During the Second World War, Baba Saheb was appointed Labour Minister by the Viceroy. Yet he never lost contact with his roots—he never became corrupt or crooked. He said that he had been born of the poor and had lived the life of the poor, he would remain absolutely unchanged in his attitudes to his friends and to the rest of the world.

The All-India Scheduled Castes Federation was formed in 1942 to gather all 'untouchables' into a united political party.

Architect of the Constitution: After the war Baba Saheb was elected to the Constituent Assembly to decide the way that India—a country of millions of people—should be ruled. How should elections take place? What are the rights of the people? How are laws to be made? Such important matters had to be decided and laws had to be made. The Constitution answers all such questions and lays down rules.

When India became independent in August 1947, Baba Saheb Ambedkar became First Law Minister of Independent India. The

Constituent Assembly made him chairman of the committee appointed to draft the constitution for the world's largest democracy.

All his study of law, economics, and politics made him the best qualified person for this task. A study of the Constitutions of many countries, a deep knowledge of law, a knowledge of the history of India and of Indian Society—all these were essential. In fact, he carried the whole burden alone. He alone could complete this huge task.

On July 15, 1947, the British Parliament passed the act of Indian Independence and on August 15, 1947, India became free. The Constituent Assemble of Independent India appointed a Drafting Committee with Dr. Ambedkar as its Chairman to draft the Constitution of India. Dr. Ambedkar was also invited to join the Cabinet as the Minister of Law. Ambedkar toiled over the Constitution while he took care of his ministry. In February 1948, Dr. Ambedkar presented the Draft Constitution before the people of India.

After completing the Draft Constitution, Baba Saheb fell ill. At a nursing home in Bombay he met Dr. Sharda Kabir and married her in April 1948. On November 4, 1948 he presented the Draft Constitution to the Constituent Assembly, and on November 26, 1949 it was adopted in the name of the people of India. On that date he said: I appeal to all Indians to be a nation by discarding castes, which have brought separation in social life and created jealousy and hatred."

Later Life—Buddhist Conversion: In 1950, he went to a Buddhist conference in Sri Lanka. On his return he spoke in Bombay at the Buddhist Temple. In order to end their hardships, people should embrace Buddhism. I am going to devote the rest of my life to the revival and spread of Buddhism in India."

Why did he choose Buddhism?: Ambedkar told his friend Dattopant Thengadi: "I am in the evening of my life. There is an onslaught of ideas on our people from different countries from the four corners of the world. In this flood our people may be confused. There are strong attempts to separate the people struggling hard, from the main life-stream of this country and to attract them towards other countries. This tendency is fast growing. Even some of my colleagues who are disgusted with 'untouchability', poverty and inequality are ready to be washed away by this flood. What about the others? They should not move away from the main stream of the nation's life; and I must show them the way. At the same time, we have to make some changes in the economic and political life. That is way I have decided to follow Buddhism." There is a way of life which has come down as a steady stream in India for thousand of years. Buddhism is not opposed to it. The backward people must rebel against the injustice done to them; they must wipe it out. But 'untouchability' is a problem of the Hindu Society. To solve this, a path which does not harm the culture and the history of Bharat must be followed. This is the basis of his resolution.

He did not believe in the theory that Aryans came from a different land and that they defeated the Dasyus' (the Dravidians) of this country. There is no foundation for this in the Vedas. The word 'Arya' appears some 33 or 34 times in the Vedas. The word has been used as an adjective meaning 'the noble' or 'the elder'. It is said in the Mahabharata that 'Dasyus' can be found in all 'varnas' (castes) and 'ashramas' (stage of life). In this way Ambedkar used to support this view.

On 14th October 1956 at a big function in Nagpur, Ambedkar, with his wife, embraced Buddhism. In May 1956, on Buddha's Anniversary, Dr. Ambedkar announced that on October 14 he would embrace Buddhism. With him his wife and some three lakh followers also converted to the faith. When asked why, Dr. Ambedkar replied, "Why can't you ask this question to yourself and... your forefathers...?"

For the next five years Baba Saheb carried on a relentless fight against social evils and superstitions. On October 14, 1956 at Nagpur he embraced Buddhism. He led a huge gathering in a ceremony converting over half a million people to Buddhism. He knew that Buddhism was a true part of Indian history and that to revive it was to continue India's best tradition. 'Untouchability' is a product only of Hinduism.

Bhim was an average student. He became fond of gardening and, whenever he could, he bought saplings and with great devotion nurtured them to full growth. While studying in Satara, many of his classmates left for good jobs in Bombay. He too wanted to go to Bombay and get a job and become independent. He realized that if he ever were to be successful, he would have to concentrate more on his studies. He became interested in reading. He read not just the prescribed books in school but any book in general. His father was too pleased when he digressed from school books but he never said "no" when Bhim wanted a book.

Fight against Untouchability: As a leading Dalit scholar, Ambedkar had been invited to testify before the Southborough Committee, which was preparing the Government of India Act 1919. At this hearing, Ambedkar argued for creating separate electorates and reservations for Dalits and different religious communities. In 1920, he began the publication of the weekly *Mooknayak* (*Leader of the Dumb*) in Mumbai. Attaining popularity, Ambedkar used this journal to criticize orthodox Hindu politicians and a perceived reticence in the Indian political community to fight caste discrimination. His speech at a Depressed Classes Conference in Kolhapur impressed the local state ruler Shahu IV, who shocked orthodox society by dining with Ambedkar and his untouchable colleagues. Ambedkar exhorted his Mahar community to abandon the idea of sub-castes, and held a joint communal dinner in which the principle of segregation was abandoned. Upon his return from Europe, Ambedkar established a successful legal practise, and also organised the Bahishkrit Hitakarini Sabha (*Group for the Wellbeing of the Excluded*) to promote education and socioeconomic upliftment of the depressed classes.

In the same vein, he was highly critical of the practice of untouchability in Indian Muslim Society, lending credence to the view that he was not exclusively against Hindus or Hinduism, but was speaking of reforming social evils. In his illustrious publication "Pakistan and the Partition of India", he writes that, while Islam speaks of "brotherhood", the practice of slavery and caste discrimination were rampant in Muslim society in South Asia, such as the Ashraf/Ajlaf caste divide and the severe discrimination against the *Arzal* castes or Dalit Muslim untouchables. With the help of Shahu Maharaj of Kolhapur, a sympathizer of the cause for the upliftment of the depressed classes, Bhimrao started a fortnightly newspaper, the Mooknayak (Leader of the Dumb) on January 31, 1920. The Maharaj also convened many meeting and conferences of the "untouchables" which Bhimrao addressed. Impressed by Ambedkar, the Maharaj declared at a meeting, "You have found your saviour in Ambedkar. I am confident he will break your shackles."

In July 1924, Ambedkar founded the Bahishkrut Hitkarini Sabha. The aim of the Sabha was to uplift the downtrodden socially and politically and bring them to the level of the others in the Indian society. The Sabha aimed at scrapping the caste system from the Hindu religion. The Sabha started free school for the young and the old and ran reading rooms and libraries. Dr. Ambedkar took the grievances of the "untouchables" to court and gave them justice. Soon he became a father-figure to the poor and downtrodden and was respectfully called "Baba Saheb."

On March 19-20, 1927 a conference of the depressed classes was held at Mahad. Ten thousand delegates attended, workers and leaders attended. Baba Saheb condemned the British for banning the recruitment of "untouchables" into the military. He declared:

"No lasting progress can achieved unless we put ourselves through a threefold process of purification. We must improve the general tone of our demeanour, re-tone our pronunciation and revitalize our thoughts. I, therefore, ask you now to take a vow to renounce eating carrion, the... flesh of... animals, from this moment....Make an unflinching resolve not to eat the thrown away crumbs. We will attain self-elevation only if we learn self-help, regain our self respect and gain self-knowledge."

On December 25 of the same year, thousands responded to Ambedkar's call. Speaker after speaker spoke, passions rose and the vast gathering waited for the satyagraha to begin with intense anticipation. The satyagraha was deferred when the matter was referred to the court. At the end of conference, a copy of the Manusmruti, the age-old code of the Hindus that gave rise to the caste system, was ceremoniously burnt. In a thundering voice, Ambedkar demanded in its place a new smruti, devoid of all social stratification. This act sent shockwaves through the nation. On October 13, 1935, at a conference at Nasik, Dr. Ambedkar reviewed the progress made on the condition of the "untouchables" in the decade since Ambedkar started his agitation. Ambedkar declared that their efforts had not borne the kind of results he had expected. He then made a fantastic appeal to the "untouchables." He encouraged them to forsake the Hindu religion and convert to a religion where they would be treated with equality. The nation was shocked.

The British Government agreed to hold elections on the provincial level in 1937. The Congress, Muslim League and Hindu Mahasabha started gearing up for the elections. Dr. Ambedkar set up the Independent Labour Party in August 1936 to contest the elections in the Bombay province. On February 17, 1937, Ambedkar and many of his candidates won this a thumping majority. Around the same time, the Chavdar Taley water dispute which was referred to the Bombay High Court in 1927 finally handed down its verdict in favour of the depressed classes. The Constituent Assemble adopted the Draft Constitution as the Constitution of India on November 26, 1949 with all its 356 Articles and eight Schedules and Article 11 which abolished untouchability in all forms.

A Legacy Marking Indian Sociopolitical History: Ambedkar's legacy, as a sociopolitical reformer, has been long-lasting on modern India. In post independence India his sociopolitical thought has acquired respect across political spectrum and influenced various spheres of life like socioeconomic, education and Government policies of affirmative action by socioeconomic and legal incentives.

Ambedkar organized untouchable political parties and social organizations, and served in the legislative councils of British India. He would intensify his criticism of orthodox Hindu society, as well as his criticism of slavery and exclusivism in Islam. Despite this, his reputation as a scholar led to his appointment as free India's first law minister, and chairman of the committee responsible to draft a constitution. Ambedkar's work would guarantee political, economic and social freedoms for untouchables and other ethnic, social and religious communities of India.

His polemical condemnation of Hinduism and attacks on Islam would make him unpopular and controversial, although his conversion to Buddhism sparked a revival in interest of Buddhist philosophy in India. In 1926, he became a nominated member of the Bombay Legislative Council. By 1927 Dr. Ambedkar decided to launch active movements against untouchability. He did begin with public movements and marches to open up & share public drinking water resources to which until then untouchable communities had no access; also he put up a struggle for entry in Hindu Temples which was not allowed by upper caste communities.

Poona Pact: Ambedkar had become one of the most prominent untouchable political figures of the time. He had grown increasingly critical of mainstream Indian political parties for their perceived lack of emphasis for the elimination of the caste system. Ambedkar criticized the Indian National Congress and its leader Mahatma Gandhi, whom he accused of reducing the untouchable community to a figure of pathos. Ambedkar was also dissatisfied with the failures of British rule, and advocated a political identity for untouchables separate from both the Congress and the British. At a Depressed Classes Conference on August 8, 1930 Ambedkar outlined his political vision:

> *"...Safety of the Depressed Classes hinged on their being independent of the Government and the Congress" both: "We must shape our course ourselves and by ourselves... Political power cannot be a panacea for the ills of the Depressed Classes. Their salvation lies in their social elevation. They must cleanse their evil habits. They must improve their bad ways of living.... They must be educated.... There is a great necessity to disturb their pathetic contentment and to instill into them that divine discontent which is the spring of all elevation."*

Born in a class considered low and outcast. Dr. Ambedkar fought untiringly for the downtrodden. The boy who suffered bitter humiliation became the first Minister for Law in free India, and shaped the country's Constitution. A determined fighter, a deep scholar, human to the tips of his fingers.

We Need Dharma—But Casteism Should Go: 'Undouchablity' is a branch of casteism; until casteism is wiped out 'untouchability' will not go – this was Ambedkar's firm belief. He argued that to wipe out casteism, political power was very necessary. He believed that Dharma was essential for men. But he revolted against those who, in the name of Dharma, treated some of their fellowmen like animals. Many people criticised him. Some newspapers also wrote against him. There were many occasions when his life was in danger. Also, Ambedkar knew from his own experience that even a bright man could not come up in life vacuse of casteism. People give his cast importance and make him powerless. Ambedkar fought casteism. He was disgusted to find how difficult it was to secure justice and to find how many men were still narrow-minded. He even said that it would be better to give up the Hindu Dharma itself.

Muslim and Christian priest and missionaries learnt about this declaration; they tried very hard to attract Ambedkar. They met and assured him that the 'untouchables' who changed their religion would be given equal status in their society.

THE MODERN MANU

Today Ambedkar's name is remembered in the history of India also because of the role he played in framing the Constitution of India. Ambedkar became the first Minister of Law in independent India. With one voice all India welcomed his appointment. He took oath as a minister.

The country, no doubt, got freedom. It was to be decided how a country with crores of people should be rules. How should elections take place? What are the rights of the people? How are laws to be made? How should the government works? How should courts of law function?—Such important matters had to be decided, and laws had to be made. The Constitution answers all such questions and lays down rules.

It was a very difficult task to prepare the Constitution. A study of the Constitutions of many countries, a deep knowledge of law, knowledge of the history of India and of the Indian society, the patience and wisdom to weigh different opinion-all these were essential. On 29th August 1947, a committee was constituted to frame the Constitution of India. Ambedkar was chosen as its Chairman. Shri T. T. Krishnamachari, a member of the committee, himself has said:

> *"Though a committee of seven members was formed, one of then resigned. Another was nominated in his place. Another member died. No one took his place. One of the members was very busy*

with government work. Owing to ill health two other members were far away from Delhi. As a result, Dr. Ambedkar alone had to carry the entire burden of preparing the draft of the Constitution. The work he has done is admirable".

As the Minister for Law, Dr. Ambedkar placed the draft Constitution before the Constituent Assembly on 4th November 1948.

He gave satisfactory answers to many questions about the Constitution.

The part of the Constitution wiping out 'untouchanblity' was approved on 29th November 1948. Ambedkar's struggle bore fruit in his own life time. A new chapter began in social life. We should remember the words of Ambedkar in answer to the debate on the Indian Constitution:

"India has lost her freedom only owing to treason of her own people. Raja Dahir of Sindh was defeated by Muhammad Bin Qasim. The only reason for this defeat was that the generals of the Sindh army took bribes from Jasim's men and did not fight for the king. It was Raja Jaichand of India who invited Muhammad Ghori to fight against Prithviraj. When Shivaji was fighting for the freedom of the Hindus, other Maratha leaders and Rajputs were fighting for the Mughals. When the Sikhs were fighting against the British, their leader did nothing.... Such things should not happen again; therefore, everyone must resolve to fight to the last drop of his blood, to defend the freedom of India"

The Constituent Assembly accepted the draft India Constitution on 26th November 1949.

A Life of Fulfilment: Ambedkar's entire life was dedicated to one purpose – securing justice and equality to those people who are called 'untouchalbes'. He had said many times "God will spare me till I complete my work for the 'untouchables'. "He lived to see 'untouchability' declared a crime. The 'untouchables' had secured political equality. They should enjoy social equality also – this feeling was beginning to grow in the country.

As early as in 1951, Ambedkar's health had begun to fail. Yet he continued to work saying that he would not succumb to ill health when there was work to be done. On 6th December 1956 he breathed his last. Thousand and thousands of people watched the funeral procession and expressed their sorrow and admiration. Five hundred thousand people witnessed the last rites.

Ambedkar was very fond of books. He had set apart a part of his house "Rajagriha' for them. When he suffered from an eye trouble, he was particularly unhappy that he could not read. Whenever he went abroad, he used to buy books. Once he bought more than two thousand books in New York, "untoucalbes', 'Buddha and His Gospel', 'Revolution and Counter – Revolution in India', 'Buddha and Karl Marx' and 'The Riddle of Hinduism'– these are some of the books he wrote. His books show how widely he had read, how he had gathered information, and how he could think for himself.

It appears that anger and perseverance are the two most important qualities that stand out in Ambedkar's life. This is true from one point of view. The Hindus had called some people 'untouchables' and treated them very unjustly. This went on for hundreds of years. Ambedkar struggled hard to strengthen his people; he knew that those who are weak are bound to suffer. Once he said," Goats are sacrificed, not lions.' He attacked like lightening those who practised injustice. He opposed the British, he opposed the Hindu that were victims of the past, he opposed even Gandhiji, he opposed the Government of free India; he brought justice to the 'untouchables'. At times his own life was in danger; but he gave no thought to it. It is important to notice another aspect of his Himalayan personality. He was very learned. At school he was not allowed to study Sanskrit, but later in life he did learn Sanskrit.

As the president of the people's Education Society he opened a number of schools and colleges; as a result people of backward classes could get education. He spent some days in Aurangabad. He saw that there were no plants or trees in the bit compound of the college. He said that any one who wanted to meet him should plant a sapling; otherwise he (Ambedkar) would not see him. In a few days more than a hundred saplings appeared inside the compound. Once in front of a hostel he saw shrubs. He himself began to clean the ground with a pickaxe and shovel. The root of his anger was kindness. It is no wonder that at the end he turned to Buddha, 'the ocean of compassion'. His heart melted in pity when he saw those who, born as men, lived worse than animals, without the respect and the justice every man should receive. That is why he opposed 'untouchability'. He felt that men need Dharma. "Food alone is not enough. Man has a mind, which also requires food. Dharma gives man hope and makes him active" he said. Once he went to Ambedkar. He said he had made avow to God and he begged for Ambedkar's permission to carry out the vow. Ambedkar asked with a smile, "Who told you that I have no faith in God? Go, do as you wish." Once an old lady knocked at his door at early in the morning. Weeping, she said, "My husband is very sick. I tried for 12 hours to admit him to the hospital. They said that there was no room in the hospital." Ambedkar himself went with her and admitted her husband to the hospital. Once, when Dr. Ambedkar resigned as Principal, a boy came to him crying. He was a Brahmin boy. He was very poor. He had a scholarship for two years. He was doubtful whether he would get it during the last year of his stay.

Ambedkar was grieved at his story. He comforted him. He made him sit with him for food. Then he gave him fifty rupees. He patted him on his back and said "if you are in trouble again, come and tell me." When Ambedkar himself was in poor health, he heard that his gardener was not well. He took another man with him and, using a stick for support, went to see the gardener. "Who will look after my wife, if I should die?" – this thought troubled the gardener. Ambedkar comforted him. He said "Do not cry, everyone has to die one day or the other. I too have to die one day. Be brave. I will send you medicine. You will be all right." He sent the medicine. The very next day Ambedkar died in his sleep.

A Lion Among Men: Ambedkar was born in a cast which was considered as the lowest of the low. People said that it was a sin if they offered him water to drink, and that if he sat in a cart it would become unclean. But this very man framed the Constitution for the country. His entire life was one of struggles. And his personal life was too misirable; he had lost his first wife and sons. But even though he did not lost hid dareness. It is no wonder that everyone called him 'Baba Saheb', out of love and admiration. Bhimrao Ambedkar was the lion-hearted man who fought for equality, justice and humanity.

"Inequality is the soul of Hinduism," wrote Ambedkar. He characterized the oppressive caste system as the tyranny of Hinduism. After spending a lifetime in a crusade against the oppressive Hinduism, Ambedkar finally renounced Hinduism, and converted to Buddhism and exhorted his followers to do the same. It is an irony that BJP and other Sangh Parivar outfits are trying to appropriate such a historic personality as Dr. B.R. Ambedkar.

They have started unveiling Ambedkar photos and statues. Some Sangh ideologies have torn some quotations of B.R. Ambedkar on Islamic invasions out of context and misinterpreted them to fit Ambedkar in their own anti-Islamic framework. Vinay Katiyar took out an Ambedkar Yatra in UP. Mayawati unveiled a statue of Ambedkar's wife even though her party, the BSP, shamelessly betrayed the Ambedkar tradition by aligning with his arch ideological-political foes, the Hindutva brigade, in a coalition for the sake of power.

To attract dalits to its fold, the BJP made Bangaru Laxman its ornamental chief but he had to ignominiously bow down from office for accepting Tehelka cash bundles. But before his resignation he made a speech in the Nagpur session of the BJP National Council almost equating Ambedkar with Hedgewar. In fact, the actual history convincingly refutes the dirty tricks of the Sangh Parivar.

During the freedom movement, because of the failures and neglect of the Congress a few political streams arose independent of it. Because of the Congress neglect of Muslims and the influence of Hindu conservatism and Hindu dominance in Congress leadership, Muslims rallied independently under the Muslim League. For similar reasons, Sikhs also rallied under the Akali Dal. Brahminical upper caste forces dominated the Congress leadership and the party turned a blind eye to the aspirations of nationalities. In Tamil Nadu, Periyar E.V. Ramasamy fought against this, first through the anti-Brahmin movement and then went on to represent the nationality aspirations of Tamils.

It was Ambedkar who squarely put social reform on the agenda during the freedom struggle and launched a simultaneous movement against untouchability and the caste order that were the hallmarks of Hinduism, and championed the interests of dalits. In this he was far to the left of Gandhi. On the other hand, far to the right of Gandhian leadership there was first Hindu Mahasabha and later RSS streams, which often collaborated with the British and considered, with open hostility, even Gandhi too liberal. This hostility finally culminated in the assassination of Gandhi by an RSS man Nathuram Godse. Ambedkar was lifelong at loggerheads with the Hindu fundamentalists. Even in his Thoughts on Pakistan, (on which Katiyar's portrayal of him as an anti-Muslim Hindutva figure rests), he ruthlessly critiques the Hindu Mahasabha and Savarkar. He writes: "The Hindu nationalist who hopes that Britain will coerce the Muslims into abandoning Pakistan, forgets that the right of nationalism to freedom from an aggressive foreign imperialism and the right of a minority to freedom from an aggressive majority's nationalism are not two different things, nor does the former stand on a more sacred footing than the latter."

This clearly illustrates his criticism of aggressive majorotarian nationalism. He further criticizes Savarkar, commenting that "strange as it may seem, Mr. Savarkar and Mr. Jinnah instead of being opposed to each other on the two nations issue, are in complete agreement about it". But Ambedkar exposes Savarkar's authoritarian intent: "Mr. Savarkar wants the Hindu nation to be the dominant nation and the Muslim nation to be the subservient nation under it."

Such being the historical evolution of different political streams in India, it is clear that the legacy of Ambedkar and Hindu fundamentalism are irreconcilably hostile to each other. Hindutva forces today are trying to delink Ambedkar from his entire legacy, cover up their hostility towards him and try to appropriate him for electoral use.

The fundamental hostility of the Sangh Parivar against Ambedkar was clearly brought to the fore by the vile campaign unleashed against him by RSS ideologue and a BJP minister in Vajpayee's cabinet Arun Shourie through his book Worshipping

False Gods. Shiv Sainiks, the soul mates of Hindutva forces, also launched a struggle against Ambedkar's book The Riddles of Hinduism. This is the actual record of Hindutava forces vis-a-vis the heritage of Ambedkar, which they are trying to hide now in order to appropriate his glorious image for their own vested interests.

Ambedkar was the architect of the constitution of India. Sangh Parivar is even opposed to the marginal secular and liberal features of this Constitution and that is why they have formed a committee to tinker with it. While Ambedkar had total enmity towards Hindu Mahasabha and RSS and other Hindu fundamentalists, he was generally pro-left and, befitting a true democrat in a semi-feudal society, he had a positive attitude towards Marxism though it was unfortunate that the communists in those days failed in their united front tactics and failed to develop a proper relationship with Ambedkar. This was part of their general weakness and shortcomings in India.

The Contrast between Ambedkar and Savarkar: Savarkar's strategy of dissolving more than 3,000 castes into one pan-Hindu identity involves pan-Hindu temples, pan-Hindu dinners, inter-caste marriages, anti-untouchability programmes and the removal of injunctions on caste-ridden vocations and sea-voyage. Thus, Savarkar seems to have admonished Hindus to break off the seven shackles that according to him hindered the progress of the Hindu society. Did this programme really denounce Hinduism? The answer to this question has to be in the negative because the anti-caste programme particularly relating to injunctions against inter-caste marriage and advocating vedic rights for the sudras and ati-sudras given by Savarkar did not have vigour and genuine thrust to attack the Hindu shastras and caste system.

Savarkar's contention regarding inter-caste marriages looked to be so casual that he offered only a qualified support to such marriages, thus replacing the need for creating any conscious motivation necessary for the radical mobilisation of the people towards reaching the desired end. Similarly, Savarkar's attempt to grant the study of vedas and vedic rituals to non-Brahmins though apparently liberal may effectively lead to the Brahminisation of the non-Brahmin castes thus according legitimacy to Hindu shastras. On the contrary, Ambedkar considers inter-caste marriages as the effective means for abolishing caste system. But Ambedkar is also aware that inter-caste dining or even inter-caste marriages are not enough to eliminate casteism. He was of the opinion that for realising the desired goal of casteless society through inter-caste marriages it is necessary to destroy the belief in the sanctity of Hindu shastras.

And for destroying this belief, Ambedkar suggests that people should not only discard the shastras, but they should deny their authority as Buddha and Nanak did. Thus; it can be argued here that socially radical Ambedkar was very unlikely to be attracted by Savarkar whose proposal, according to one of the sincere Savarkarites, contained reformative zeal aimed at revival of Hinduism rather than its denunciation.

Ambedkar was never a Marxist. He could not carry forward his struggle for thorough going abolition of semi-feudalism and against imperialism through a democratic revolution like Mao did in China. He focused mainly on the petty bourgeois and bourgeois intelligentsia from the oppressed communities and worked largely within the system representing their interests in the form of reservation etc. Nevertheless, despite this limitation, he remained an outstanding bourgeois revolutionary democrat who was head and shoulders above many in the Congress leadership and was clearly far more radical than Gandhi.

In the course of his differences against the Congress, he never made any concession to the Hindu Right and always remained hostile to them.

Against Brahminical Hinduism During his boyhood Ambedkar had to suffer lots of personal humiliation due to untouchability. In Chowder Tank satyagraha led by Ambedkar in 1927, the upper caste Hindus attacked him and physically injured him. During the freedom movement Ambedkar emerged as the tallest leader of social reform in India.

Ambedkar asserted: "I was born a Hindu, but never will die a Hindu. What is required is to get rid of the doctrine of 'Chatuvarna'. That is the root cause of all inequality and is also the parent of the case system and untouchability, which are merely other forms of inequality". It is relevant to note here that while both Hedgewar and Golwalkar upheld Manu and thus rationalised the caste system inherent to the Hindu religion, Ambedkar even burnt copies of Manusmruti through a campaign. On December 25, 1927 Ambedkar observed a "Manu Smruti Dahan Din", and publicly burnt Manusmruti. The struggle was known as the "Maha-Sangharsha" of Mahad Satyagraha, and it is an important milestone in Dalit struggle against Brahmanism and Brahminical Hinduism.

Manuvadis had conspired so that Ambedkar did not get a ground for the meeting, but a Muslim gentleman, Mr. Fattekhan, gave his private land to observe this protest. There was a strong reaction in the Brahmanical press, Baba Saheb was called "Bheemaasura" by one paper. Dr. Ambedkar justified the burning of Manusmruti in various articles.

Ambedkar made a scathing attack on Hinduism: "I tell you, religion is for man and not man for religion. If you want to organise, consolidate and be successful in this world, change this religion. The religion that does not recognise you as a human being, or give you water to drink, or allow you to enter temples is not worthy to be called a religion. The religion that forbids you to receive education and comes in the way of your material advancement is not worthy of the appellation 'religion'. The religion that does not teach its followers to show humanity in dealing with its co-religionists is nothing but a display of a force. The religion that teaches its followers to suffer the touch of animals but not the touch of human beings is not a religion but a mockery. The religion that compels the ignorant to be ignorant and the poor to be poor is not a religion but a visitation!"

He added this on the upper castes: "It is your claim to equality which hurts them. They want to maintain the status quo. If you continue to accept your lowly status ungrudgingly, continue to remain dirty, filthy, backward, ignorant, poor and disunited, they will allow you to live in peace. The moment you start to raise your level, the conflict starts. Untouchability is not a transitory or temporary feature; it is eternal, it is lasting. Frankly it can be said that the struggle between the Hindus and the Untouchables is a never-ending conflict. It is eternal because the religion which assigns you the lowest status in society is itself divine and eternal according to the belief of the so-called high caste Hindus. No change warranted by change of time and circumstances is possible." Such being the views of Ambedkar, those who offer political patronage to outfits like Ranvir Sena can have no claim over Ambedkar. The ideologies of Hindutva are trying to rationalise caste system saying that it is a division of labour. Ambedkar refuted this saying, "Caste System is not merely a division of labour.

It is also a division of labourers. It is an hierarchy in which the divisions of labourers are graded one above the other." While the Hindutva brigade is known for defending Manu and the caste system, Ambedkar made a trenchant criticism of the caste system associated with Hinduism: "There cannot be a more degrading system of social organisation than the Chaturvarna. It is the system which deadens, paralyses and cripples the people from helpful activity." He further added, "Caste in the hands of the orthodox has been a powerful weapon for persecuting the reforms and for killing all reform." Relating the inseparable relation between caste system and Hinduism, Ambedkar wrote, "Hinduism is a veritable chamber of horrors. The sanctity and infallibility of the Vedas, Smritis and Shastras, the iron law of caste, the heartless law of karma and the senseless law of status by birth are to the untouchables veritable instruments of torture which Hinduism has forged against untouchables."

In Buddha and His Dhamma, Ambedkar has enumerated the evils of Hinduism in the following manner:

1. It has deprived moral life of freedom;
2. It has only emphasized conformity to commands; and
3. The laws are unjust because they are not the same for one class as of another.

Besides, the code is treated as final. According to Ambedkar, "what is called religion by Hindus is nothing but a multitude of commands and prohibitions." The Sangh Parivar is out to make this code the official code in India under their scheme of authoritarian Hindu rashtra.

Sensing the alienation of dalits, many people, from Savarkar to Gandhi, made token gestures against casteism. The RSS was also forced to come out with some tokenist pronouncements. But Ambedkar put things in the right perspective by saying, "Caste cannot be abolished by inter-caste dinners or stray instances of inter caste marriages. Caste is a state of mind. It is a disease of mind. The teachings of the Hindu religion are the root cause of this disease. We practice casteism and we observe untouchability because we are enjoined to do so by the Hindu religion. A bitter thing cannot be made sweet. The taste of anything can be changed. But poison cannot be changed into nectar."

Ambedkar even made a sarcastic comment against Gandhi: "There have been many mahatmas in India whose sole object was to remove untouchability and to elevate and absorb the depressed classes, but everyone has failed in their mission. Mahatmas have come, mahatmas have gone but the untouchables have remained as untouchables." Ambedkar told dalits that, "You must abolish your slavery yourselves. Do not depend for its abolition upon god or a superman. Remember that it is not enough that a people are numerically in the majority.

They must be always watchful, strong and self-respecting to attain and maintain success. We must shape our course ourselves and by ourselves." He further stressed that, "What you have lost others have gained. Your humiliations are a matter of pride with others. You are made to suffer wants, privations and humiliations not because it was preordained by the sins committed in your previous birth, but because of the overpowering tyranny and treachery of those who are above you. You have no lands because others have usurped them; you have no posts because others have monopolised them. Do not believe in fate; believe in your strength."

It may be recalled that Advani recently raised a controversy over a Buddhist symbol like Ashoka chakra figuring in the national flag and a Buddhist symbol being the national emblem. Regarding their origin Ambedkar explained, "Even though Buddhism is almost extinct in India, yet it has given birth to a culture, which is far better and richer than the Brahminic culture. When the question of the national flag and the national emblem was being considered by the Constituent Assembly we could not find any suitable symbol from the Brahminic culture. Ultimately, the Buddhist culture came to our rescue and we accepted the Wheel of Law (Dhamma-Chakra) as the national symbol." No wonder, a Brahminical high-priest of Hindutva like Advani wanted to do away with these symbols introduced by Ambedkar and his colleagues.

In his slanderous campaign against Ambedkar, the RSS ideologue Arun Shourie questioned the patriotism of Ambedkar. Ambedkar, however, defined patriotism thus, "I do not want that our loyalty as Indians should be in the slightest way affected by any competitive loyalty whether that loyalty arises out of our religion, out of our culture or out of our language. I want all people to be Indians first, Indian last and nothing else but Indians." And despite all his differences with the Congress, Ambedkar remained a staunch nationalist.

For Ambedkar, the conception of a secular state is derived from the liberal democratic tradition of the West. In contrast to the Gandhian misinterpretation of secularism as 'sarva dharma samabhava', Ambedkar said, "No institution, which is maintained wholly out of state funds, shall be used for the purpose of religious instruction irrespective of the question whether the religious instruction is given by the state or by any other body". He further explained the corruption of the concept of secularism in India, "This country has seen the conflict between ecclesiastical law and secular law long before Europeans sought to challenge the authority of the Pope. Kautilya's Arthshastra lays down the foundation of secular law. In India unfortunately ecclesiastical law triumphed over secular law. In my opinion this was the one of the greatest disasters in the country."

Ambedkar effectively punctured the false supremacy of the narrow Brahminical elite: "In every country the intellectual class is the most influential class. This is the class which can foresee, advise and lead. In no country does the mass of the people live the life for intelligent thought and action. It is largely imitative and follows the intellectual class. There is no exaggeration in saying that the entire destination of the country depends upon its intellectual class. If the intellectual class is honest and independent, it can be trusted to take the initiative and give a proper lead when a crisis arises. It is true that the intellect by itself is no virtue. It is only a means and the use of a means depends upon the ends which an intellectual person pursues. An intellectual man can be a good man but he may easily be a rogue. Similarly an intellectual class may be a band of high-souled persons, ready to help, ready to emancipate erring humanity or it may easily be a gang of crooks or a body of advocates of narrow clique from which it draws its support."

Though changing one's religion through conversion is not going to abolish the semi-feudal inequalities, Ambedkar's decision to convert to Buddhism in the evening of his life—just a couple of months before his demise on 6 December 1956—only underlined his disgust and bitterness with the highly iniquitous Hinduism. About 2 lakh dalits converted to Buddhism along with him in October 1956. Since then neo-Buddhism has remained a trend. This clearly rattled the Hindutva bosses who are clamouring for anti-conversion legislation in every state.

A THOROUGH DEMOCRAT

Though Ambedkar headed the committee that drafted the Constitution of the democratic republic of India, he was never fully satisfied with the democracy which came to be established in India. In his opinion, "A democratic form of government presupposes a democratic form of a society. The formal framework of democracy is of no value and would indeed be a misfit if there was no social democracy. It may not be necessary for a democratic society to be marked by unity, by community of purpose, by loyalty to public ends and by mutuality of sympathy. But it does unmistakably involve two things.

The first is an attitude of mind, and attitude of respect and equality towards their fellows. The second is a social organisation free from rigid social barriers. Democracy is incompatible and inconsistent with isolation and exclusiveness resulting in the distinction between the privileged and the unprivileged." "Democracy is not a form of government, but a form of social organisation", he asserted.

He further elaborated, "What we must do is not to content ourselves with mere political democracy. We must make our political democracy a social democracy as well. Political democracy cannot last unless there is at the base of it, a social democracy."

Ambedkar underlined the limitations of formal law and Constitution: "The prevalent view is that once the rights are enacted in law then they are safeguarded. This again is an unwarranted assumption. As experience proves, rights are protected not by law but by social and moral conscience of the society. If social conscience is such that it is prepared to recognise the rights which law proposes to enact, rights will be safe and secure. But if the fundamental rights are opposed by the community, no law, no parliament, no judiciary can guarantee them in the real sense of the world. What is the use of fundamental rights to the untouchables in India?" "If I find the constitution being misused, I shall be the first to burn it," he declared.

Ambedkar also had certain premonitions about the rise of authoritarian forces in India which is coming true before our eyes: "On the 26th January 1950, we are going to enter into a life of contradictions. In politics we will have equality and in social and economic life we will have inequality. In politics we will be recognising the principle of one-man-one-vote and one-vote-one-value. In our social and economic life, we shall by reason of our social and economic structure, continue to deny the principle of one-man-one-value. How long shall we continue to live this life of contradictions? How long shall we continue to deny equality in our social and economic life? If we continue to deny it for long, we will do so only by putting our political democracy in peril". The Sangh Parivar outfits rally tribals and dalits only to use them to attack Christian missionaries as witnessed in Orissa or to launch pogroms against Muslims as seen in Gujarat, and thereby endanger democracy. To frustrate the designs of the Sangh Parivar it is necessary that today communists and genuine Ambedkarites should come together to defend democracy from communal fascists, a democracy to establish which Ambedkar fought so hard.

In his last days, Ambedkar raised a note of warning: "The point is that India once lost the independence she had. Will she lose it a second time? It is this thought which makes me most anxious for the future. What perturbs me greatly is the fact that not only India has once before lost her independence, but she lost it by treachery of some of her own people...Will history repeat itself? It is this thought which fills me with anxiety.. Will Indians place the country above their creed or creed above their country? I do not know, But this much is certain that if the parties place creed above country, our independence will be put in jeopardy a second time and probably be lost forever. This eventuality we all must resolutely guard against. We must be determined to defend our independence with the last drop of our blood!" The rise of Hindutva forces who totally cringe before the US imperialism but at the same time are bent upon establishing a fascistic Hindu rashtra has proved how correct this warning was. As Ambedkar called upon us, we must defend this freedom and democracy with the last drop of our blood.

Baba Saheb Ambedkar has undoubtedly been the central figure in the epistemology of the Dalit universe. It is difficult to imagine anything serious or important in their collective life that is totally untouched by Ambedkar. For the Dalit masses he is everything together; a scholar par excellence in the realm of scholarship, a Moses or messiah who led his people out of bondage and ignominy on to the path of pride, and a Bodhisatva in the pantheon of Buddhism. He is always bedecked with superlatives, quite like God, whatever may be the context in Dalit circles.

It is not difficult to see the reason behind the obeisance and reverence that dalits have for Ambedkar. They see him as one who devoted every moment of his life thinking about and struggling for their emancipation, who took the might of the establishment head on in defence of their cause; who sacrificed all the comforts and conveniences of life that were quite within his reach to be on their side; who conclusively disproved the theory of caste based superiority by rising to be the tallest amongst the tall despite enormous odds, and finally as one who held forth the torch to illuminate the path of their future. Few in the history of millenniums of their suffering had so much as looked at them as humans and empathised with them as fellow beings.

He was their own among these few. It was he, who forsook his high pedestal, climbed down to their level, gave them a helping hand and raised them to human stature. It is a commonplace occurrence to see dalits right from the humble landless labourer in villages to the highly placed bureaucrat in corridors of power, emotionally attributing their all to him. They all believe that but for him, they would still be living like their forefathers, with spittoons around their necks and broom sticks to their behind.

It is thus natural for dalits to place him at the centre as their beacon and conduct their collective affairs as directed by its beam. This beam however is not monochromatic like a laser beam, to use an analogy from physics, but is composed of many light frequencies, the filters for which are controlled not by the masses but by some others. They manipulate this beam as per their desire, sometimes letting some frequencies pass and some times some other. They could selectively amplify some part and de-amplify the other and present an entirely different spectrum. What reaches the masses, thus, is not the holistic and true picture of 'Ambedkar' but its part, sometimes a distorted part, carefully filtered out and amplified by the 'technicians'.

This fragmented and false Ambedkar is what reaches the masses. For them, Ambedkar is no more a historical personality named Bhimrao Ramji Ambedkar. He is already metamorphosed into a symbol—a symbol for their collective aspiration, an icon for the thesis of their emancipation. Because for the masses icons come handy. They are sans complexity of the main body, practical useable artefacts. Iconisation of the great heroes and their ideas at the hands of masses is thus inevitable. Human history is replete with such icons; rather it is largely made of them. The Dalit politicians who never let the masses see the material aspects of their problems and kept them entangled in the cobweb of emotional issues have moreover promoted iconisation of Baba Saheb Ambedkar.

The history of post-Ambedkar Dalit movement is largely influenced by the icons of Ambedkar that were produced by the sociopolitical dynamics of post-independence India. The process of iconisation, whatever be the motivations, has to have the basis, howsoever tenuous, in the material reality, in the facts about the subject. Being essentially a simplification of a complex reality, it involves the playing up of facts as per one's proclivities and propensities. The icons in Ambedkar himself and simultaneously highlights the motive force behind the underlying distortions that they embody. While it largely holds these icons responsible for the current sorry State of the Dalit movement based on the near-monotheistic devotion of dalits towards Baba Saheb Ambedkar, it still considers that the conceptual framework that he reflects could be used, not only to further the emancipatory struggles of dalits to its logical end but also to promote a true democratic revolution in India, provided it is seen in a radical light.

The first part reviews the post-Ambedkar Dalit movement, essentially in relation to certain significant milestones or trends and attempts to trace the specific icon of Ambedkar that underscores each. The second part discusses the general limitations of transpositioning the ideologies, characterising specific episodes in the history across the historical periods and in specific reviews the predominant profiles of the Ambedkar-icons.

It outlines the need to redefine Ambedkar, if he is to be the ideological icon to guide the Dalit movement to its logical end. The third part discusses certain predominant issues that will have to be essentially resolved in the redefinition project and gives clues for profiling 'Ambedkar' for the future Dalit movement. The fourth and final part sums it up, emphasising the relevance and validity of the basic framework implied in Ambedkar's work—to view the contradictions in the society from the standpoint of the worst victim and work for their resolution, to bring about a democratic revolution in India.

NEED FOR A REVIEW

Various icons that the post-Ambedkar movement of dalits appear to have built up, characterise Ambedkar as the maker of the Indian Constitution, provider of the present order, a Bodhisatva, a constitutionalist, a messiah, a saviour, an SC leader, a liberal democrat, a staunch anti-Communist, a social engineer who believed in the reform process and disliked revolutions. It is heavily sculpted by the petty-bourgeoisie outlook that has completely hegemonised the Dalit movement. It rarely reflects the dreamer in him who was perpetually in search of ways and means to see the human society sans exploitation, injustice and humbug.

Many students of the Dalit movement are influenced by these post-Ambedkar reflections in characterising Ambedkar as the bourgeoisie liberal democrat. Does it really project what Ambedkar stood for? Does it capture the full essence of his movement? More importantly, is that the Ambedkar whom we are going to use as the weapon in the emancipatory struggle of dalits?

Dalits as a social group, are still the poorest of poor. A negligible minority has managed to escape poverty limits and to locate itself on to a continuum ranging up to a reasonable level of prosperity with the help of certain State policies like reservation and political patronage. In social terms however, all dalits, irrespective of their economic standing, still suffer oppression. This social oppression varies from the crudest variety of untouchability, still being practised in rural areas, to the sophisticated forms of discrimination encountered even in the modern sectors of urban life. Although, the statistics indicate that dalits have made significant progress on almost all parameters during the last five decades, the relative distance between them and non-dalits seems to have remained the same or has increased.

More than 75 per cent of the Dalit workers are still connected with land; 25 per cent being the marginal and small farmers and the balance 50 per cent being landless labourers. The proportion of dalits landless labourers to the total labourers has shown a steady rising trend.

In urban areas, they work mainly in the unorganised sector where the exploitation compares well with that of a feudal rural setting. Out of the total Dalit population of 138 million, the number of dalits in services falling in the domain of reservations does not exceed 1.3 million including sweepers; less than even a percent. And this too would be grossly misleading, as out of this 1.3 million the relatively well-off group A and B officers (in which most of the clerical staff of the PSUs also come), count only 72,212 as against 131,841 sweepers.

With the new politico-economic order emerging in the world, the grammar of the Dalit liberation struggle is going to be totally different from that familiar to dalits. The onslaught of the adversarial forces is being felt world over by all the oppressed people and it would be folly for dalits not to feel a part of the latter. Their objective situation as a social block is not represented by the minuscule minority that managed to find themselves in the organised sectors of economy, but by the vast majority who are left behind in the villages or the numbers who toil in the unorganised sectors in towns and cities. They need the weaponry for battling out their salvation. This battle is to be waged simultaneously on two fronts, marked by the caste and class. These terms under segmented and sectarian usage came to bear an erroneous exclusivity.

Since, Ambedkar still provides a better framework for their problems than any other, and since he commands an unchangeable place in their hearts, the weapons in his armoury needs dusting and sharpening. They will need a review for their effective application in the changing context and possibly, substantial supplementation and replenishment. Ambedkar, quite similar to Buddha in his own hands, needs redefinition. The folklore 'Ambedkar' needs to be replaced by the radical 'Ambedkar', who would inspire people to claim the whole world as theirs and not to beg for petty favours from the robbers.

It is the responsibility of all those who are capable of seeing the reality, to contribute to this task. For, without such a redefinition, Ambedkar could be fossilised as god but would fail in the emancipation project; he might be raised to the highest pedestal by the vested interests but then he would be unable to reach out to where he is most needed; he would lose out to the parody of history.

VISIONS AND ICONS OF GREAT PERSON

Every great person has a vision that impels all her/his works. Its discernibility may vary from case to case, generally being the function of the degree of turbulence around her/him, her/his relative position within the power structure in the given environment, her/his own equipment and conception of self-role. Marx, for instance, offers an articulate vision in clearest terms as he assumed the primary role of a philosopher to bring about revolutionary change, whereas Ambedkar had donned the mantle of mass-leadership in his primary role to spearhead the change; the degree of turbulence in the work domain of Marx had been minimal as he basically struggled in the realm of thought spanning complete human history whereas Ambedkar situated himself in the political turbulence that obtained in India as his strategy;

Ambedkar's position in the power structure that bounded his work domain was certainly weak relative to Marx's.

This is neither to undermine the role of Marx as the activist constantly trying out his philosophy in the realm of practice nor to belittle the problems he suffered in life. With regard to personal equipment, both Ambedkar as well as Marx, could be taken to be equally equipped to undertake their respective tasks that they had undertaken. Marx had started off with philosophy and adopted the class-consciousness of the proletariat quite unlike Ambedkar, in whose case it was his own consciousness—the consciousness of an untouchable built up through concrete experience that had propelled his philosophical search.

Marx was well aware of his role in the revolutionary project, that he had to provide requisite tools and tackles for the working class for bringing about a change in the overall interest of humanity. But, Ambedkar was always loaded with anxiety as he had to strategize his way through the political maze around him, winning for dalits the maximum he could in a short span of time. In process, his role also underwent transformation with the expanse of the battleground. Inevitably, his thoughts and action always remained context-laden, polemical and pragmatically purposeful. It is therefore a relatively difficult task to discern a coherent vision underscoring the life work of Baba Saheb Ambedkar.

It is a moot point as to what extent a great person, who is essentially anchored in her/his space and time, could transcend these barriers and be equally effective in a different situation. A great person basically is the product of prevailing social relations. It is a particular moment in history that reflects an acute demand for such a person. Depending upon her/his location in the social setting, she/he imparts her/his individual feature to the historical moments and movements in terms of working out specific means for resolving contradictions that engender them and releasing the forces of history in a specific direction.

The masses whose cause she / he espouses throng around her/him in this process, depending upon the level of their collective consciousness. The longevity of the ideas a great person propounds in a historical setting depends upon the nature of contradictions, the size and expanse of problems and the time domain in which they are situated.

Generally, the classes that share the vision and ideology of such persons tend to iconise them with specific attributes of their class choice, in an attempt to institutionalise the latter. In this process, they would de-contextise some of the ideas and proffer them as universal theorems, if they perceive a pay-off for themselves in the sphere hegemonised by them.

This phenomenon becomes clear only over a long time horizon. For instance, the religious principles that were sprouted in the soil of certain specific social relations have basically blossomed in an alien soil with the help of the nutrients of class interests. Very broadly speaking, the trend of iconisation of great persons and the attempt of institutionalising their ideas is a gauge to assess the forces of status quo in the society.

COMMITMENT AND CONSTRAINT

In the case of Baba Saheb Ambedkar, iconisation was inevitable. The combination of factors like his high stature, his devotion to the cause of his people; the historical setting in which he lived, the low level of literacy and political consciousness in masses; and the vested interests of internal as well as external people have been its cause. The problem is not with iconisation as it is with its multiplicity. A question may be pertinently asked can Ambedkar be uniquely represented by a single icon? As Prof. Upendra Bakshi had outlined in one of his articles during the centenary year of his birth anniversary that there were many Ambedkars and had questioned as to which Ambedkar do we commemorate? When he said so, Prof. Bakshi was referring to different facets of Ambedkar's personality that could be virtually segregated.

One can even periodise some of them. For example, the pre-1942 Ambedkar as a young, untouchable man endowed with highest scholastic distinctions, struggling within and without for the emancipation of his people is a grossly different personality than the Ambedkar as a member of the viceroy's Executive Council or the Ambedkar as the law minister in the Nehru cabinet in the post-independence India or the Ambedkar as the chairman of the drafting committee for the Indian Constitution or even the

Ambedkar of still later years who had completely identified himself with Buddhism and in a way completely spiritualised himself.

What comes clearly however, is that the changes in his outlook and role were essentially driven by his unstilted commitment to the cause of emancipation of oppressed humanity in general and dalits in particular. He might not have had appropriate methodological tools to deal with the problem at hand. With the equipment that basically belonged to a school of social engineers, he tried to dissect history. Paradoxically, he attempted to demolish the establishment with the very tools that were forged to serve the ruling classes. By training he did not have the facility to look at history as the continuum of human struggle with a certain inherent logic. He did use history as a repertoire of human episodes and attributed even logic to it but its source was externalised.

NON-DIALECTICAL SOLUTION: STATE AND RELIGION

It appears that Baba Saheb Ambedkar had really internalised the doctrine of momentariness (*Anityatawad* and later *Kshanikwad*) of Buddha and therefore even refused to care for consistency in his views and opinions. This doctrine states that every thing changes every moment, that things are constantly becoming. It follows that in this situation of flux not even mental processes could be static, they had essentially to match the dynamicity of the material world. He thus never hesitated in changing his thoughts or strategy as per the unfolding situation. Viewed another way, these changes can be understood in relation to foci of control.

The degree of consistency in thought and action is generally inversely proportional to the distance of the subject from the foci of control of its surrounding. Ambedkar had nil or little control over his situation. He had to consistently create space for himself and strategize to influence the situation to his advantage. (The dynamics of the situation was propelled by the forces that were variously placed in the adversary camps.) The framework within which he conceived his struggle had exposed him to his lot to respond to this dynamics. The hallmark of Ambedkar's thoughts is the dynamic rationale, which he has consistently employed to comprehend situations and to strategize his response thereto. 'Ambedkar' therefore cannot be captured in static terms. His icon will have to represent the dynamism that he lived. Since, this is an infeasible proposition; we will have to discern the underscoring vision behind his works, the intransient essence of his entire mission to create a suitable icon. This icon, even if it does not resemble the familiar Ambedkar, alone could be the beacon of the Dalit movement.

The concept of *Anityawad* in Buddhism essentially belongs to dialectics that has made Buddha an early dialectician philosopher. The dichotomy that creeps in can only be resolved by dialectical method. It may be questioned whether Ambedkar's method was dialectical. It appears that while he accepts constant becoming of things as the principle underscoring the universe, he faces a dilemma with respect to the conception of order in this State. It could be resolved dialectically in terms of systemic attribute of self-regulation—a characteristic of internal control. But the conventional conception of order, essentially a non-dialectical conception, leads to externalisation of control. Ambedkar, having experienced the brutal aspects of history and unbridled exploitation of man by man, appears in need of a control mechanism operating at two levels, *viz.*, internal and external, so as to maintain the societal order in the desired State. His internal control mechanism is the moral code provided by the religion and the one for external control is the State.

If this moral code is internalised by all individuals and in turn by society as the summation of the latter (as the liberal tradition held), society is expected to have an internal order. If however the baser instincts of some people or group of people defy this order, either as a result of conflicting codes they follow or for any other reason, then in such case the State will step in and restore the order. The will of the collective is supposed to be embodied in the State by the Constitution. It is therefore that Ambedkar has reservation in agreeing with Marx that 'religion was the opium of masses' or the 'State shall eventually wither away'. Ambedkar certainly did not know that the order could be the attribute of the system itself. It is only in the sixties that Cybernetics principles came to lime light that the complex probabilistic systems, which the social systems certainly are, do have the inherent capability of self-regulating and self-organising control.

CHRONOLOGICAL: THE STRUGGLE FOR AN EDUCATION

Born in 1891, the young Ambedkar had (for his caste, for his time and place) a relatively comfortable upbringing. But his mother died when he was only five, and his early childhood brought other painful experiences as well, as he began to experience the full degradation of his place in the subbasement of the caste system.

1891, April 14: Bhimrao Ramji Ambedkar was born in the British-founded town of Mhow, an important military centre near Indore, Madhya Pradesh. He was the fourteenth and last child of Ramji Sankpal and Bhimabai Murbadkar Sankpal. The family's ancestral town was Ambavade (in the Ratnagiri District of Maharashtra).

1894: Gopal Baba Walangkar, retired and living in Dapoli, created the first public petition of the Untouchable movement: it asked the British colonial army to resume its recruitment of from the Untouchable castes.

1894-1896: When Bhimrao's father retired from his career with the British Army in 1894, he settled for a time in Dapoli (in Ratnagiri District). The young Bhimrao had his earliest education there: "At Dapoli in Bombay Presidency, however, there was a government-aided school, and the elder Ambedkar insisted his boys be allowed to attend on the ground that he was an army officer. It was finally arranged that thev and four other "untouchables" might go to the school on the condition that they stay in a room by themselves and never come in contact with the caste children, and above all that they never take a drink from the school water supply. Those terms were accepted, and the future Doctor of Philosophy of Morningside Heights had his first conscious experience in ostracism and in learning at the same time. He was then 6 years old. The Hindu teacher at the school never entered the room in which the outcast children were struggling with their lessons. But occasionally he went to the door, whereupon the six small boys placed their slates on the ground, where he could see them, and then retreated to a far corner to listen to any comment the teacher might have to make. They could ask no questions. If they did not understand the lesson, there was no help from the teacher.... he was the only one of the group who got beyond the first school."

1896:-The family moved to Satara, where Ramji Sakpal found a job with the Public Works Department in Goregaon; Bhimrao was enrolled in school in Satara.

1896: Bhimabai Sakpal died; of her fourteen children, only three sons (Balaram, Anandrao, Bhimrao) and two daughters (Manjula, Tulasa) survived her. The children were cared for by their paternal aunt Mira, who had a disabling hunchback but did her best to look after them.

"Our family came originally from Dapoli Taluka of the Ratnagiri District of the Bombay Presidency. From the very commencement of the rule of the East India Company, my forefathers had left their hereditary occupation for service in the Army of the Company. My father also followed the family tradition and sought service in the Army. He rose to the rank of an officer, and was a Subhedar when he retired. On his retirement my father took the family to Dapoli with a view to settling down there. But for some reason my father changed his mind. The family left Dapoli for Satara, where we lived till 1904."

"My father was a military officer, but at the same time a very religious person. He brought me up under a strict discipline. From my early age I found certain contradictions in my father's religious way of life. He was a Kabirpanthi, though his father was Ramanandi. As such, he did not believe in Murti Puja (Idol Worship), and yet he performed Ganapati Puja—of course for our sake, but I did not like it. He read the books of his Panth. At the same time, he compelled me and my elder brother to read every day before going to bed a portion of Mahabharata and Ramayana to my sisters and other persons who assembled at my father's house to hear the Katha. This went on for a long number of years."

A guarded gateway, but with a gap Bhimrao studied at Satara and then in Bombay, where he did so well on his exams that he was admitted to Bombay University—a unique feat for a member of the Mahar caste in his time and place. His marriage was arranged; amidst any amount of turmoil, he focused firmly on his studies.

Bhimrao entered the Government Middle School at Satara: "His second experience was at Satara, where he was the only untouchable pupil. He was allowed to sit in the same room with other boys, but always on the floor by himself in a remote corner. None could play with him or speak to him." "There was another Brahmin teacher in the High School. His surname was Ambedkar. Obliging and humane, he was a very irregular teacher. He loved Bhim very much. He dropped daily a part of his meal—boiled rice, bread and vegetables—into the hands of Bhim during recess. This teacher has left his impress on the life of his pupil. The original surname of Bhim's father was Sakpal.

It was a family name. Bhim drew his surname Ambedkar from his native village of Ambavade, as Maharashtrian surnames are often derived from the names of the ancestral villages. The teacher took so much fancy to the boy that he even changed his surname from Ambedkar to his own surname Ambedkar in the school records.... Ambedkar gratefully remembered this teacher."

"This incident gave me a shock such as I had never received before, and it made me think about untouchability—which, before this incident happened, was with me a matter of course, as it is with many touchables as well as the untouchables."…. "The incident, which I am recording as well as I can remember, occurred in about 1901, when we were at Satara. My mother was then dead. My father was away on service..."

1901: Ramji Sakpal, who had remarried in 1898, moved his family from Satara to Bombay, the capital city of Bombay Presidency. They found housing in the Dabak Chawl, Lower Parel. Bhimrao soon entered Elphinstone High School in Bombay: "At the age of 13 he went to the government high school at Elphinstone, becoming its [one] untouchable student. Here also he was ostracized, but was allowed to sit alone on a back bench. By this time his abilities with his lessons began to attract attention."

"One day it so happened that the class teacher called upon Bhim to come to the black board to solve an example. Instantaneously there was an uproar in the class. The caste Hindu children used to keep their tiffin-boxes behind the blackboard. Since they feared that their food would be polluted by Bhim's presence near the board, they dashed to the blackboard and hurled their tiffin-boxes aside before Bhim could reach and touch the blackboard. During his high school days both Bhim's elder brother and he were not allowed to take up Sanskrit as the second language. It was the key to the study of the Vedas which were neither to be heard nor to be read by the Sudras and the Atisudras—the Untouchables."

1902: The progressive-minded Shahu I (1884-1922), Maharaja of Kolhapur ordered 50% of the posts in the Kolhapur state services to be reserved for the backward classes. In 1907 he started two hostels open to Depressed Class boys.

1903: Shivram Janba Kamble, a Mahar from Poona, convened a meeting of Mahars from 51 villages at Saswad, near Poona; the result was a petition sent to the Governor of Bombay that requested admission into government jobs, public schools, the police, and the army.

1906: Bhimrao's marriage was arranged, with Ramabai, nine-year-old daughter of Bhiku Dhutre of Wanand, near Dapoli. Some accounts have it that she was related to Gopal Baba Walangkar.

1907: Bhimrao passed the Matriculation Examination that entitled him to enrol in a college affiliated with Bombay University; his marks were average, his best subject was Persian (which he studied in place of Sanskrit).

> *"My community people wanted to celebrate the occasion by holding a public meeting to congratulate me. Compared to the state of education in other communities, this was hardly an occasion for celebration. But it was felt by the organisers that I was the first boy in my community to reach this stage; they thought that I had reached a great height. They went to my father to ask for his permission. My father flatly refused, saying that such a thing would inflate the boy's head; after all, he has only passed an examination and done nothing more. Those who wanted to celebrate the event were greatly disappointed. They, however, did not give way. They went to Dada Keluskar, a personal friend of my father, and asked him to intervene. He agreed. After a little argumentation, my father yielded, and the meeting was held. Dada Keluskar presided. He was a literary person of his time. At the end of his address he gave me as a gift a copy of his book on the life of the Buddha, which he had*

written for the Baroda Sayajirao Oriental Series. I read the book with great interest, and was greatly impressed and moved by it."

1908: Bhimrao entered Elphinstone College, a college affiliated with Bombay University.

1910: Shivram Janba Kamble, another early caste reformer, organized a second Mahar conference at Jejuri; this resulted in a memorandum sent to the British government. Young Bhimrao met the reform-minded Gaikwar of Baroda, Sayaji Rao III (r.1875-1939) who then approved a scholarship of Rs. 25 a month for his education.

Off to Columbia, and on to London: The great escape! At the age of 22, the young Ambedkar came to Columbia, and began to make the intellectual and personal connections that shaped the rest of his life. He experienced what it was to be free—for a time—from the stigma of untouchability.

1912: Bhimrao passed the B.A. Examination (special subjects: Economics and Politics) from Bombay University, and prepared to take a position in the administration of Baroda State. His oldest son, Yashwant, was born.

1913: He had barely begun at his new post when he learned by telegram that his father was gravely ill; he rushed home just in time for a last farewell. "It was February 2, 1913, the saddest day in Bhimrao Ambedkar's life."

1913: The Gaikwar of Baroda announced his decision to offer scholarships to send students for higher education at Columbia University. A scholarship of 11.50 British pounds a month, for three years, was awarded to the young Ambedkar.

Receives Baroda State Scholarship to join the Political Science Department of the Columbia University as a Post Graduate Student where he worked under Professors Seligman, Clark, Seager, Moore, Mitchell, Chadwick, Simkovitch, Giddings, Dewey and Goldenweiser."

1913: Arriving in New York during the third week in July, Bhimrao was housed in Hartley Hall. But he didn't care for the food, and only stayed for a week. In August he moved from

Hartley Hall to "Cosmopolitan Club" (554 West 114th Street), a housing club maintained by a group of Indian students. He finally settled in a dormitory, Livingston Hall (since renamed Wallach Hall, with his friend Naval Bhathena, a Parsi; the two remained friends for life. "'The best friends I have had in life,' Dr. Ambedkar says, 'were some of my classmates at Columbia and my great professors, John Dewey, James Shotwell, Edwin Seligman, and James Harvey Robinson.'"

At Columbia: Prof. John Dewey: One of the major philosophers of education of the twentieth century, John Dewey (1859-1952) became one of the young Ambedkar's heroes. Writing in 1936, Ambedkar referred to the work of "Prof. John Dewey, who was my teacher and to whom I owe so much."

Profs. Shotwell and Robinson: Another of the young Ambedkar's mentors, Prof. James Shotwell (1874-1965) was a Barnard historian who specialized in international relations, and a former student of Prof. James Harvey Robinson (1863-1936), Barnard's first historian—who himself was another of the mentors named by Dr. Ambedkar. Prof. Edwin Seligman: A friend of Lala Lajpat Rai, the well-known economist Edwin R. A. Seligman (1861-1939) became a particularly sympathetic mentor to the young Ambedkar, who continued to correspond with him for years.

During his three years at Columbia (including summers) 29 courses in economics, 11 in history, 6 in sociology, 5 in philosophy, 4 in anthropology, 3 in politics, and 1 each in elementary French and German. (Source: Office of the Registrar, Columbia University.)

"Parents can mold the destiny of children, and if we but follow this principle, be sure that we shall soon see better days; and our progress will be greatly accelerated if male education is pursued side by side with female education, the fruits of which you can very well see verified in your own daughter," Ambedkar wrote from New York in a Marathi letter to a friend of his father. "Let your mission therefore be to educate and preach the idea of education to those at least who are near to and in close contact with you."

1915: The young graduate student passed his M.A. exam in June, majoring in Economics, with Sociology, History, Philosophy, and Anthropology as other subjects of study; he presented a thesis, "Ancient Indian Commerce". For his outstanding achievement, he was honoured by students and professors of the Faculty of Arts at a special dinner. In 1916 he offered another M.A. thesis, "National Dividend of India—A Historic and Analytical Study"; it was this one that later became the nucleus of his Ph.D. dissertation.

1916: On May 9th, he read his paper "Castes in India: Their Mechanism, Genesis, and Development" before a seminar conducted by the anthropologist Prof. Alexander Goldenweiser (1880-1940). Dr. Ambedkar was very proud of this paper, and remained so. He promptly got it published in the Indian Antiquary (May 1917). As late as 1936 he wrote that only shortage of time prevented him from reworking Annihilation of Caste so as to include in it this early seminar paper.

1916: In June he went to London, and in October he was admitted to Gray's Inn for Law, and to the London School of Economics and Political Science for Economics, where he was allowed to start work on a doctoral thesis. He often worked in the British Library Reading Room.

1917: The term of his scholarship from Baroda ended, so that he was obliged to come back to India in June with his work unfinished; he was, however, given permission to return and finish within four years. He sent his precious and much-loved collection of books back on a steamer—but it was torpedoed and sunk by a German submarine. He was appointed Military Secretary to the Gaikwar of Baroda; he had agreed to join the Baroda service as a condition of his scholarship. But this experience was not a happy one. Even to reach Baroda, he had to pay his own expenses; he used the damages paid by Thomas Cook and Company for his torpedoed luggage. And when he arrived in Baroda, things went from bad to worse:

> *"My five years of staying in Europe and America had completely wiped out of my mind any consciousness that I was an untouchable, and that an untouchable wherever he went in India was a problem to himself and to others. But when I came out of the station, my mind was considerably disturbed by a question, 'Where to go? Who will take me?'*

1917: Meeting in Calcutta with Annie Besant as its President; for the first time in its history the Indian National Congress adopted a resolution endorsing "the justice and righteousness of removing all disabilities imposed by custom upon the Depressed Classes."

1918: After the Baroda fiasco, he tried to find ways to make a living for his growing family. With the help of Parsi friends, he became a private tutor, and found some work as an accountant. He also started an investment consulting business, but it failed when his clients learned that he was an untouchable.

Finally he became Professor of Political Economy in the Sydenham College of Commerce and Economics, in Bombay. (This position came about through the recommendation of his London acquaintance, Lord Sydenham, former Governor of Bombay.) He was mostly successful with his students, but some of the other professors objected to his sharing the same drinking-water jug that they all used.

In the new *Journal of Indian Economics* (1-1), he reviewed a book by Bertrand Russell: "Mr. Russell and the Reconstruction of Society". And in the new *Journal of the Indian Economic Society* (1,2-3) he published "Small Holdings in India and Their Remedies".

1919: He testified both orally and in writing before the Southborough Committee, which was investigating franchise matters in the light of the planned Montagu-Chelmsford reforms. He demanded separate electorates and reserved seats for the untouchables: "The real social divisions of India then are: (1) Touchable Hindus. (2) Untouchable Hindus. (3) Mohammedans. (4) Christians. (5) Parsees.

1920: Dr. Ambedkar started a weekly paper, "Mooknayak" ("Leader of the Voiceless"), in Marathi, with the help of the reform-minded Shahu I (1884-1922), Maharaja of Kolhapur. In the first issue he called India a "home of inequality," and described Hindu society as "a tower which had several storeys without a ladder or an entrance. One was to die in the storey in which one was born." The Depressed Classes must be saved "from perpetual slavery, poverty, and ignorance"; herculean efforts must be made "to awaken them to their disabilities." In March, he spoke at a Depressed Classes conference in Mangaon in Kolhapur State; it was attended by the Maharaja of Kolhapur, who publicly praised him as a future national leader. At the end of the conference the Maharaja and his courtiers shocked the tradition-minded by actually dining with Ambedkar and his caste members.

In May, the Maharajah of Kolhapur convened another such conference, in Nagpur, a town later to acquire a major symbolic significance in Dr. Ambedkar's life. "At the conclusion of the conference, Ambedkar made an attempt in the direction of consolidating the forces of the Depressed Classes. In the Central Provinces the Mahar community had eighteen sub-castes. He called the leaders of the community together and gave a dinner in which they all participated. It should be noted that with great persuasion Ambedkar could get all the sub-castes of the Mahar community, and not all the Untouchable communities, to dine together. It was not possible yet to make all the communities belonging to the Untouchables participate in an intercaste dinner!"

Having resigned from his teaching position, in July he returned to London, relying on his own savings, supplemented by loans from the Maharaja of Kolhapur and his friend Naval Bhathena. He returned to the London School of Economics, and to Gray's Inn to read for the Bar. He lived in poverty, and studied constantly in the British Museum.

1922: Through unremitting hard work, Ambedkar once again over fulfilled all expectations: he completed a thesis for a M.Sc. (Econonics) degree at London School of Economics, and was called to the bar, and submitted a Ph.D. thesis in economics to the University of London.

1923: His Ph.D. thesis at the University of London, "The Problem of the Rupee", was challenged on political grounds (for its allegedly subversive, anti-British implications), but was resubmitted and finally accepted; it was at once published in London (by P. S. King and Son, Ltd.), and was "dedicated to the memory of my father and mother, as a token of my abiding gratitude for the sacrifices they made and the enlightenment they showed in the matter of my education."

1924: Back in India, Dr. Ambedkar began to practice as a barrister in Bombay, and also began to lecture part-time at Batliboi's

Accountancy Training Institute. He founded the "Bahishkrit Hitakarini Sabha" (Group for the Wellbeing of the Excluded), to help the Depressed Classes mobilize. Its motto was "Educate, Agitate, Organise."

1925: He published his London School of Economics M.A. thesis as "The Evolution of Provincial Finance in British India", it was dedicated to the Gaikward of Baroda ("for his help in the matter of my education"), and had an introduction by Prof. Seligman. He also gave testimony before the Royal Commission on Indian Currency and Finance.

> *"There is no use pretending that I and my wife have recovered from the shock of our son's death, and I do not think that we ever shall. We have in all buried four precious children, three sons and a daughter, all lively, auspicious, and handsome children. The thought of this is sufficiently crushing, let alone the future which would have been theirs if they had lived....My last boy was a wonderful boy, the like of whom I have seldom seen. With his passing away life to me is a garden full of weeds. But enough of this, I am too overcome to write any more."— A letter to a friend, Aug. 16, 1926.*

1926: The Governor of Bombay nominated him as a member of the Bombay Legislative Council; he took his duties seriously, and often delivered speeches on economic matters.

He led the satyagraha at Mahad to exercise the right of Untouchables to draw water from the Chavdar Tank. He ceremonially took a drink of water from the tank, after which local caste Hindus rioted, and Brahmins took elaborate measure for the ritual purification of the tank.

1927: On January 1st, he held a meeting at the Koregaon Victory Memorial, 17 miles from Poona, which commemorates the defeat of the Peshwa's forces and the inauguration of British rule. The names of Mahar soldiers who fought with the British are inscribed there on a marble tablet. Such meetings still take place annually there on that day.

On June 8, he was formally awarded the Ph.D. degree from Columbia University. His Ph.D. thesis was "The Evolution of Provincial Finance in British India".

On December 24th, he addressed a second Depressed Classes Conference in Mahad; he attacked the *Laws of Manu*, and then a copy of this ancient text was publicly burned, to the shock and horror of many caste Hindus.

1928: Dr. Ambedkar was appointed Professor at the Government Law College, Bombay; his term of appointment ended in 1929.

Dr. Ambedkar was selected as a member of the Bombay Presidency Committee to work with the Simon Commission, drafting guidelines for political change in India. Congress decided to boycott the Simon Commission because it had no Indians on it. Dissenting from the views of many of his colleagues, Dr. Ambedkar prepared a detailed report setting out his own recommendations.

1929: Dr. Ambedkar closed his second journal, "Bahiskrit Bharat" ("Excluded India"), which he had started in 1927, and replaced it with the "Janata" ("The People"), which was published until 1956, when it took on the name "Prabuddha Bharata" (after his conversion).

On Oct. 23, during a visit to Chalisgaon, he had a bad accident, and was confined to bed until the last week of December:

> *"At Chalisgaon I got down to go to a village on the Dhulia line, to investigate a case of social boycott which had been declared by the caste Hindus against the untouchables of that village. The untouchables of Chalisgaon came to the station and requested me to stay for the night with them..."*

The year was 1929. The Bombay Government had appointed a Committee to investigate the grievances of the untouchables. I was appointed a member of the Committee. The Committee had to tour all over the province to investigate the allegations of injustice, oppression and tyranny. The Committee split up. I and another member were assigned the two districts of Khandesh. My colleague and myself, after finishing our work, parted company. He went to see some Hindu saint. I left by train to go to Bombay. At Chalisgaon I got down to go to a village on the Dhulia line, to investigate a case of social boycott which had been declared by the caste Hindus against the untouchables of that village. The untouchables of Chalisgaon came to the station and requested me to stay for the night with them. My original plan was to go straight to Bombay after investigating the case of social boycott. But as they were keen, I agreed to stay overnight. I boarded the train for Dhulia to go to the village, went there and informed myself of the situation prevailing in the village, and returned by the next train to Chalisgaon.

I found the untouchables of Chalisgaon waiting for me at the station. I was garlanded. The Maharwada, the quarters of the untouchables, is about two miles from the Railway Station, and to reach it one has to cross a river on which there is a culvert. There were many horse carriages at the station plying [available] for hire. The Maharwada was also within walking distance from the station. I expected immediately to be taken to the Maharwada. But there was no movement in that direction, and I could not understand why I was kept waiting.

After an hour or so a *tonga* (one-horse carriage) was brought close to the platform, and I got in. The driver and I were the only two occupants of the tonga. Others went on foot by a short cut. The tonga had not gone 200 paces when there was almost a collision with a motor car. I was surprised that the driver, who was hired for driving every day, should have been so inexperienced. The accident was averted only because on the loud shout of the policeman the driver of the car pulled it back.

We somehow came to the culvert on the river. On it there are no walls as there are on a bridge. There is only a row of stones fixed at a distance of five or ten feet. It is paved with stones. The culvert on the river is at right angles to the road we were coming by. A sharp turn has to be taken to come to the culvert from the road. Near the very first side stone of the culvert, the horse, instead of going straight, took a turn and bolted. The wheel of the tonga struck against the side stone so forcibly that I was bodily lifted up and thrown down on the stone pavement of the culvert, and the horse and the carriage fell down from the culvert into the river.

So heavy was the fall that I lay down [=there] senseless. The Maharwada is just on the other bank of the river. The men who had come to greet me at the station had reached there ahead of me. I was lifted and taken to the Maharwada amidst the cries and lamentations of the men, women and children. As a result of this I received several injuries. My leg was fractured, and I was disabled for several days. I could not understand how all this had happened. The tongas pass and repass the culvert every day, and never has a driver failed to take the tonga safely over the culvert.

On enquiry I was told the real facts. The delay at the railway station was due to the fact that the tongawalas were not prepared to drive the tonga with a passenger who was an untouchable. It was beneath their dignity. The Mahars could not tolerate that I should walk to their quarters. It was not in keeping with their sense of my dignity. A compromise was therefore arrived at. That compromise was to this effect: the owner of the tonga would give the tonga on hire, but not drive. The Mahars may [could] take the tonga, but must find someone to drive it.

The Mahars thought this to be a happy solution. But they evidently forgot that the safety of the passenger was more important than the maintenance of his dignity. If they had thought of this, they would have considered whether they could get a driver who could safely conduct me to my destination. As a matter of fact none of them could drive, because it was not their trade. They therefore asked someone from amongst themselves to drive. The man took the reins in his hand and started, thinking there was nothing in it. But as he got on, he felt his responsibility and became so nervous that he gave up all attempt to control.

To save my dignity, the Mahars of Chalisgaon had put my very life in jeopardy. It was then I learnt that a Hindu tongawalla, no better than a menial, has a dignity by which he can look upon himself as a person who is superior to any untouchable, even though he may be a Barrister-at-law.

In the year 1934, some of my co-workers in the movement of the depressed classes expressed a desire to go on a sightseeing tour, if I agreed to join them. I agreed. It was decided that our plan should at all events include a visit to the Buddhist caves at Verul. It was arranged that I should go to Nasik, and the party should join me at Nasik. To go to Verul we had to go to Aurangabad. Aurangabad is a town in the Mohammedan State of Hyderabad, and is included in the dominion of His Exalted Highness, the

Nizam. On the way to Aurangabad we had first to pass another town called Daulatabad, which is also in the Hyderabad State. Daulatabad is a historical place and was, at one time, the capital of a famous Hindu King, by name Ramdeo Rai. The fort of Daulatabad is an ancient historical monument,, and no tourist while in that vicinity should omit a visit to it. Accordingly our party had also included in its programme a visit to the fort of Daulatabad.

We hired some buses and touring cars. We were about thirty in number. We started from Nasik to Yeola, as Yeola is on the way to Aurangabad. Our tour programme had not been announced—and quite deliberately. We wanted to travel incognito, in order to avoid difficulties which an untouchable tourist has to face in outlying parts of the country. We had informed only our people at those centres at which we had decided to halt. Accordingly, although on the way we passed many villages in the Nizam's State, none of our people had come to meet us. It was naturally different at Daulatabad. There our people had been informed that we were coming. They were waiting for us and had gathered at the entrance to the town. They asked us to get down and have tea and refreshment first, and then to go to see the fort. We did not agree to their proposal. We wanted tea very badly, but we wanted sufficient time to see the fort before it was dusk. We therefore left for the fort, and told our people that we would take tea on our return. Accordingly we told our drivers to move on, and within a few minutes we were at the gate of the fort.

The month was Ramadan, the month of fast for the Mohammedans. Just outside the gate of the fort there is a small tank of water full to the brim. There is all around a wide stone pavement. Our faces, bodies and clothes were full of dust gathered in the course of our journey, and we all wished to have a wash. Without much thought, some members of the party washed their faces and their legs on the pavement with the water from the tank. After these ablutions, we went to the gate of the fort. There were armed soldiers inside. They opened the big gates and admitted us into the archway.

We had just commenced asking the guard the procedure for obtaining permission to go into the fort. In the meantime an old

Mohammedan with [a] white flowing beard was coming from behind shouting "The Dheds (meaning untouchables) have polluted the tank!" Soon all the young and old Mohammedans who were near about joined him and all started abusing us. "The Dheds have become arrogant. The Dheds have forgotten their religion (*i.e.* to remain low and degraded). The Dheds must be taught a lesson." They assumed a most menacing mood. We told them that we were outsiders and did not know the local custom. They turned the fire of their wrath against the local untouchables, who by that time had arrived at the gate. "Why did you not tell these outsiders that this tank could not be used by untouchables?" was the question they kept on asking them. Poor people! They were not there when we entered [the] tank [area]. It was really our mistake, because we acted without inquiry. The local untouchables protested that it was not their fault.

But the Mohammedans were not prepared to listen to my explanation. They kept on abusing them and us. The abuse was so vulgar that it exasperated us. There could easily have been a riot, and possibly murders. We had, however, to restrain ourselves. We did not want to be involved in a criminal case which would bring our tour to an abrupt end. One young Muslim in the crowd kept on saying that everyone must conform to his religion, meaning thereby that the untouchables must not take water from a public tank. I had grown quite impatient, and asked him in a somewhat angry tone, "Is that what your religion teaches? Would you prevent an untouchable from taking water from this tank if he became a Mohammedan?" These straight questions seemed to have some effect on the Mohammedans. They gave no answer, and stood silent.

Turning to the guard I said, again in an angry tone, "Can we get into the fort or not? Tell us; if we can't, we don't want to stay." The guard asked for my name. I wrote it out on a piece of paper. He took it to the Superintendent inside, and came out. We were told that we could go into the fort, but we could not touch water anywhere in the fort; and an armed soldier was ordered to go with us to see that we did not transgress the order.

I gave one instance to show that a person who is an untouchable to a Hindu is also an untouchable to a Parsi. This will show that a person who is an untouchable to a Hindu is also an untouchable to a Mohammedan.

The next case is equally illuminating. It is a case of an Untouchable school teacher in a village in Kathiawar, and is reported in the following letter which appeared in the Young India, a journal published by Mr. Gandhi, in its issue of 12th December 1929. It expresses the difficulties he [=the writer] had experienced in persuading a Hindu doctor to attend to his wife, who had just delivered, and how the wife and child died for want of medical attention. The letter says:

> *"On the 5th of this month a child was born to me. On the 7th, she [the writer's wife] fell ill and suffered from loose stools. Her vitality seemed to ebb away and her chest became inflamed. Her breathing became difficult and there was acute pain in the ribs. I went to call a doctor—but he said he would not go to the house of a Harijan, nor was he prepared to examine the child. Then I went to [the] Nagarseth and Garasia Darbar and pleaded [with] them to help me. The Nagarseth stood surety to the doctor for my paying his fee of two rupees. Then the doctor came, but on condition that he would examine them only outside the Harijan colony. I took my wife out of the colony along with her newly born child. Then the doctor gave his thermometer to a Muslim, he gave it to me, and I gave it to my wife and then returned it by the same process after it had been applied. It was about eight o'clock in the evening and the doctor, on looking at the thermometer in the light of a lamp, said that the patient was suffering from pneumonia. Then the doctor went away and sent the medicine. I brought some linseed from the bazar and used it on the patient. The doctor refused to see her later, although I gave the two rupees fee. The disease is dangerous and God alone will help us.*

The lamp of my life has died out. She passed away at about two o'clock this afternoon." The name of the Untouchable school teacher is not given. So also the name of the doctor is not mentioned. This was at the request of the Untouchable teacher, who feared reprisals. The facts are indisputable. No explanation is necessary. The doctor, in spite of being educated, refused to apply the thermometer and treat an ailing woman in a critical condition. As a result of his refusal to treat her, the woman died. He felt no qualms of conscience in setting aside the code of conduct which is binding on his profession. The Hindu would prefer to be inhuman rather than touch an Untouchable.

There is one other incident more telling than this. On the 6th of March 1938, a meeting of the Bhangis was held at Kasarwadi (behind Woollen Mills), Dadar, Bombay, under the Chairmanship of Mr. Indulal Yadnik. In this meeting, one Bhangi boy narrated his experience in the following terms:

> *"I passed the Vernacular Final Examination in 1933. I have studied English up to the 4th Standard. I applied to the Schools Committee of the Bombay Municipality for employment as a teacher, but I failed, as there was no vacancy. Then I applied to the Backward Classes Officer, Ahmedabad, for the job of a Talati (village Patwari), and I succeeded. On 19th February 1936, I was appointed a Talati in the office of the Mamlatdar of the Borsad Taluka in the Kheda District."*

Although my family originally came from Gujarat, I had never been in Gujarat before. This was my first occasion to go there. Similarly, I did not know that untouchability would be observed in Government Offices. Besides in my application the fact of my being a Harijan was mentioned and so I expected that my colleagues in the office would know beforehand who I was. That being so, I was surprised to find the attitude of the clerk of the Mamlatdar's office when I presented myself to take charge of the post of the Talati.

The Karkun contemptuously asked, "Who are you?" I replied, "Sir, I am a Harijan." He said, "Go away, stand at a distance. How dare you stand so near me! You are in office, if you were outside I would have given you six kicks. What audacity to come here for service!" Thereafter, he asked me to drop on the ground my certificate and the order of appointment as a Talati. He then picked them up. While I was working in the Mamlatdar's office at Borsad I experienced great difficulty in the matter of getting water for drinking. In the verandah of the office there were kept cans containing drinking water. There was a waterman in charge of these water cans. His duty was to pour out water to clerks in office whenever they needed it. In the absence of the waterman they could themselves take water out of the cans and drink it. That was impossible in my case. I could not touch the cans, for my touch would pollute the water, I had therefore to depend upon the mercy of the waterman. For my use there was kept a small rusty pot No one would touch it or wash it except myself. It was in this pot that the waterman would dole out water to me. But I could get water only if the waterman was present. This waterman did not like the idea of supplying me with water. Seeing that I was coming for water, he would manage to slip away, with the result that I had to go without water; and the days on which I had no water to drink were by no means few.

I had the same difficulties regarding my residence. I was a stranger in Borsad. No caste Hindu would rent a house to me. The Untouchables of Borsad were not ready to give me lodgings, for the fear of displeasing the Hindus who did not like my attempt to live as a clerk, a station above me. Far greater difficulties were with regard to food. There was no place or person from where I could get my meals. I used to buy 'Bhajhas' morning and evening, eat them in some solitary place outside the village, and come and sleep at night on the pavement of the verandahs of the Mamlatdar's office. In this way, I passed four days. All this became unbearable to me. Then I went to live at Jentral, my ancestral village. It was six miles from Borsad. Every day I had to walk eleven miles. This I did for a month and a half.

Thereafter the Mamlatdar sent me to a Talati to learn the work. This Talati was in charge of three villages, Jentral, Khapur and Saijpur. Jentral was his headquarters. I was in Jentral with this Talati for two months. He taught me nothing, and I never once entered the village office. The headman of the village was particularly hostile. Once he had said, "Your fellows, your father, your brother are sweepers who sweep the village office, and you want to sit in the office as our equal? Take care, better give up this job!" One day the Talati called me to Saijpur to prepare the population table of the village. From Jentral I went to Saijpur. I found the Headman and the Talati in the village office doing some work. I went, stood near the door of the office, and wished them "good morning," but they took no notice of me. I stood outside for about fifteen minutes. I was already tired of life, and felt enraged at being thus ignored and insulted. I sat down on a chair that was lying there. Seeing me seated on the chair, the Headman and the Talati quietly went away without saying anything to me.

A short while after, people began to come, and soon a large crowd gathered round me. This crowd was led by the Librarian of the village library. I could not understand why an educated person should have led this mob. I subsequently learnt that the chair was his. He started abusing me in the worst terms. Addressing the Ravania (village servant) he said, "Who allowed this dirty dog of a Bhangi to sit on the chair?" The Ravania unseated me and took away the chair from me. I sat on the ground.

Thereupon the crowd entered the village office and surrounded me. It was a furious crowd raging with anger, some abusing me, some threatening to cut me to pieces with the Dharya (a sharp weapon like the sword). I implored them to excuse me and to have mercy upon me. That did not have any effect upon the crowd. I did not know how to save myself. But an idea came to me of writing to the Mamlatdar about the fate that had befallen me, and telling him how to dispose of my body in case I was killed by the crowd. Incidentally, it was my hope that if the crowd came to know that I was practically reporting against them to the Mamlatdar, they might hold their hands. I asked the Ravania to give me a piece of paper, which he did. Then with my fountain pen I wrote the following on it in big bold letters so that everybody could read it:

"To,

The Mamlatdar, Taluka Borsad.

Sir,

Be pleased to accept the humble salutations of Parmar Kalidas Shivram. This is to humbly inform you that the hand of death is falling upon me today. It would not have been so if I had listened to the words of my parents. Be so good as to inform my parents of my death."

The Librarian read what I wrote and at once asked me to tear it off, which I did. They showered upon me innumerable insults. "You want us to address you as our Talati? You are a Bhangi and you want to enter the office and sit on the chair?" I begged for mercy and promised not to repeat this, and also promised to give up the job. I was kept there till seven in the evening, when the crowd left. By then the Talati and the Mukhiya had still not come. Thereafter I took fifteen days' leave and returned to my parents in Bombay."

CONFLICT, CONTROVERSY AND CONGRESS

Dr. Ambedkar was now in the midst of his career; this was the central and perhaps most controversy-filled decade of his whole complex life. He was often at odds with Congress, and was attacked by the nationalist press as a traitor. But as always, through all difficulties and frustrations, he persevered.

1930: On Aug. 8, Dr. Ambedkar presided over the Depressed Classes Congress at Nagpur, and made a major speech: he endorsed Dominion status, and criticized Gandhi's Salt March and civil disobedience movement as inopportune; but he also criticized British colonial misgovernment, with its famines and immiseration. He argued that the "safety of the Depressed Classes" hinged on their "being independent of the Government and the Congress" both: "We must shape our course ourselves and by ourselves." His conclusion emphasized self-help: "Political power cannot be a panacea for the ills of the Depressed Classes. Their salvation lies in their social elevation. They must cleanse their evil habits. They must improve their bad ways of living.... They must be educated.... There is a great necessity to disturb their pathetic contentment and to instil into them that divine discontent which is the spring of all elevation."

Dr. Ambedkar was invited by the Viceroy to be a delegate to the Round Table Conference, and left for London in October. He participated extensively in the work of the Round Table Conference, often submitting written statements of his views. His views at the time were described in an unpublished manuscript later found among his papers: "The Untouchables and the Pax Britannica".

"Prince and Outcast at Dinner in London end Age-old Barrier: Gaikwad of Baroda is Host to 'Untouchable' and Knight of High Hindu Caste.."

"But I tell you that the Congress is not sincere about its professions. Had it been sincere, it would have surely made the removal of untouchability a condition, like the wearing of khaddar, for becoming a member of the Congress." On August 14th, 1931, Dr. Ambedkar met with Gandhi for the first time. From Gandhi's side, their discussion was an absent-minded rebuke that seemed to be more in sorrow than in anger; from Ambedkar's side, it was an outburst of passionate reproach.

1932: The All-Indian Depressed Classes Conference, held at Kamtee near Nagpur on May 6th, backed Dr. Ambedkar's demand for separate electorates, rejecting compromises proposed by others. Gandhi, in Yeravda jail, started a fast to the death against the separate electorates granted to the Depressed Classes by Ramsay McDonald's Communal Award. By September 23, a very reluctant Dr. Ambedkar was obliged by the pressure of this moral blackmail to accept representation through joint electorates instead. The result was the Poona Pact. In 1933, Gandhi replaced his journal "Young India" with a new one called "Harijan," and undertook a 21-day "self-purification fast" against untouchability.

1933: Dr. Ambedkar participated in the work of the "Joint Committee on Indian Legislative Reform", examining a number of significant witnesses.

1935: Dr. Ambedkar was appointed Principal of the Government Law College, and became a professor there as well; he held these positions for two years. In May, Dr. Ambedkar's wife Ramabai died after a long illness. Her great wish had been to make a pilgrimage to Pandharpur, but since as an untouchable she would not have been allowed to enter the temple, her husband had never allowed her to go.

On Oct. 13th, Dr. Ambedkar presided over the Yeola Conversion Conference, held in Yeola, in Nasikh District. He advised the Depressed Classes to abandon all agitation for temple-entry privileges; instead, they should leave Hinduism entirely and embrace another religion. He vowed, "I solemnly assure you that I will not die as a Hindu."

The struggle for social justice began to receive increasing attention and support from progressive writers. Mulk Raj Anand's powerful novel "Untouchable" (1935) was followed by "Coolie" (1936), with a foreword by E. M. Forster; both works called international attention to caste and class injustices. In Hindi, there was the work of Premchand.

In December, Dr. Ambedkar was invited by the Jat-Pat-Todak Mandal of Lahore, a caste-reform organization, to preside over its annual conference in the spring of 1936.

1935/36: He composed (or began to compose?), but did not publish, a brief, moving, and largely autobiographical memoir called Waiting for a Visa.

1936: On April 13-14th, he addressed the Sikh Mission Conference in Amritsar, and reiterated his intention of renouncing Hinduism.In late April, the Jat-Pat-Todak Mandal realized the radical nature of its guest's planned speech, and withdrew its earlier invitation. On May 15th, Dr. Ambedkar published the speech he would have given, with an introductory account of the whole controversy. The result, a slim little book called "The Annihilation of Caste", became famous at once.

On May 31st, Dr. Ambedkar addressed the Mumbai Elaka Mahar Parishad (Bombay Mahar Society), during a meeting at Naigaum (Dadar), in Bombay. He spoke in Marathi, to his own people, with vividness and poignancy: "What Path to Salvation?". This was the only time he addressed an audience expressly limited to Mahars.

In August, he founded his first political party, the Independent Labour Party, which contested 17 seats in the 1937 General Elections, and won 15.

The Maharaja of Travancore issued a proclamation allowing temple entry to the Depressed Classes; this was the first such event in modern India.

1937: Dr. Ambedkar published the second edition of "The Annihilation of Caste", adding a concluding appendix that featured a debate with Gandhi over the speech. This work remained a best-seller, going through many editions in the coming years—and exciting much controversy. "It was logic on fire, pinching and pungent, piercing and fiery, provocative and explosive."

1938: Over Dr. Ambedkar's vigorous protests, in January Congress adopted Gandhi's own term "Harijans" ("Children of

God") as the official name for the "scheduled castes." In protest against a term that he considered condescending and meaningless, Dr. Ambedkar and his party staged a walkout from the Bombay Legislative Assembly. Dr. Ambedkar made a number of significant speeches to the Assembly, 1938-39.

1939: In January, he delivered to the Gokhale Institute of Politics and Economics a lecture called "Federation versus Freedom".

During the debate over Congress's plan to leave the government in protest at not having been consulted about the declaration of war on Germany, Dr. Ambedkar made his own loyalties very clear: "Wherever there is any conflict of interests between the country and the Untouchables, so far as I am concerned, the Untouchables' interests will take precedence over the interests of the country. I am not going to support a tyrannising majority simply because it happens to speak in the name of the country.... As between the country and myself, the country will have precedence; as between the country and the Depressed Classes, the Depressed Classes will have precedence."

In November, Congress left the government. Jinnah arranged the celebration of a "Day of Deliverance," and Dr. Ambedkar enthusiastically joined him. Dr. Ambedkar was careful to emphasize, however, that this was an anti-Congress rather than an anti-Hindu move; if Congress interpreted it as anti-Hindu, the reason could only be, he said, that Congress was a Hindu body after all.

Dr. Ambedkar was now lecturing and writing constantly, and was heavily involved in politics. With Independence (and Partition), he joined Nehru's cabinet as India's first Minister of Law, and became the Chairman of the Drafting Committee for the Constitution. Framing the Constitution and guiding it through to adoption was his greatest political achievement.

1940: In December, Dr. Ambedkar published the first edition of his "Thoughts on Pakistan". In this work he argued that though partition would be an unfortunate thing, it wouldn't be the worst possible outcome, and if the Muslims wanted it they had a perfect right to claim it.

1942: He founded his second political party, the All-India Scheduled Castes Federation, which didn't do so well in the elections of 1946.

Dr. Ambedkar was inducted into the Viceroy's Executive Council as Labour Member, a position which he held until his resignation in June 1946. His thoughtful comments in that forum cover various topics.

Congress started the "Quit India" movement. Dr. Ambedkar severely criticized this move. He described it as "both irresponsible and insane, a bankruptcy of statesmanship and a measure to retrieve the Congress prestige that had gone down since the war started. It would be madness, he said, to weaken law and order at a time when the barbarians were at the gates."

1943: On January 19th he delivered the Presidential Address on the occasion of the 101st birth anniversary of Justice Mahadev Govind Ranade. It was published in book form in April, under the title "Ranade, Gandhi, and Jinnah".

In September he also prepared and published the vigorous memorandum, "Mr. Gandhi and the Emancipation of the Untouchables".

1944: On January 29th, he presided over the second meeting of the Scheduled Caste Federation, in Kanpur.

1945: In February, he published a revised version of "Thoughts on Pakistan"; this second, expanded edition was called "Pakistan; or Partition of India". A third edition of this book was published in 1946. On May 6th he addressed the Annual Conference of the All India Scheduled Caste Federation, held at Parel, Bombay. This speech was soon published as "The Communal Deadlock and a Way to Solve It".

In June, he published a political manifesto detailing the problems of dealing with Congress, and accusing it of many acts of betrayal: "What Congress and Gandhi Have Done to the Untouchables". The next year, he published a second edition, with major revisions in one chapter.

1946: In June, he founded Siddharth College, in Bombay; it was a project of the People's Education Society, which he had founded in 1945. In October, he published "Who Were the Sudras? How They Came to Be the Fourth Varna in the Indo-Aryan Society". He dedicated the book to the great early reformer Jotiba Phule.

1947: In March he published "States and Minorities: What Are their Rights and How to Secure them in the Constitution of Free India", a memorandum on fundamental rights, minority rights, safeguards for the Depressed Classes, and the problems of Indian states.

Dr. Ambedkar accepted Nehru's invitation to become Minister of Law in the first Cabinet of independent India. On August 29th he was appointed Chairman of the Drafting Committee for the new Constitution.

1948: In the last week of February, the Draft Constitution was submitted for public discussion and debate: Constitutional discussions and debates.

On April 15th, Dr. Ambedkar married Dr. Sharda Kabir (a Saraswat Brahmin) in Delhi; she adopted the name Savita. He was now diabetic and increasingly ill, and she took care of him for the rest of his life. In October, he prepared a memorandum on "Maharashtra as a Linguistic Province", expressing his views for submission to the Linguistic Provinces Commission. He published "The Untouchables: a Thesis on the Origin of Untouchability" (New Delhi: Amrit Book Company), as a sequel to his book on the Sudras. As always on this subject, he wrote with passion. In the Preface he said, "The Hindu Civilisation.... is a diabolical contrivance to suppress and enslave humanity. Its proper name would be infamy. What else can be said of a civilisation which has produced a mass of people... who are treated as an entity beyond human intercourse and whose mere touch is enough to cause pollution?" In November, the Draft Constitution with its 315 articles and 8 schedules was formally introduced to the Constituent Assembly. Dr. Ambedkar concluded his speech: "I feel that the Constitution is workable; it is flexible and it is strong enough to hold the country together both in peace time and in war time. Indeed, if I may say so, if things go wrong under the new Constitution the reason will not be that we had a bad Constitution. What we will have to say is that Man was vile."

1949: In November, the Constituent Assembly adopted the Constitution, including Article 11, which formally abolished untouchability.

1950: Dr. Ambedkar gave several addresses about Buddhism; in May, he flew to Colombo, in Sri Lanka, to pursue further Buddhist connections.

1951: In February, he introduced in Parliament the "Hindu Code Bill" that he had drafted, which included greatly expanded rights for women; it proved very controversial, and consideration of it was postponed: on the Hindu Code Bill.

In September, Dr. Ambedkar resigned from the Cabinet, embittered over the failure of Nehru and the Congress to back the Hindu Code Bill as they had earlier pledged to do. He became the "Leader of the Opposition".

1952: Dr. Ambedkar received an honorary L.L.D. degree from Columbia University as part of its Bicentennial Special Convocation. The President described him as "one of India's leading citizens—a great social reformer and a valiant upholder of human rights."

1953: His political thinking included analysis of the issue of linguistic states; he published "Need for Checks and Balances" on this question. In 1955, he was still working on the subject, as the preface to "Thoughts on Linguistic States" testified.

1954: In the midst of his round of (increasingly embittered) Parliamentary and other activity, his health gave way; he was confined to bed for two months.

While dedicating a new Buddhist vihara near Poona, Dr. Ambedkar announced that he was writing a book on Buddhism, and that as soon as it was finished, he planned to make a formal conversion to Buddhism. He also claimed that the image of Vithoba at Pandharpur was in reality an image of the Buddha, and said that he would write a thesis to prove this claim.

1956: Dr. Ambedkar brought the manuscript of "The Buddha and His Dhamma" to completion. "In February 1956 two new chapters are added to it: 'There is no god'; 'There is no soul'.... On March 15, 1956, Ambedkar wrote the Preface to his book in his own handwriting and dictated it to Rattu [his secretary]." Printing began in May, but was slowed by constant last-minute revisions of the proofs.

From June to October, he was bedridden in his Delhi residence. His eyes were failing, he suffered from side effects of the drugs he was given for his diabetes, he felt deeply depressed.

His formal conversion took place on Oct. 14th in Nagpur, a town selected for reasons he explained in his moving speech, "Why Was Nagpur Chosen?". Many thousands of Mahars and other Dalits accepted Buddhism along with him.

In November, he flew to Kathmandu to attend the Fourth World Buddhist Conference.

On December 2, he completed the manuscript of "The Buddha or Karl Marx", his last finished work, and gave it for typing.

On the night of December 5 or the early morning of December 6, he died quietly in his sleep; on December 7 there was a huge Buddhist-style funeral procession in Bombay, and he was cremated on the seashore.

1957: "The Buddha and His Dhamma", Dr. Ambedkar's own version of a Buddhist scripture for his people, was posthumously published, by Siddharth College Publications, Bombay.

1957 and beyond: A number of unfinished typescripts and handwritten drafts were found among his notes and papers and gradually made available. Among these were "Waiting for a Visa", which probably dates from 1935-36.

LIBERALISM AND REFORMISM

By upbringing and training Ambedkar was influenced by western liberalism. The openness and liberal values of the western society had struck him with pleasant surprise by his own admission. There is a reason to believe that he had studied Marxism. His first essay on caste reflects some amount of analytical orientation of Marxism. One of the subjects in his curriculum also happened to be related to Marxian socialism and his guide Prof. Seligman was well versed with the economic interpretation of history. However, as his later work reveals, Ambedkar reflected more closeness with the liberal tradition than Marxism. However, consciously he never identified himself with the Liberalism. Being aware of its pitfalls, he needed to declare that he was not a liberal reformist, although while having reservations with the postulations of Marxism he could never hide his attraction towards it.

The pitfall of his thinking emanates from his conception of the moral force of religion divorced from the material reality. He therefore hopes that without any bloodshed, the society based on liberty, equality and fraternity could be created. Of course as hypothesized above, he conceptualizes the constitutional State based on these principles. With this wishful thinking, he tends to ignore the fact that regardless of the pretensions of ruling classes, the impact of liberal governance in the multicentric iniquitous society is bound to result in sustaining multicentricity and inequality.

This liberalism rather promotes politics of casteism and communalism, schism among dalits, their use in political power games, subversion of their real problems and protects the interests of the few rich. It was a kind of contradiction in terms to assume that liberal democracy, which is actually the manifestation of the political power of the bourgeois, will do justice to the paupers. It might appear to extend certain concessions to the weaker sections, but its real motive is to maintain the existing rule of the ruling classes. Liberal democracy might appear better than the decadent Hindu caste system but it is incapable of bringing any real change in favour of dalits. It muffles the tension of the exploitative system and kills the revolutionary motivation of its victims.

REDEFINITION PROJECT

Many of the constructs employed by Babasaheb Ambedkar in his working have a qualified meaning. Firstly, they are not absolute as they appear. They are the derivatives of his thought process, the source of which could be traced to his basic objective of annihilation of castes and creating a society based on equality, liberty and fraternity. Even these three principles that he held so dear to his heart, bear very different meaning from the familiar ones associated with the French Revolution. He said he had them from Buddha. What Buddha said also is to be understood from his interpretation, which could be as different from the accepted version as to be disproved by the Buddhist church. His Buddha and His Dhamma, for instance, had faced this kind of disapproval initially from many Buddhists. Understanding Ambedkar thus essentially demands extra consideration and care about the specific meanings of the constructs and concepts he uses. The lack of it has already caused much misunderstanding among many people. It is one thing to have a clear understanding of what he said or meant but quite another to extrapolate it to something congruent to his basic objective or vision that may be useable in shaping the future movement.

Quite like Marx had said of philosophy, it could be said that the issue is not to understand Ambedkar as he is but to possibly think of him as a weapon in the struggle to which he devoted his life. The redefinition referred to here will have to essentially address both these issues. From the viewpoint of one seeking a revolutionary change, there are indeed many dimensions on which Ambedkar calls for critical interpretation. Many of the concepts that seem to act as the props for his formulations are rooted in the reactionary camp.

Paradoxically, he brings them to work for his emancipatory project, which potentially is no less than a revolution. Predominant among these concepts are identified as State, religion, liberal democracy, constitutionalism, revolution, socialism, violence and Marxism, that some way or the other have been the cause of misunderstandings about him.

It is important to appreciate that Ambedkar employed the search process that is essentially rational and the underlying objective undoubtedly radical. There could be flaws in the specific design or the application of the search process, depending upon the State of his knowledge and complexity of the situation to which it is applied. Besides this, the end result depends upon the repertoire of alternatives used for the search. What it means is that the specific method, thought or action of Ambedkar may constitute the historical facts but they cannot be taken in their face value if one wants to comprehend the ideological aspects of Ambedkar. In his usage of the above concepts for instance he does not always exercise the academic rigour. Besides the reason that much of his usage was addressed to the un-academic lot, most of the times he tended to impart his own meanings to the terms he used. With the changed contexts or with the change in information, he readily changed his opinions. For, hypothetically speaking, if Ambedkar had lived longer he would have certainly changed his views, looking at more information available or experiencing the undesired aftermath of some of his own beliefs and opinions.

Had he not disowned the Constitution, which he had so laboriously written and so forcefully defended, saying that he was used as the hack to write it? Whatever he had done had several limitations. He never hesitated to change his opinion or stand if he was convinced that it was right. The redefinition project proposed here, in a way, is something, which he has done himself, all his life and would have continued doing if he had been alive. It is essentially something in the nature of continuing his unfinished task.

The methodological aspects of this exercise consists in the process of conceptualisation of the core vision and ideological proclivities of Ambedkar through the analytical study of his life within its contextual parameters, oriented towards capturing its intransient content.

It should reflect the basic purpose, that is, to see whether and how he could catalyse the emancipatory movement of dalits and in turn democratise the Indian society. This process may not be free from bias. The bias could be in favour of the change craved for by the have-nots, not of the ruling classes that has necessarily been colouring the history so far.

'AMBEDKAR' FOR THE MOVEMENT OF DALITS

'Ambedkar' for the Dalit movement, first of all, should be shorn of all the sectarian outlook that unfortunately came to be associated with him. He was an iconoclast and therefore should inspire us to break such icons that are imbued with this outlook. Dalits have to demolish all the handiwork of the reactionaries and vested interests. The project of redefinition of Ambedkar should liberate him from the dens of the ruling class and bring him back to the huts in slums and villages where he rightly belongs.

The greatest thing about Ambedkar is his consistent anti-dogmatic stance. He never accepted any thing in name of authority.

He hated humbug of every kind. He always approached problems with a student's sincerity and researcher's intellectual honesty. He gave a vision that even the ideologies are bound by the tenet of impermanence and no body should claim them validity beyond their times. His followers therefore can assume absolute liberty to think through things as per their own experience in changing times.

'AMBEDKAR' AGAINST EXPLOITATION

The underscoring vision in Ambedkar's thought and action is to be found in his yearning for the end of all kinds of exploitation. Whenever and wherever he smelt exploitation, he raised his voice against it. The caste system that subjugated more than one fifth of the population to levels worse than animals' for more than two millennia and which represented institutionalisation of the most heinous inequality by the Hindu religion as ordained by its gods, became the prime target of his life. He attacked it from the standpoint of its victims—the untouchables. He waged many battles; initially targeting the citadels of Brahminism—the custodian of the Hindu religious code, and later politicised the battle, realising the ineffectiveness of the former. He did not let this objective out of sight even for a moment and worked incessantly for its achievement. This Herculean task almost completely overshadows the fact that his struggles extend well beyond the caste struggles and rather encompass all other forms of exploitation.

Even the credit for struggling against untouchability was reluctantly granted to him by the establishment which had belittled him initially as merely a leader of his own caste—Mahar. This prejudicial treatment of Ambedkar could itself be taken as a measure of the severity of the problematic of caste. The facts are clear today that not only was his struggle directed towards the emancipation of all the untouchables but also towards annihilation of the entire caste system. It was basically against the systemic exploitation that ran unabated for centuries. The protest against this inhuman system could be articulated only in a concrete situation, not in a vacuum. He did not theorise the struggle on a hypothetical plane. He built it on the basis of real problems in a concrete situation. Unlike many cases, the motive force for his life mission was provided by his experience itself. Although he pitched his tents against Brahminism, he never bore any enmity against the Brahmins or identified any one for his friend or foe by caste. The Bahishkrit Hitkarini Sabha that was the launch vehicle of his movement had majority from the forward caste people in its executive body. Even later, this intention of having a non-caste base for the organisation could be consistently seen in his movement, be it the Mahad struggle or the Indian Labour Party. He was perceptive enough to say that the Brahminism could exist in all the castes including the untouchables, for that was the essence of the casteism. It is tragic to find his legacy being monopolised today by only the scheduled castes.

Although, he considered the magnitude of the problem of emancipation of dalits is such as to warrant his sole attention, he did take cudgels for other oppressed entities like workers, peasants and women. At one occasion in response to the accusation that he did not care for the tribals, he had to squarely admit the fact that he considered the problem at hand big enough to outlast his life and provokedly put that he never claimed to fight for whole humanity. Such instances though disturbing enough could be understood within their specific context. While dealing with the socioeconomic depravation of dalits, he comprehensively exposed certain systemic dimensions that help perpetuate exploitation. For instance, he was well aware of the capitalist and imperialist oppression besides the decadent feudalism within which domain his problem lay.

CAPITALISM

During the colonial British regime, capitalism started taking root in India with the collaboration of Indian mercantile capital and British capital. Unlike Europe, it did not have to battle against feudalism; rather it was implanted on the trunk of the latter in India. As a result, even in the capitalist institutions in the cities, caste discrimination simultaneously existed. Ambedkar was quite aware of the exploitative potential of capital and hence he had declared capitalism and Brahminism as the twin enemy of his movement. Capitalism was in an infantile stage then but

Brahminism encompassed the phases of slavery, feudalism and extended its tentacles as we see to the phase of imperialism. Moreover, he noted the reactionary compradore character of rising capitalism in the contemporary sectors of the economy and the inhuman exploitation of workers that it unleashed.

His, Indian Labour Party (ILP) was an attempt to take up the question of capitalist exploitation, as well as to combine the struggle on both caste and class basis. Various workers' problems were taken up by the ILP, the leadership of combined strike of the mill workers, parliamentary fight for the workers' interest in relation to the Industrial Disputes Act, and various legal reforms that were brought about while he was in the Executive Council of the Viceroy, can be the examples of his concern for workers' exploitation. It cannot be denied that his approach to these contemporary problems was closer to that of the Fabian socialists with whom he was more familiar. But, it was a model adopted out of familiarity and pragmatism, a matter of strategy, never thought out on an ideological plane to be a theoretical plank. Although, there cannot be any doubt that he stood against capitalism, he could not articulate a sound theoretical basis for doing so. Resultantly, his efforts remained constricted with a short view of workers' welfare but could not provide them a vision of their liberation.

IMPERIALISM

Ambedkar's attitude towards imperialism has been projected in a distorted manner right from the beginning, mainly because he refused to take part in the freedom struggle or opposed Gandhi who for certain category of ignoramuses was the anti-imperialism personified. He strategically sought to maintain neutrality vis-a-vis the colonial State. As per him, it would not be possible for the resourceless dalits to fight its mighty foes all together. He did not want to dissipate and squander his extremely limited resources on several fronts. He however knew the basic exploitative character of the colonial regime. At several occasions, he burst out saying that British imperialism and Indian feudalism were the two leaches that clung to Indian people. However, there was a fundamental difference between his and others' viewpoint. For instance, he did not approve equating opposition to imperialism with opposing the British. He noted that the opposition to imperialism couldn't be effective until its supporters within the country are left untouched.

The then leader of the Communist Party of India--Manabendranath Roy once met him at his residence and during discussions insisted that destruction of imperialism had to be the first and foremost objective of Indian politics. Ambedkar's response to him summarised his outlook towards this problem. He replied to Roy in explicit terms that without struggling against the landlords, mill owners, moneylenders—the friends of imperialism within the country, it was not possible to wage an effective fight against imperialism. It may be a matter of research but a priori his anti-imperialist attitude pervades even his writings as a student.

The validation of his stand comes from an entirely unrelated corner and nearly half a century later. Suniti Kumar Ghosh, (1985 and 1995) in his books has shown in great detail how the Congress representing landlords and capitalists had played a compradore role to serve the interest of imperialism during the so-called freedom struggle and how even after the transfer of power in 1947 the grip of imperialism instead of weakening became stronger. Does it not indicate that he was more correct than any of his contemporary politicians? The ones who biasedly wish to pronounce their half baked verdict that Ambedkar was a stooge of British merely on the basis of his acceptance of membership of Viceroy's Executive Council or talking to the Simon Commission, not only display their ignorance of history but also their casteist fangs. They ought to rethink the comparison between Ambedkar who, even being apparently a part of the imperialist apparatus was perhaps striking at its roots by empowering the people and many others, so called nationalists, who after wearing the mask of anti-imperialism were indirectly strengthening its pillars.

In relation to British rule, Ambedkar basically makes two points. The first is that he questions the so-called freedom struggle launched under the leadership of Congress as an anti-imperialist struggle. He contended that the Congress basically represented the class of feudal lords and the urban capitalists—the two some exploiters of Indian masses. Although, it succeeded through the charismatic leadership of Gandhi in galvanising masses in its support, it essentially relied on bargaining with the colonial rulers for securing itself more share of power.

It always throttled the mass-spontaneity as in the case of 1942-uprisings and actively opposed the genuine anti-imperialist struggles of the revolutionaries like Bhagat Singh. Ambedkar reflects the understanding of true character of the Congress in his own way, when he says that if Congress was fighting a real anti-imperialist war, he would whole heartedly support it. The rhetoric of such statement apart, for he never appears to even take a note of other truly anti-imperialist struggles like the one referred to above, it is enough to reveal his attitude towards imperialism and understanding of the class character of the Congress. He knew that the class character of the Congress would not permit it to don this role in reality. Ambedkar could see through the anti-imperialist masks the real fangs of an exploiter of masses.

He thus not only saw no point in siding with this more real exploiter of people than perhaps the colonial rulers, but also did not hesitate to openly oppose it when it came in the way of Dalit liberation. He smelt rot in all such struggles that refused to notice existence of inhuman exploitation of some of their own people within their precincts and tended to over-externalise their woes. Here lay his second point when he raised a question of Hindu imperialism perpetrated through its caste system that was certainly seen as more vicious by its victims than the British rule. It may be pertinent to ask of those who raise the issue of Ambedkar's attitude and conduct towards imperialism, to answer as to why the problem of untouchability or caste system that reduced its one—fifth of the population to subhuman levels did not find a mere mention in the lofty discussions of freedom struggle that predated Ambedkar's raising it. The anti-imperialist aspiration also could be seen in the context of the class/caste division in the society.

The battle for the lost kingdom waged by the vanquished lords also could be camouflaged as an anti-imperialist struggle and at the same time the genuine peoples' anti-imperialist aspiration manifested in the form of say anti-feudal struggle could be condemned as the pro-imperialism, merely because it directed its gun towards the props of the imperialism. The real anti-imperialist aspirations belong to the masses of people the manifestation of which is possible only through the peoples' war. Whatever anti-imperialist struggle people waged were soon hijacked by the phoney war whose real intent was to extract political power to native ruling classes. While the scenes of anti-British struggles were being enacted for the 'mother' India of exploiters, Ambedkar busied himself to liberate the other India-the India of the exploited and oppressed.

OPPRESSION OF WOMEN

Besides these mainstream forms of exploitation even the subaltern forms like women's exploitation, could not escape his agenda. He viewed them as the most oppressed of all. His approach to the problems was typically that of a liberal democrat constitutionalist. This certainly constrained his articulation of this problem as in many others. This issue will have to be seriously rethought by dalits under the redefinition project. But suffice here to say that at any opportunity, he raised his voice against women's discriminatory situation in the society.

His basic law of social engineering was that the social revolutions must always begin from the standpoint of the most oppressed or the ones on the lowest rung of the society. Right from the days of Mook Nayak and Bahiskrit Bharat, he appears to take cudgels for women. He always involved women in his struggles and tended to give them vanguard positions. For example, about 500 women had marched at the head of the historical procession at Mahad to assert the untouchables' right to drink water from the public tank. He was immensely pained to see the permanent denial of education and religious rights to women ordained in the Shastras of the Hinduism (*e.g.* Manusmriti). His democratic consciousness never reconciled with any thing lesser than the equality of men and women though its expression was acutely constrained perhaps by his anxieties about the possibilities, so much so that it might even be mistaken as the male centric tactic.

While he asked women to be good mothers so as to shape up their son or to be good wives to their husbands or be a carrier of community's cultural baggage, he did struggle for their equal rights as in the case of Hindu Code Bill. He described sacramental marriages (Mathew, 1991) as polygamy for men and perpetual slavery for women because under no circumstances within that system the latter would get liberty from their husbands, however bad or undesirable they may be. He insisted that women should have the freedom to break this contract.

ON REVOLUTION

Revolution, on the face of it, appears to be an anathema to Ambedkar who seems to dread it and instead advocates reforms. But it would be disaster to take it at face value. For, like many other terms, his usage of the term 'revolution' does not bear the same meaning as is in vogue, particularly in Marxist circles. What Ambedkar seems to detest in revolution is the violence. At many places he tends to equate rebellion, revolution and revolt with violence. He also seems to disagree with the method of insurrection. He thought that without mass consciousness being ripe enough for revolutionary change, insurrectionary methods would not succeed.

Moreover, he appears to be sceptical of the justness of revolutions as they invariably represent the triumph of the collective over the individual. It may be attributed to the influence of liberal democracy in which he got his indoctrination in his formative days. Liberal democracy always put an individual on a high pedestal and considered it precious. His concern for the individual is not again doctrinaire but emanates from the value that any and every human being is precious and the belief that alone can act as the best guarantee against the collective tyranny and totalitarian excesses any time. In the context of the collapse of erstwhile Soviet block, where the totalitarian states that came into being in the name of dictatorship of proletariat and played havoc with people, this human-centric value assumes importance. One needs to be however reminded that even the values do need to have some material bases. They do not fall from sky. The contradiction between collective and individual has thus to be resolved in the concrete situation. As for Ambedkar, apart from this scepticism, he does not seem to have any dispute with the general aim and object of revolution.

Revolution, inasmuch as it seeks to bring about a fundamental change in the social relations in the society, will always be opposed by the forces of status quo, whose material interests are directly threatened by this change. In corollary, it becomes imperative for the forces of revolution to overcome this resistance whatever be the means. Whereas, the antagonist camp will always project codes of ethics and morality for their tactical defence in face of the onslaught of revolution, the revolutionaries discard them as decadent; for them revolution itself represents the highest value. Being the upsurge of the suppressed ones, revolutions do have a tendency to be bloody, but it is always in response to the resistance of its opponents.

Therefore it is a representation only by the vested interest to associate violence or moral turpitude with revolutions. On the contrary, it would be more logical to say about the revolutionaries that being propelled by an external motivation to deliver mankind from the existing traps at the risk of their own lives; they cannot be bloodthirsty people. The revolutionary violence is almost an inevitability that arises at the instance of the oppressors.

In that sense Marx called "violence as the midwife of history", emphasising its inevitability. It is the inevitability that marks the compulsion of the vast majority of people to resist the antirevolutionary violence of the minority. The prerequisite here is that the revolution truly represents the majority consciousness. If it does not, then the violence of the few exercised with howsoever a lofty objective could transform into its antithesis, fortifying itself against the majority will. In this sense and insofar as the recent history showed the scepticism that revolutions trample upon individual's rights therefore cannot be dismissed as baseless.

Historically, revolution is the process of identifying and destroying the obstacles in the existing order to take productive forces to the qualitatively next higher level, for the overall progress of human race. The progress achieved by mankind so far is basically due to the qualitative transformation from quantitative continuum that characterises revolutions. The qualitative transformations always need concentrated inputs, akin to latent heat in the case of phase transformation of water. In social transformation it takes the form of revolutionary energy that in turn may manifest into violence. Ambedkar does not neglect the necessity of violence. As he himself said that if dalits wanted to be effective they would need the canons.

It is erroneous to construe that his opposition to violence was idealistic or doctrinaire. Violence was not a taboo for him; it could be practised when it was absolutely necessary. Even his mentor Buddha, who is respected as the greatest apostle of non-violence had the same pragmatic approach towards violence. Ambedkar was not obsessed either with the idea of non-violence or the value of individualism professed by the classical school of liberal democracy. His reservations were against the possibility of the cunning of a few overriding the will of majority as had happened in the case of caste institution. He would hate to see any thing like caste getting institutionalised again. In his scheme of things he therefore was not ready to compromise the value of democracy, the will of majority of people, whatever may be the end.

Ambedkar did not juxtapose reform against revolution, as many people tend to do. He does not reflect comprehension of technicality of dialectical materialism in his usage of these terms. Often his revolution is the violent overthrow of the existing rule and establishment of the new rule. Likewise, he does not seem to mean that reforms will not entail a qualitative transformation. What he certainly means by revolution is the change brought about in a 'big bang' manner. Notwithstanding what Ambedkar said about his own work, revolution does not always entail a 'big bang'; it is not a point concept as mistakenly regarded in common parlance, but a line concept. Mao's Great Proletarian Cultural Revolution may be a good example of this.

There could be many bits of work, which contributes to taking society to a qualitatively higher rung in the ladder of progress that qualify to be the revolutionary work. The qualitative change itself occurs over a discrete time horizon and not a moment. The moment that marks out transformation of power and looks like a 'big bang', alone is not the revolution. The particular phase of history puts constraints on the kind of changes that can be conceived in its womb. Some one dreaming of a socialist revolution in the slave society would only at best be a daydreamer; a romanticist but he cannot be a revolutionary. Likewise, certain phase of history demands a lot of quantitative preparation before a revolutionary change can be planned for. Ambedkar largely reflects these kinds of concerns while dealing with the issue of revolution. He did not see Indian situation ripe enough for any revolutionary change. Any change without resolution of the caste question, according to him, would not only be detrimental to dalits but also be an extremely short-lived.

The importance of Ambedkar's work can be gauged in relation to contemporary social situation and its transitional social context. Indian society was ridden with a peculiar brand of feudalism, the most prominent feature of which was caste. Caste had incapacitated over 15 per cent of its population and maintained them at the subhuman level. The large part of the balance population also suffered the degradation in a varying degree. This decadent institution had far outlived its minimal utility and as a result for centuries kept Indian society in a fossilised form. It served the material needs of a handful of people but all perceived varying stakes in the system on account of its hierarchical structure and faithfully practised it because they internalised it as their *Dharma* ordained by none other than God.

The possible exception in generic terms were dalits who were placed at the lowest rung of the caste ladder and had hardly anything to their share. However, in particular terms only a few castes from the Dalit castes, who did not have any specific caste profession and hence little stake in the system and consequently who as the general workmen of villages had better exposure to the changing urban life than any one else came out of the hegemony of Brahmins to articulate the challenge to the system. The hierarchy among dalits however prevented them to come together and consequently this challenge had to be articulated caste by caste. Capitalism that took root in India in big cities also had struck compromise with the caste institution like its harbingers, the British imperialism. It was an arduous task, as it still is, to conceive a model for this struggle and still more difficult to build.

During the colonial times for various reasons these struggles had germinated largely in Maharashtra and Southern states where the social structure reflected sharper polarisation between dalits and balance society. Ambedkar's advent in the Indian sociopolitical scene marked their zenith. It articulated its attack on Brahminism and capitalism that accepted its alliance, focused its organisation on dalits and gave a clarion call for annihilation of castes for achieving the ultimate aim of society based on Liberty, Equality and Fraternity to provide wider umbrella for all progressive forces to work. It reflects the distinct historical need to democratise Indian society without which it was bound to suffer constriction of its productive forces. This work had to have large content in the sociocultural realm; it is a credit to Ambedkar's acumen that he gave it a political dimension.

It had to be approached as reform. Ambedkar clearly found the talks of communist revolution as out of phase with the history although he never fully accepted the tenets of historical materialism as he thought it negatived human ingenuity and carried it through a predetermined channel. He insisted that India did not provide congenial soil for germination of class-consciousness because of castes. Their annihilation therefore constituted the first task in the revolutionary agenda. It is unfortunate that many communist revolutionaries still parrot the same characterisation of his work as in years back their predecessors proclaimed using the spoon fed theories from the West.

One day it is hoped that the contributions of all the caste struggles to democratisation of Indian society would be restored as a native revolutionary heritage by these well meaning people. Till then it will always sound puerile to pigeonhole the historical work as reform or revolution merely on the basis of syntax and not the content. However, it is much more unfortunate for Ambedkarite dalits to deny themselves the credit for this historical contributions by dissociating from the revolutionary agenda, mistakenly thinking that it something alien to them. Effectively, not only they are denying themselves a historical opportunity to contribute to revolution but also delaying their own emancipation.

Dalits have to rethink their position vis a vis revolution. Ambedkar's dream of a society based on liberty, equality and fraternity cannot be realised except through revolution. They will have to understand Ambedkar's life and mission only from this perspective. His contribution to Indian revolution lies in the fact that he tried to comprehend Indian reality independently and tried to contribute to the resolution of its contradictions in his own way. Indian history held out the gauntlet of fossilised Indian feudalism for so long to the Indian revolutionaries but every one conveniently wished it away, initially as a superstructural matter that would disappear automatically when the material base is revolutionised and now after seven decades as a problem belonging to both structure and superstructure, that could be solved through revolutionary practice. It still lacks the clarity and courage to hold the bull by horn.

Ambedkar did not confuse issues, he saw clearly that the annihilation of caste will have to be consciously worked for before taking up any revolutionary project. He went beyond and found out the institutional base of castes in the Indian village whose economic support lay in the land-relations and caste division of labour. But, unlike many communists who still use the stereotype of land reform—a slogan of land to the tiller as the only revolutionary programme, he did not hamper on it because he knew that firstly it was economically impossible to satisfy the land hunger of the landless in the country, secondly the likely transformation of landless to a marginal farmer through land reforms was unlikely to solve the problems of dalits and thirdly, as the later empirical data showed, contrary to expectations the land reforms could aggravate the problem of caste. Instead, he proposed nationalisation of land and co-operativisation of farming.

He realised the necessity of detaching substantial village population from land and absorbing it into the industrial sector that was to be mainly under State sector. Even in retrospect, these points could have constituted a viable agenda for democratic revolution. As one naxalite scholar—(Ashok Kumar, 1995) perceptively puts it, for having independently seen the question of annihilation of castes linked with the question of land one could unhesitatingly call Ambedkar as the torchbearer of the people's democratic revolution.

'AMBEDKAR' AS THINKER

Dalits are never tired of projecting Ambedkar as the greatest of all the leaders. That unfortunately smacks of sectarian attitude and of their blind devotion to him. They need to understand that the measure of greatness of any person could only be her / his contribution to better the human situation, in terms of correct understanding of its ailment and contribution to cure it. What Ambedkar did could be seen in relation to the broad five currents in Indian politics of his times:

- The Reformists current that wanted to bring about development on the western pattern, possibly with the support of British imperialism,
- Congress, that represented Indian capital and which demanded self-rule under the domination of British imperialism,
- The Terrorist Nationalists who had taken up arms in their fight for freedom against British imperialism,
- The Communists who were trying to implant Bolshevik revolution in India, and
- The Muslim League which opened up a separatist front of Muslims.

All of them scarcely reflected an understanding of the Indian situation. For instance, none showed even a cursory concern about the problems of one fourth of their countrymen who were forced to live worse than animals as ordained by their decadent religion. It was indeed surprising that although all craved for self-rule from the British, none concerned with the caste-system which basically was responsible in pushing the country repeatedly into slavery. None seemed to attempt an objective analysis of either the history or the present of this country. It could circumstantially be said that their motivations came from their narrow class-caste interests. These movements were motivated by the desire of an abstract freedom for country and a refusal to see the concrete slavery of their own people. Granted that the problems before the country were really intricate, still no one would dare say that the need for democratisation was in anyway subordinate.

The real people's movement in the country was required to wage simultaneous war against imperialism, internal compradore bourgeoisie, landlords and Brahminism. It was only Ambedkar who clearly indicated this requirement. In this light, he was certainly ahead of all others. His own bitter experiences with untouchability had stood him in good stead in seeing this more clearly than any other. He strove to build his movement along this understanding but unfortunately it was neither in his power to deal comprehensively with all the issues, nor was there an ideological and programmatic clarity required therefore. He inevitably had to focus his attention on dalits who were the worst victims of this multifaceted oppression. It was the misfortune of Indian history that this struggle progressed in a constricted manner and eventually got dissolved into regressive statist politics. It reflected both the limitation of Ambedkar as well the situational compulsion on him.

The anti-caste movements before Ambedkar were mainly welfare oriented. Some wanted a higher rank for their own caste in the caste hierarchy and some taking the inferior culture of their caste to be the reason for their suffering, aimed at improving the same. Mahatma Phuley's movement was an exception to this trend insofar as it attempted to unite the Sudra and Ati-Sudra castes against the exploitation by the parasitic castes of Shetjis (capitalists) and Bhatjis (priests). While Ambedkar accepted the lineage/inheritance of this movement and held Phuley in greatest esteem as his one of the three *Gurus,* he went beyond to declare annihilation of caste to be the object of his movement in the direction of the goal of 'liberty, equality and fraternity'. In the historical context it certainly was a radical step. He rightly diagnosed that the caste system is basically sustained by the peculiar economic constitution of the Indian village of which the land relations were the main features. Towards breaking this link he toyed with an idea of separate settlement for dalits at one time and at another exhorted them to leave villages for cities.

He had clearly understood that castes stood on multiple props, *viz.,* the religio-cultural relations, feudal relations in village setting of which land relations constituted the crux and the sociopolitical nexus with the State. Annihilation of castes thus needed destruction of all of them. He soon realised the necessity of political power for this multi-fronged attack. Even to bring about the residual change in the belief system either through the cultural or religious route, he stressed the necessity of political power. In this way, for the first time he brought the problem of untouchability and caste out of the confines of culture to the political agenda. Unfortunately, this political agenda got lost into the maze of parliamentary politics that soon became be-all-end-all with Dalit leaders. Even during Ambedkar's times the economic aspects of the problem remained largely untouched giving the impression to his followers as though they did not count. In the overall context it can be seen that they could not be as easily dealt with as the religio-cultural and political aspects of the problem. Moreover, it meant direct confrontation with the State for which Ambedkar was certainly not prepared. Alternately, the feudal relations in villages could be destroyed only if the private ownership of land is abolished and co-operativisation of farming is introduced. He thought, this structural change could be effected through the Constitution. It was a folly that he would soon realise when even as the 'chief architect' of the Constitution he failed so much as to bring this point on the agenda of the Constituent Assembly.

CONCEPTION OF AN IDEAL

Babasaheb Ambedkar envisioned his ideal in the famous three principles: liberty, equality and fraternity. They were the basis for the ideal society of his conception. He denied that he had adopted them from the French Revolution. He said he had derived them from the teachings of Buddha. These principles were the clarion call of the French Revolution but later became the ideological props of the liberal bourgeoisie in Europe. Since Marx had ridiculed these principles as the fantasy of the bourgeois society, many people tended to stereotype Ambedkar as the petty-bourgeois liberal democrat. As according to Ambedkar the source of these principles is different from the French Revolution, familiar to Marx, there is a prima facie scope to argue that Marx's ridicule does not apply to him. His conception of these principles is indeed substantially different from that associated with the liberal bourgeoisie. Actually, what Marx refers to are the slogans of liberty and equality of the bourgeois parliamentary democracy.

There, 'liberty' is the liberty to contract and 'equality' refers to equality in market. Ambedkar insists that the conception of the ideal society ought to have them all the three together. Absence of any would not be acceptable to him. The ideal society of his dream could only be seen within a kind of spiritual frame. It would be interesting to compare this society with the communist society of Marx's conception. Marx reached his inference following the dialectical track of historical materialism. In Ambedkar' case it was just his vision. Inevitably, he had to attribute the origin of them to some spiritual source.

For Ambedkar they meant to denote the State of society sans exploitation and with an emotive ambience of fellow feeling. It was beyond him to describe this State further in concrete terms and much so to indicate the forms of struggle to reach it. Known for his obsession with pragmatism and belief that any definitive laws could not bind the flow of human history, he would avoid the speculative construction of this distant stage of human society.

Not even Marx could describe what his dream communist society would be like beyond that it would be freed of the familiar contradictions. It essentially reflected a contradiction between human desire and material reality. It would be disaster to derive the meaning of this ideal State of Ambedkar's conception from what he did. He left that to posterity to decide as per their circumstances. But, rationally there could be little doubt that the vision of Ambedkar can only be realised in the communist society of Marx's conception where most (not all) of the contradictions in human society would have been resolved.

Dalits ought to internalise this vision and strive for its realisation. Ambedkar had a radical enough interpretation of his principles of liberty, equality and fraternity so as to feel inadequacy even in Marxism. He said that Marxism supported only equality. He was in need of a body of thought that would give equal importance to all these three principles. He met it with a convenient conceptualisation of religion. It is paradoxical that a person who is rational enough not to bind the posterity with his vision volitionally binds himself with what is said more than 25 centuries before.

It is natural to find ideals better articulated in spiritual spheres but it is equally true that these dream worlds are incapable to provide any clue for their realisation on the earth except for their pet prescription to ignore the material reality and imagine it happened in the mind. They run away from the fact that the evil humans suffer from are the attributes of the divisions in human society, and their abolition essentially calls for struggles by the sufferers against those who perpetrate sufferings. Howsoever, inherently rational the religion may be or radical its interpretation may be it cannot fully escape these limitations.

It can be seen in relation to Buddhism handed down by Babasaheb Ambedkar with his radical interpretation. Notwithstanding the familiar quibbling around the Dhamma and Dhamma among dalits, what remained of Buddhism with them is what would happen to any religion. It is a different question whether Marxism embodied Ambedkar's ideals or not but it is certain that they are neither realisable neither through any kind of constitutional acrobatics nor through any religious practice.

STATE

Ambedkar's conception of State reflects some amount of autonomy from the hegemony of the ruling classes. It is why he expected it to act as per the constitutional structure and endeavoured to incorporate the pro-Dalit bias into the Constitution. He must have realised the true nature of it, the boundaries of the autonomy and basic class bias of the State, when he actually reached not only the Constituent Assembly but also became the chairman of its Drafting Committee.

In his anxiety to secure some provisions in favour of dalits, he accepted to be the 'hack' to write what was acceptable to the ruling caste-class representatives. He must have thought that within the given constraints he had done a good job of making the Constitution responsive to the needs of the downtrodden people. Indeed, many of the provisions in the directive principles and elsewhere apparently bear clear imprint of his zeal and owe their existence to him. But, even they had to be within the strategic space provided by the rulers. His realisation of the folly was near complete when he had to burst out in utter dejection at its ineffectual implementation, that he would be the first man to burn the Constitution as it was of no good to any one. He was inaccurate, as the Constitution had proved good enough to the upper caste-class combine who had hegemonised complete political space in post-1947 India. He attributed it to the 'devils' in the Congressmen who had occupied the constitutional 'temple' he and others had built.

Ambedkar could not reach the point of understanding that the State is a mere instrument in the hands of the ruling classes to coerce the ruled ones into submission to their interests. Until the downtrodden themselves become the ruling class, they cannot expect the State to do good to them. Whatever good that appears to come to their share, in ultimate balance accrues to the other side in multiple measure.

The post-1947 State, which has never tired of propagandising its concern for dalits and poor, has in fact been singularly instrumental in aggravating the caste problem with its policies. Even the apparently progressive policies in the form of Land Ceiling Act, Green Revolution, Programme of Removal of Poverty, Reservations to Dalits in Services and Mandal Commission etc. have resulted against their professed objectives. The effect of the Land Ceiling Act, has been in creating a layer of the middle castes farmers which could be consolidated in caste terms to constitute a formidable constituency. In its new incarnation, this group that has traditionally been the immediate upper caste layer to dalits, assumed virtual custody of Brahminism in order to coerce Dalit landless labourers to serve their socioeconomic interests and suppress their assertive expression in the bud. The Green Revolution was the main instrument to introduce capitalisation in agrarian sector.

It reinforced the innate hunger of the landlords and big farmers for land as this State sponsored revolution produced huge surplus for them. It resulted in creating geographical imbalance and promoting unequal terms of trade in favour of urban areas. Its resultant impact on dalits has been far more excruciating than that of the Land Ceiling Act. The much publicised programme for Removal of Poverty has aggravated the gap between the heightened hopes and aspirations of dalits on one hand and the feelings of depravation among the poorer sections of non-dalits in the context of the special programmes especially launched for upliftment of dalits. The tension that ensued culminated in increasingly strengthening the caste—based demands and further aggravating the caste-divide. The reservations in services for dalits, notwithstanding its benefits, have caused incalculable damage in political terms. Reservations created hope, notional stake in the system and thus dampened the alienation; those who availed of its benefit got politically emasculated and in course consciously or unconsciously served as the props of the system. The context of scarcity of jobs provided ample opportunity to reactionary forces to divide the youth along caste lines. Mandal Commission, that enthused many progressive parties and people to upheld its extension of reservation to the backward castes, has greatly contributed to strengthen the caste identities of people. Inasmuch as it empowers the backward castes, actually their richer sections, it is bound to worsen the relative standing of dalits in villages.

Thus, the State, its welfare mask notwithstanding, has viciously and consistently acted against dalits and poor people. It is a complete contra-evidence to hopes of Ambedkar who strove to maximise and make use of the autonomous space of the State for the benefits of the have-nots, particularly dalits. It is one thing to assume autonomous space but quite another to equate it with caste-class neutrality. Unfortunately, the Dalit political behaviour always reflected this erroneous notion of caste-class neutrality of the State. It has already caused great damage to the Dalit interests. The radical Ambedkar might have strategy to use State for Dalit cause but would never see it as caste-class neutral.

SOCIALISM

Despite his ambivalence and reservations about the emphasis on the economic dimension in socialism, Ambedkar broadly remained a socialist. Some scholars do find little scope for suspecting his socialist credentials because of his disapproval of Russell's criticism of property, his non-acceptance of Marxian formulations and his placement of social issues higher than the economic and political issues. He called the complaint against love of money as 'philosophy of sour grapes' and ridiculed materialism as 'the ideology of pigs'. This impression is moreover strengthened by his reservations to accept the economic interpretation of history. But, in all fairness it may be said that what he appears to mean is the integrative consideration of all the factors that are needed for any society to be based on liberty, equality and fraternity. Notwithstanding his variant conception, there should not bc any doubt about his socialistic antecedents.

His conception of socialism also underwent evolution. Once he had stated that there was hardly any difference between his socialism and communism. As such, his disagreement with the communists was about the means and not about the aim. He warns the communists that the classless society can emerge only after the emergence of a casteless society. It implies that his quarrel with the then communists was over the stages of revolution. In the 1920s and 30s, these people had borrowed the communist dogma and parroted class struggle in utter disregard of the reality.

Ambedkar, on the contrary, was firmly rooted in it. They believed that the soviet Russian model of revolution was importable for bringing about a socialist revolution into India whereas Ambedkar realistically postulated that unless the consciousness of the working class was congenial for revolution, there was no question of it materializing. And, unless the caste system is destroyed, creation of the pro-revolution consciousness was out of question. His annoyance with the Bombay communists was largely because of their dogmatic behaviour. It is unfortunate that the ideal of classlessness that was latent in his agenda never really surfaced during his lifetime.

Ambedkar relies on the concept of 'State' for materialisation of his conception of socialism. His conception of State is largely idealist. He wanted the State to intervene in the economic structure and its monitoring. He wanted to constitutionalise this State intervention so that it would not be subject to change any time with the whims of simple majority vote in the legislation.

Ambedkar who taught, "The lost rights cannot be regained by making appeals or requests to the robbers; it needs struggles"; did not say anything on how the oppressed people will get such strength as to create the constitutional provisions, that would put the class structure upside down. On behalf of his party—Scheduled Caste Federation, he had submitted a draft for the future constitution to the Constituent Assembly for the independent India. It was published later as "States and Minorities". This book has really aided students in understanding some aspects of his conception of socialism.

Nevertheless, one cannot afford to forget the constraints placed by the context in which it was written. The context was that he had failed to get into the Constituent Assembly and was therefore anxious to strike a feasible and still radical note that could find the support of the vast majority of the have-nots which might then create some pressure either for its inclusion in the Constitution or for his entry into the Constituent Assembly. For some years, during the preceding turbulence of negotiations for transfer of power, he found himself totally marginalised. Notwithstanding the probable limitations of this draft, its provisions in operational terms were still very radical. The main provisions are:

- All important industries and services shall belong to the nation.
- Insurance industry shall be in public sector and insurance will be compulsory for every citizen.
- Private sector and entrepreneurs shall have a role in the economy but it shall not be dominating.
- Nationalisation of land and promotion of cooperative farming on a collective principle.

These provisions, if implemented, would have gone a long way towards supporting democratic revolution in the country. It would have limited inequality and exploitation in the economic and political sphere. Politically, it would have had far-reaching impact. Ambedkar till the end could not completely remove the Fabian influence (which he might have gathered while in England) on him. In his times, particularly before World War II, few people in India were well versed in Marxist philosophy. The knowledge of Marxism seldom exceeded some broad principles and 'Stalin's dictatorship' painted by imperialists or the 'revolt of the workers, the insurgency of the poor. Ambedkar also does not seem to have gone very far from this point. Without indulging into the debate of ifs and buts, there should not be any iota of doubt that the ideal society of his conception could materialise only through socialism.

DEMOCRACY

Ambedkar had unshakeable faith in democracy. In his conception of an exploitation-less society, democracy has an extraordinary role. Democracy means 'one person, one vote'; and 'one vote, one value'. Democracy means empowerment of any person for participating in the process of decision-making relating to her/him, democracy means liberty, equality and fraternity—Ambedkar's definition of democracy had such a tone. Because he presided over making of the Constitution and is being projected as its chief architect, there is a misunderstanding that parliamentary democracy is what he wanted. But nothing could be farther from the truth than this. He himself spoke against parliamentary democracy. For instance, he defined parliamentary democracy as "voting by the people in favour of their owners and handing over the rights of ruling over themselves". This provides a glimpse of the expanse of his ideal, which certainly was much beyond the Indian Constitution or any common place understanding about him.

His conception of democracy appears to be purely people oriented. He showed that the bookish concepts of equality are detrimental to the disabled sections of society in the prevailing social setting and proposed a fundamental change in the concept of equality. It envisaged complete abolition of inequality. His principle of positive discrimination is based on this very concept of equality. But the operational aspects of this concept involved the need for some kind of autonomous institution, which was met by 'State' and 'religion'. It is necessary to stress that his greatness lies in the radicality of his conceptions, his vision of a human society sans any kind of exploitation; not in the remedies or apparatus he proposed in the circumstances prevailing in his time.

ASPECTS OF THE STRATEGY AND TACTICS

In the context of strategy, some of Ambedkar's contributions are really noteworthy. He brought the struggle against Brahminism into the political battlefield. He inferred that without political power the social and religious structures will collapse and motivated his followers to capture political power. But his conception of political power being acutely constrained by the parliamentary framework where bargaining is the predominant medium of securing political power, inevitably it made way for all kinds of aberrations and perversities to creep in. The prevailing politics being the game of possibilities, he was soon sucked into its vortex. Politics came to dominate the other aspects of his personality. Slowly, the impact of politics started becoming visible everywhere. This phase significantly contributed to multiplication of his inconsistencies out of tactical imperatives. Dalits have taken this legacy of parliamentary politics very seriously, almost as the be all and end all of their political being. It may be, interesting to probe how much damage this kind of political orientation inflicted on the Dalit movement.

It is altogether a different question whether Ambedkar had any other alternative to parliamentary politics for political practice. It may be argued that in the context of his resources, adversarial environment and to some extent his personal limitations, he had none. Even if it is taken as correct, it should not be forgotten that it was a matter of strategy and tactic that presuppose contextual variables: it cannot be taken as the lasting value.

The fundamental source of most of Ambedkar's political thoughts and action is his conception of State and religion, that he had adopted as the extraneous instruments to reconcile the state of flux of things and the necessity of order in them. It is necessary to understand that both, the State as well as religion, are the products of the evolutionary process of the human society. There is nothing inevitable about them. Marx took State as the instrument of coercion in the hands of ruling classes and religion as the opium of the masses. Dalits have a long experience of nearly five decades with the so-called welfare State of Ambedkar's design. What does it say? Does the State side with them in their conflict with the landlords? Does it come to their rescue when every day three or four of their daughters are raped?

Does it come to save the shame of their women when they are paraded naked in the streets? Does it take their side when they come in conflict with landlords, moneylenders in villages or with management in the modern settings? Does it really ensure they get their dues as provided in the Constitution or punish the defaulting management for noncompliance? To all of such questions the answer could only be in the negative. It is not a matter of 'devils occupying the temples' as Ambedkar lamented seeing the people occupying the Constitutional positions. The

State possesses the characteristics of its master class. In India the upper caste capitalists, landlords, top bureaucrats, etc. being the ruling class, the State can never have saints who would favour dalits. It is a fact that even the government by a Dalit party like the BSP could not transform it into a Dalit State.

Religion, in Ambedkar's conception is necessary to maintain the moral order of the society. It may be interesting to examine to what extent it conforms to this idealistic expectation. Buddhism, which undoubtedly is the most rational of all the religions, does not have any evidence of having created over its near millennium long tenure in India such an order of the society which could claim liberty, equality and fraternity of Ambedkar's conception. Ambedkar's argument that the Bhikku Sangha in Buddhism was the prototype of this kind of society becomes invalid once we call into question the role of Sangha in the production process.

Before that, the order that envisaged nostalgically to recreate the value of the vanishing *Gana Rajya* in microcosm against the evil of rising monarchies, cannot just sublimate to the era of capitalism without being an alley of exploiters unless it transforms itself in some way as a catalyst for the revolution. The moral tenets of Buddhism likewise cannot submerge the lure of surplus extraction, that is its dominating ethos. If at all, it may help it become more pronounced by weakening the resistance of the exploited masses. As we empirically see, the Buddhism of his conception could not produce even a trace of morality in its adherents. On the contrary, for the masses it presents the distorted, if not inverted, worldview; it orients them to look inwards for their misery and be blind to the reality that some one exploits him. He could certainly derive mental peace and pleasure but it is a state of an intoxicated mind. Keeping in mind the causal links in Ambedkar's adoption of these instruments, the redefinition project needs to address these issues afresh.

The strategy of the ruling class always stresses on diversion of peoples' attention from their real problems and their disarmament—both in physical and ideological terms. They invariably have a multilayered strategy in place for this purpose. The vanguard parties of the ruling classes open up sentimental fronts and attempt to divert the attention of people as their real problems get aggravated. Secondly, their time-tested methods of adulterating radical ideas with the masses are always in operation. Towards this end, we see all the ruling parties vying with each other in co-opting Ambedkar. 'Ambedkar' represents a potentially dangerous ideological weapon in the hands of the Indian proletariat and so the ruling class will be hell bent on blunting its edge. They will do everything to eulogise him not only for wooing dalits for their immediate electoral gains but also to neutralise him as the radical ideological force by propagandising a distorted version of the latter. Dalits will have to exercise vigil over their ideological assets even after redefining Ambedkar.

Conclusion

For at least over last four decades Dalits have devotedly followed Ambedkar as their ideal, as a virtual God and zealously practised, as they claim, his teachings. Their social being could be seen to be totally imbued with what they call Ambedkarism—the veritable science of their emancipation. If it is true, and no one would deny it is not, it should be pertinent to ask why despite this flawless following of Ambedkar they continue to be in a pathetic state in every sense. Barring a handful dalits in the government and public sector services and of course politicians, they continue to occupy the lowest rung in the social as well as economic hierarchy of Indian society. Their politics, notwithstanding the media hype, gauged by the measure of general empowerment, continues to be in shambles. Over these decades, their relative situation either shows stagnation or decline. The insinuation to relate this State with their faith in Ambedkar itself would be distasteful for many dalits. But, it is vital for ones that are committed to their liberation to squarely face the facts and dispassionately find out where the rot lay.

Generally, beyond the first burst of anger in reaction to this question, one would face the defensive arguments to discount this relationship. Typically, they tend to attribute their miserable situation to the lack of competent leadership after Babasaheb Ambedkar, to the educated dalits who they think have become Dalit Brahmins and have deserted the community; and sometimes to the people themselves for their extreme self- centredness. Sometimes, the finger is raised at the high caste hegemony that has neutralised the impact of the Constitution that Ambedkar created. Some, particularly the leadership, even would dismiss the basic premise itself that there is something wrong with the Dalit movement. They might even go so far as to claim net achievements indicating the prosperity of themselves or some others of their like. More sober may argue that what is seen is the transition state. Conceding them all some amount of validity even would not erase the stark fact that the general situation of the vast majority of Dalit masses remains still alarmingly pathetic. Externalisation of the reasons for this state has not helped dalits wee bit. The time has come for dalits to self-critically see whether anything was wrong with their ideology and / or with their practice thereof.

Reviewing the post-Ambedkar Dalit movement at some significant milestones, one finds a queer underscoring behaviour, believed to be in accordance with the teachings of Babasaheb Ambedkar, that is certainly incongruent with the essence of what he taught. This dichotomy between the essential Ambedkar and the 'Ambedkar' in the faith of Dalit masses—the icon of Ambedkar, comes out as the problematic in this review. In relation to almost every aspect of his teaching there emerged an icon that represented varying amount of distortion.

Insofar as they constituted the ideology that gripped the masses, these icons can be seen to be at the root of the Dalit pathos. Among the myriad sources for these icons, Ambedkar himself might come out as the major source. Because, even a myth can not sustain for long without some material base. The icons of Ambedkar thus could be linked to some such bases, howsoever tenuous, within his own life. The rationalist in Ambedkar never hesitated to change his opinions and behaviour if the facts so warranted. They appear to be inconsistencies to the ones who see it sans context.

His distance from the focus of control in his sociopolitical environment, the vastly varying target audience (ranging from the Englishmen to the illiterate dalits) to whom he had to communicate, the exigency to respond to the dynamics of communities set in motion by the pre-independence politics, his anxiety to accomplish as many gains for dalits as he could in his life time, the exigencies for 'short' actions at the expense of 'long' vision inevitably led to mark patterns that could support array of behaviours. The first to take advantage of it were his own lieutenants for serving their personal ambitions that set the trends of distortion of Ambedkar in the minds of gullible Dalit masses.

The ruling classes that always look for the grounds to divide masses had severally reinforced this distortion and accelerated fragmentation of dalits in every field. They, along with willing collaboration of Dalit politicians and emerging elite, promoted and sustained the particular icons of Ambedkar that would prevent political coalescence of dalits and suck them into the vortex of parliamentary politics in order to bring the establishment much needed legitimacy. Dalits failed to note this cunning and let themselves flow in the currents of confusion the ruling classes deliberately created. Today, with increasing political crises the ruling classes seem vying with each other in co-opting Ambedkar, as though that may be their last chance of survival. If dalits stood their grounds well, that might have proved to be their last act.

But, unfortunately dalits are giving them new leases of life by blinding themselves to the reality. Not only that they have not resisted these ruling class machinations but on the contrary they are curiously seen to swell the cadres of these castiest, communalist and anti-poor groups and parties. These parties who openly profess the ideology of Hindu revivalism and represent all that is decadent in Indian tradition show the temerity to project Ambedkar among their ideologies. Apart from the reasons of security that propel Dalit youth into their fold, the compradore behaviour of Dalit elite certainly has influenced the phenomenon. What is common in all the attempts by the ruling classes is to sap 'Ambedkar' of its rebellious content.

It is advantageous for them to show that he was the chief architect of the Indian Constitution, committed to parliamentary democracy and opposed to any ideology that propagates violence or revolution. He is projected to favour gradual change implying that dalits should patiently wait and strive persuasively to better their own lives. He is projected as the Bodhisatva that inspires *nirvana*—the State of total detachment from worldly matters. All these images have caused significant damage to the emancipatory struggles of dalits. Some of these images might be the purposeful and blatant disfiguring of Ambedkar but some of them represent genuine dilemma arising from Ambedkar's own stands on various issues. From the viewpoint of the comprehensive pro-people change in the present historical phase a democratic revolution is an imperative. The motive force for this revolution ought to sprout from dalits. The history provides a strong testimony that any radical movement in the country could be sustained by dalits and tribals at its base. Ambedkar as a symbol for Dalit aspirations holds a key to the barrage that has so far bound the revolutionary upsurge in India below the alarming levels. If one concedes that Ambedkar's framework is going to haunt revolutionary commitment till the Indian Democratic Revolution actually happens and that Ambedkar represents the ideological weaponry in the hands of dalits who along with other oppressed people are going to be the axis of this revolution, then one would clearly see the need to redefine Ambedkar in radical terms commensurate with this purpose.

Many aspects of confusion with regard to the facts could be cleared with rational interpretation of his thoughts. But much might need the logical extrapolation of his basic thinking which for some reason appears to have settled in erroneous forms. As he himself showed the way in the case of his redefinition of Buddha's Dhamma, dalits will have to undertake this task, for giving themselves a powerful ideology. Their future as a social group almost hinges on this task. There are enough clues left behind by Ambedkar himself that point to this need.

There is no doubt that he was frustrated at the end of his life seeing the undesired aftermath of his lifelong struggle. He had to lament over the betrayal of the educated dalits in whom he had seen the crusaders of his mission. He had to weep with remorse that he could not do anything for his people in the villages. He had to disown the Constitution for working on which he had cut short his life at least by a few years. He had to swallow the frustration of not being able to pilot the Constitution of his conception (States and Minorities). He had to regret the anti-people State that emerged in republican India. He obviously lacked the analytical tools to see through the reasons for these happenings.

His excessive religiosity and spirituality at the fag end of his life perhaps could be taken as the manifestation of this frustration.

The social engineer could only be busy with problems; he is unlikely to come to grip with the design defects in the system. Almost every thing that Ambedkar pinned his hopes on can be found today in antithetical shambles. His educational society, his vision of Buddhism, the political party of his conception, the social reforms could be some of the examples. These tragic aftermaths also would denote the necessity of a critical review of Ambedkar's thoughts if they were to be used as the ideology to further the Dalit movement towards its logical end. If this process is sincerely followed, there cannot be any doubt that this 'redefined Ambedkar' would be a revolutionary icon, organically linking the Dalit struggle to the revolutionary struggle in the world. It will truly globalize the Dalit struggle.

POLITICAL CAREER

Between 1941 and 1945, he published a large number of highly controversial books and pamphlets, including *Thoughts on Pakistan*, in which he criticized the Muslim League's demand for a separate Muslims state of Pakistan. With *What Congress and Gandhi have Done to the Untouchables*, Ambedkar intensified his attacks on Gandhi and the Congress, charging them with hypocrisy. In his work *Who were the Sudras?*, Ambedkar attempted to explain the formation of the Sudras *i.e.* the lowest caste in hierarchy of Hindu caste system. He also emphasised that how Sudras are separate from Untouchables. Ambedkar oversaw the transition of his political party into the All India Scheduled Castes Federation, although it performed poorly in the elections held in 1946 for the Constituent Assembly of India. In writing a sequel to *Who were the Sudras?* in 1948, Ambedkar lambasted Hinduism in the *The Untouchables: a Thesis on the Origins of Untouchability*:

> *Ambedkar was also critical of Islam and its practices in South Asia. While justifying the Partition of India, he condemned practices of Child-Marriage in Muslim society, as well as the mistreatment of women. He also condemned the Caste practices carried out by Muslims in South Asia. He was also critical of slavery in Muslim communities. He said:*

> *"No words can adequately express the great and many evils of polygamy and concubinage, and especially as a source of misery to a Muslim woman." "Take the caste system. Everybody infers that Islam must be free from slavery and caste. While slavery existed, much of its support was derived from Islam and Islamic countries. While the prescriptions by the Prophet regarding the just and humane treatment of slaves contained in the Koran are praiseworthy, there is nothing whatever in Islam that lends support to the abolition of this curse. But if slavery has gone, caste among Musalmans has remained."*

He wrote that Muslim Society is "even more full of social evils than Hindu Society is" and criticized Muslims for sugar-coating their sectarian Caste System with euphemisms like "brotherhood". He also criticized the discrimination against the Arzal classes among Muslims who were regarded as "degraded", as well as the oppression of women in Muslim society through the oppressive *purdah* system. He alleged that while Purdah was also practised among Hindus, only in Muslims was it sanctioned by religion. He criticized their fanaticism to Islam on the grounds that their literalist interpretations of Islamic doctrine made their society very rigid and impermeable to change. He further wrote that Indian Muslims have failed to reform their society unlike Muslims in other countries like Turkey.

In a "communal malaise," both groups [Hindus and Muslims] ignore the urgent claims of social justice. While he was extremely critical of Muhammad Ali Jinnah and the communally divisive strategies of the Muslim League, he argued that Hindus and Muslims should segregate and the State of Pakistan be formed, as ethnic nationalism within the same country would only lead to more violence. He cited precedent with historical events like the dissolution of the Ottoman Empire and Czechoslovakia to bolster his views regarding the Hindu-Muslim communal divide.

However, he questioned as to whether the need for Pakistan was sufficient and it might be possible to resolve Hindu-Muslim differences in a less drastic way. He wrote that Pakistan must "justify its existence" accordingly. Since other countries such as Canada also have had communal issues with the French and English and have lived together, it may not be impossible for

Hindus and Muslims to live together. He warned that the actual implementation of a two state solution would be extremely problematic with massive population transfers and border disputes. This claim was almost prophetic in its realization with the violent Partition of India after independence.

Architect of India's constitution despite his increasing unpopularity, controversial views and intense criticism of Gandhi and the Congress, Ambedkar was by reputation an exemplary jurist and scholar. Upon India's independence on August 15, 1947, the new Congress-led government invited Ambedkar to serve as the nation's first law minister, which he accepted. On August 29, Ambedkar was appointed chairman of the constitution drafting committee, charged by the Assembly to write free India's constitution. Ambedkar won great praise from his colleagues and contemporary observers for his drafting work.

The text prepared by Ambedkar provided constitutional guarantees and protections for a wide range of civil liberties for individual citizens, including freedom of religion, the abolition of untouchability and the outlawing of all forms of discrimination. Ambedkar argued for extensive economic and social rights for women, and also won the Assembly's support for introducing a system of reservations of jobs in the civil services, schools and colleges for members of scheduled castes and scheduled tribes, a system akin to affirmative action.

India's lawmakers hoped to eradicate the socioeconomic inequalities and lack of opportunities for India's depressed classes through this measure, which had been originally envisioned as temporary on a need basis. The constitution was adopted on November 26, 1949 by the Constituent Assembly. Speaking after the completion of his work, Ambedkar said:

> *Ambedkar resigned from the cabinet in 1951 following the stalling in parliament of his draft of the Hindu Code Bill, which sought to expound gender equality in the laws of inheritance, marriage and the economy. Although supported by Prime Minister Nehru, the cabinet and many other Congress leaders, it received criticism from a large number of parliament members. Ambedkar independently contested an election in 1952 to the lower house of parliament, the Lok Sabha but was defeated.*

He was appointed to the upper house of parliament, the Rajya Sabha in March 1952 and would remain its member until his death.

AMBEDKAR, GANDHI AND CONGRESS

Ambedkar was a fierce critic of Mahatma Gandhi and the Indian National Congress. He was also criticized by his contemporaries and modern scholars for his opposition to Mahatma Gandhi, who had been one of the first Indian leaders to call for the abolition of untouchability and discrimination.

Gandhi had a more positive, arguably romanticised view of traditional village life in India, whereas Ambedkar had a much more negative view. Ambedkar encouraged his followers to leave their home villages, move to the cities and get an education.

Limitations, Criticism and legacy: Most of contemporary sociopolitical leaders across political spectrum joined in condemnation evil social practice of untouchability, many times their priorities on the ground in eliminating these evil practices did not match to expectation of Ambedkar. While it took long time, curse of untouchability and forms of overt discrimination got removed eventually from most of Indian social life over the years.

Structure of Indian Caste system specially so of Hindu's, and their superstitions were so complex and intermingled, that those religions which in principal were not supposed to have caste system, in many instances were practising the same indirectly. While in sharing of food together by different caste people became more common, practice of marriage among same caste and political voting lines based on caste achieved very little change over the years.

The whole situation was so frustrating that while progressive people agreed with his cause, he could not get unanimous and unequivocal support from even all depressed classes at one time. So he could not get enough mileage of vote bank in actual number of parliamentary seats, in post independence era.

Benefits of Governments affirmative action did not reach adequately to affected population due to ever growing population, practices of child labour and child marriage, discrete forms of discrimination, castism among even oppressed classes themselves.

At the same time, some economically poor sections of society got disenchanted because of affirmative action as their castes or communities were not among selected few.

Above factors have been polarising Indian politics, at times, with extreme POVs. This aspect is more of reason in accusing Ambedkar as a controversial and polarizing figure in Indian politics even after his death.

While Ambedkar's supporters argue that he was working to secure Dalit and Backward Caste political rights. Contemporary and modern scholars also questioned Ambedkar's research and point of view regarding origin of the caste system and racial theories.

He acquired sympathy and criticism both about his mass conversion of Buddhism as a political stunt, from his opponents. Ambedkar was also criticised for his intensely anti-Hindu views, though his supporters argue that he was only opposed to "Orthodox Brahminism" rather than to all Hindus. He came in touch with many progressive people belonging to Brahmin and other upper classes.

Because of oppressive traditional caste system many scholars including that of affected castes took a view that Britishers are more even handed in respect of Indian caste system, and continuance of British rule can help in eradicating some of evil practices. This political thought believed that let the social improvement happen first and then only we should go for political independence, and was shared by quite a number of social activists including that of Mahatma Jyotiba Phule and Ambedkar. So this earned criticism from certain quarters like writer Arun Shourie, who questioned Ambedkar's contributions to the Indian Independence struggle.

His criticism about certain aspects of Islam and Islamic society in India and his favour in form of benefit of affirmative action to limited sections; limited support among many Muslims.

Legacy: Ambedkar's legacy has been long-lasting on modern India. He is widely regarded as the "father of the Indian constitution" for his role in creating the document. His political philosophy has given rise to a large number of Dalit political parties, publications and workers unions that remain active across India, especially in Maharashtra. His promotion of the Indian Buddhist Movement has rejuvenated interest in Buddhist philosophy in many parts of India. Mass conversion ceremonies have been organized by Dalit activists in modern times, emulating Ambedkar's Nagpur ceremony of 1956.

Cost of Change: However, frequent violent clashes between Dalit groups and orthodox Hindus have occurred over the years. When in 1994 a garland of shoes was hung around a statue of Ambedkar in Mumbai, sectarian violence and strikes paralysed the city for over a week. When the following year similar disturbances occurred, a statue of Ambedkar was destroyed. In addition, some Dalits who converted to Buddhism have rioted against Hindus and desecrated Hindu temples, often incited into doing so by anti-Hindu elements and replacing deities with pictures of Ambedkar.

Humans as the Homo sapience evolved on this planet about 150,000 years before present. Some of the oldest civilizations known in the history of humanity have been dated 10,000 years old. Human Being is a social animal. Social animal has a tendency to govern and to be governed by a set of rules framed by the society itself. There are two fundamental types of human nature. Creative and possessive. Creative humans use human intellect for creative endeavours which enriches human thought; knowledge and wealth thereby contribute to the development of human heritage for the posterity. Possessive people, on the other hand do not believe in the use of human intellect for creative purpose. Rather, they believe in appropriation, amassing and even usurpation of the products of the labour of the creative people.

This type of people posses a strong urge to become the governing class by all means in order to achieve their aims. Lesser the degree of civilization in the society, greater is the probability of succeeding this type of people in becoming the governing class. However, in a more civilized society the creative people can offer resistance to possessive people and try to safeguard their interests. This is a continuous process in the human society. Karl Marx has scientifically analysed this conflict by applying the principles of dialectical materialism to the sphere of social phenomenon and described it as the historical materialism. Slavery, apartheid, gender bias and caste system are the abominable creations of possessive peoples for the exploitation of creative people. These are man made evils created by man for the exploitation of man. Those, who have raised their voices against these evils and given a relentless fight against the prevailing social order of their times in order to free the creative peoples from the shackles imposed on them have become immortal personalities in the human history.

Some of these great persons are better known as founders of religions. Gautama Buddha, Jesus Christ and Guru Nanak for example. Some have become famous as saints as Kabirjee, Ravidasjee and Tukarama. Some have become source of inspiration and guidance to the underprivileged classes as Krantiba Jotiba Phoolay and Periyar Ramaswamy Naicker and some are revered even more than gods as Bharatratna Dr. Bhimrao Ramjee Ambedkar. Gautama Buddha, Jesus Christ, Guru Nanak Kabir, Ravidas, Tukarama, Krantiba Jotirao Phoolay, Periyar and Dr. Babasaheb Ambedkar they all belong to the great class of exalted Homo sapience called as Humanists.

Dr. Babasaheb Ambedkar was truly a multifaceted personality. A veritable emancipator of Dalits, a great national leader and patriot, a great author, a great educationist, a great political philosopher, a great religious guide and above all a great humanist without any parallel among his contemporaries. All these facets of Dr. Baba Saheb Ambedkar's personality had strong humanistic underpinnings. It is only regrettable that the press in the past as well as the contemporary has projected Ambedkar mainly as a great social rebel and a bitter critic of the Hindu religion. Critics of Dr. Ambedkar have ignored his basic humanistic instincts and strong humanitarian convictions behind his every act or speech through out his life. It is important to trace the origin and consolidation of his humanistic convictions.

Origins of Dr. Ambedkar's Humanistic Convictions: Dr. Ambedkar's father, Subhedar Ramji was a known follower of the Kabirpanth. Many of the Kabir's Dohas are the veritable gems of rationalism and the most daring expressions of the humanitarian beliefs. Dr. Ambedkar's mind was thus deeply imbued with Kabir's philosophy in the childhood days. On passing his matriculation examination, he was felicitated by his teacher and was presented with a copy of a book on the life of Buddha. This gift must have made a profound impact on the mind of young Ambedkar. Dr. Ambedkar stayed in America, the land of liberty, for his higher studies. There he studied the western liberal thought and the humanitarian philosophy expounded by great thinkers such as Prof. John Dewey, who was also his teacher, John Stuart Mill, Edmund Burke, and Prof. Harold Laski to name a few. The impact of this original thinker on Dr. Ambedkar's mind is evident from the frequent quotations one comes across in his writings and speeches. The contrast between the social milieu which he lived in, and the liberal academic thought he studied could not have resulted in anything but making him an ardent humanist.

Fundamental rights assured to all citizens of our country is a great leap towards establishing the basic human values in the society that was based on graded inequality. As the chairperson of the constitution drafting committee Dr. Ambedkar was instrumental in the incorporation of the principle of fundamental rights in the constitution.

Dr. Ambedkar was a firm believer in the parliamentary democracy. That is why when the fear of fascism represented by Hitler was looming large over the world, he decided to cooperate with the British government in its fight against the fascism. Because as a humanist he could foresee the dangerous consequences of the victory of the fascism. Today some myopic people criticize Dr. Ambedkar for this. However, by criticizing Dr. Ambedkar on this score, they inadvertently expose their fascist leanings.

A few months before his Mahaparinirvana he embraced Buddhism. It was a great tribute of a great humanist to the greatest humanistic philosophy of Buddha. By initiating millions of his follower in to the Buddhist fold, he asserted his faith in the humanistic values preached by Buddha in alleviating the sufferings of his lot. He thus reached the pinnacle of the humanism by becoming a Bodhisattva.

Ambedkar and his patrons were dealt a humiliating blow by the elections of 1937. There were a total of 1,585 seats in the 11 assemblies in 'British India'. Of these 777 were 'tied'—in the sense that they were to be filled by communal or special representation from Chambers of Commerce, plantations, labour etc. Of the 808 'general' seats, the Congress, which Ambedkar, Jinnah and others denounced from the house tops, won 456. It secured absolute majorities in 5 assemblies—those of Madras, United Provinces, Central Provinces, Bihar and Orissa. And was the largest single party in 4 others—Bombay, Bengal, Assam and the NWFP.

From the point of view of Ambedkar and the British—who had been holding him up to counter the Congress claim that it represented the harijans as much as any other section of Indian society—worse was the fact that the Congress did extremely well in the seats which had been reserved for harijans. Thirty seats were reserved for harijans in Madras Presidency, the Congress contested 26 and won 26. In Bihar there were 24 reserved seats—in 9 of these Congress candidates were returned unopposed; of the remaining 15 reserved seats, it contested 14, and won 14.

In Bombay of the 15 reserved seats, it secured 1 unopposed, contested 8 and won 5. In the United Provinces there were 20 reserved seats; two of its candidates were returned unopposed; it contested 17 seats and won 16. In Bengal of the 30 reserved seats, it contested 17 and won 6. In the Central Provinces of the 19 reserved seats, it contested 9 and won 5.

The lesson was there for all to see. Reporting to the Viceroy on the result in the Bombay Presidency, the Governor, Lord Brabourne wrote, "Dr. Ambedkar's boast of winning, not only 15 seats which are reserved for the harijans, but also a good many more—looks like being completely falsified, as I feared it would be."

The electorate, including the harijans, may have punctured his claims but there was always the possibility of reviving one's fortunes through politicking and manoeuvres. Efforts of all these elements were focused on the objective of installing non-Congress ministries in Bombay and wherever else this was a possibility. Brabourne reported to the viceroy that Jamnadas Mehta, the finance minister "who is chief minister in all but name", was telling him that the ministry in Bombay would survive motions on the budget and may even get through the motion of no-confidence:

"His calculations are based on the fact that he expects to get the support of the bulk of the Muhammadans, the whole of Ambedkar's Scheduled Castes Party, and of half a dozen or so of those individuals who stood as Congressmen merely to get elected," he reported. But added, "I gather that he is in touch with Ambedkar, who is carrying on negotiations for him, but, as you will find from the next succeeding paragraph, it rather looks to me as if Ambedkar is playing a thoroughly double game, in which case Jamnadas Mehta's hopes are likely to be rudely shattered."

The governor went on to report that he had also had a long conversation with Jinnah, and that Jinnah had told him that, in the event of the ministry being defeated, the Muslim League would be prepared to form a ministry provided they could secure a majority of even two or three in the assembly. "He (*that is, Jinnah*) went on to say that Ambedkar and his party were prepared to back him in this," Brabourne reported, "and that he expected to get the support of ten or a dozen of the so-called Congress MLAs mentioned above.

He made it quite clear to me that they would not support the present ministry. The governor was sceptical about the claims and assurances of all of them. He wrote, "It is, of course, quite impossible to rely on anything that Jinnah tells me, and the only thing for me to do is to listen and keep silent. I obviously cannot tell Jamnadas Mehta what Jinnah told me, or vice versa, as both of them are hopelessly indiscreet. The only thing that is clear is that a vast amount of intrigue is going on behind the scenes, but, in the long run, I cannot see anything coming out of it at all, as none of these people trust each other round the corner. Were to hazard a guess, it would still be that the present ministry will be defeated on the budget proposals and the alternative will then lie between Congress or Section 93"—the equivalent of our present-day governor's rule.

Congress ministries were formed. And in 1939 they resigned in view of the British government's refusal to state what it intended to do about Indian Independence after the War. Jinnah announced that the Muslim League would celebrate the resignations as 'Deliverance Day.' Guess who was at his side in these 'celebrations' addressing meetings from the same platforms? Ambedkar, of course. Nationalist leaders were neither surprised that Ambedkar was on the platforms with Jinnah, nor had they any doubts about the inspiration behind these celebrations. Addressing the Congress Legislature Party in Bombay on 27 December, 1937, Sardar Patel noted, "We cannot forget how Sir Samuel Hoare set the Muslims against the Hindus when the unity conference was held at Allahabad. The British statesmen in order to win the sympathy of the world, now go on repeating that they are willing to give freedom to India, were India united.

The 'Day of Deliverance' was evidently calculated to make the world and particularly the British public believe that India was not united and that Hindus and Muslims were against each other. But when several sections of Muslims were found to oppose the 'Day of Deliverance', the proposed anti-Hindu demonstrations were converted into a Jinnah-Ambedkar-Byramji protest against the Congress ministries and the Congress high command.

That rout in the election remained a thorn in the heart of Ambedkar for long. A large part of *What Congress and Gandhi Have Done to the Untouchables* which Ambedkar published in 1945 is a tortuous effort to explain that actually the Congress had not done well in the election, that in fact, while groups such as his which had opposed Congress had been mauled even in reserved constituencies, they had triumphed, and the Congress, in spite of the seats having gone to it, had actually been dealt a drubbing!

Though this is his central thesis, Ambedkar gives reasons upon reasons to explain why he and his kind have lost and why the Congress has won! One of the reasons he says is that the people in general believe that the Congress is fighting for the freedom of the country. This fight for freedom, Ambedkar says, "has been carried on mostly by Hindus." It is only once that the Mussalmans took part in it and that was during the short-lived Khilafat agitation. They soon got out of it, he says. The other communities, particularly the untouchables, never took part in it.

A few stray individuals may have joined it—and they did so, Ambedkar declares, for personal gain. But the community as such has stood out. This is particularly noticeable in the last campaign of the "Fight For Freedom", which followed the 'Quit India Resolution' passed by the Congress in August 1942, Ambedkar says. And this too has not been just an oversight, in Ambedkar's reckoning it was a considered boycott. The Untouchables have stayed out of the Freedom Movement for good and strong reasons, he says again and again.

Traditionally, according to the Hindu code of conduct, the untouchables were placed at the bottom of the caste hierarchy and were known by different names in different parts of the country. They were called *Sudras, Atisudras, Chandalas, Antyajas, Pariahs, Dheds, Panchamas, Avarnas, Namasudras, Asprusthas,* etc.

The hierarchical and inegalitarian structure of Indian society came into existence during the period of *manusmriti*. The manusmriti set the tenor of social discrimination based on birth. This, in turn led to economic degradation and political isolation of the untouchables now popularly known as Dalits. Dalits are the poor, neglected and downtrodden lot. Their social disabilities were specific, severe and numerous. Their touch, shadow or even voices were considered by the caste Hindus to be polluting. They were not allowed to keep certain domestic animals, use certain metals for ornaments, eat a particular type of food, use a particular type of footwear, wear a particular type of dress and were forced to live in the outskirts of the villages towards which the wind blew and dirt flowed. Their houses were dirty, dingy and unhygienic where poverty and squalor loomed large. They were denied the use of public wells. The doors of the Hindu temples were closed for them and their children were not allowed into the schools attended by the children of caste Hindu. Barbers and washer men refused their services to them. Public services were closed to them. They followed menial hereditary occupations such as those of street sweepers, scavengers, shoe makers and carcasses removers.

Generally the term *Dalit* includes those who are designated in administrative parlance as Scheduled Castes, Scheduled Tribes and other backward classes. However, in common political discourse, the term Dalit is so far mainly referred to Scheduled Castes. The term Scheduled Caste was used for the first time by the British officials in Government of India Act, 1935. Prior to this, the untouchable castes were known as depressed classes. Mahatma Gandhi gave them the name *Harijans* meaning children of God. Gandhi himself did not coin the name. He borrowed the name from a Bhakti movement saint of the 17th century Narsinh Mehta. The name *Harijan* became popular during 1931 amid conflicts between Gandhi and Ambedkar on the issue of guarantying communal political representation to the dalits. Gandhi took this move as a step towards the disintegration of Hindu society. By terming the untouchables as *Harijans,* Gandhi tried to persuade caste Hindus to shed their prejudices against the *achchutas i.e.* untouchables.

The purpose to adopt this new nomenclature of *Harijan* for the untouchables was to induce change in the heart and behaviour of the Hindus towards untouchables. At the same time, it was hoped that this new name would be accepted by the untouchables who would too try to cultivate the virtues which it connotes. To quote Gandhi "...probably, Antyaja brethren would lovingly accept that name and try to cultivate the virtues which it connotes... may the Antyaja become Harijan both in name and nature" (Gandhi 1971: 244-5). The term *Harijan* got further recognition as an emancipatory nomenclature in the formation of *Harijan Sewak Sangh,* an organisation established for the purpose of upliftment of the dalits under the aegis of the Congress. A weekly *'Harijan'* was also started by Gandhi to provide voice for the cause of the downtrodden. However, Ambedkar did not find any substance in the change of name for the redressal of the structural hindrances that stood menacingly in the way of the their all around amelioration. To him it did not make any difference whether the downtrodden were called *achchuta* or *Harijan,* 'as the new nomenclature did not change their status in the social order'.

The term *Dalit* was used by no less a person than Ambedkar in his fortnightly called *Bahishkrit Bharat.* Though Ambedkar did not popularise the word Dalit for untouchables, his thoughts and actions have contributed to its growth and popularity. The word Dalit is a common usage in Marathi, Hindi, Gujarati and many other Indian languages, denoting the poor and oppressed persons. It also refers to those who have been broken, ground down by those above them in a deliberate way. "It includes all the oppressed and exploited sections of society. It does not confine itself merely to economic exploitation in terms of appropriation of surplus. It also relates to suppression of culture – way of life and value system – and, more importantly, the denial of dignity. It has essentially emerged as a political category. For some, it connotes an ideology for fundamental change in the social structure and relationships". The word Dalit indicates struggle for an egalitarian order and provides the concept of pride to the politically active dalits. The word Dalit gained currency through the writings of Marathi writers in the early 1970s. "Dalit writers who have popularised the word have expressed their notion of Dalit identity in their essays, poems, dramas, autobiographies, novels and short stories. They have reconstructed their past and their view of the present. They have expressed their anger, protest and aspiration".

"Dalit" is a by-product of the Ambedkar movement and indicates a political and social awareness. Ambedkar adopted a different approach and philosophy for the emancipation of Scheduled Castes. He wanted to liberate the dalits by building an egalitarian social order which he believed was not possible within the fold of Hinduism whose very structure was hierarchical which relegated the dalits to the bottom. Initially, he tried to seek emancipation of the dalits by bringing transformation within the structure of Hinduism through his efforts for opening the temples for the dalits and multi-caste dinners. However, Ambedkar came to realise soon that such an approach would not bring the desired result for the amelioration of the inhuman condition of the dalits. He asserted that the dalits should come forward and fight for their own cause. He gave them the *mantra* – educate, organise and agitate. He did not have faith in the charitable spirit of the caste Hindus towards the untouchables as it failed to bring any change in the oppressive social order. Ambedkar did not have any faith in Mahatmas and Saints whose main emphasis was not on the equality between man and man. Their philosophy, according to him, was mainly concerned with the relation between man and God.

Baba Saheb Dr. B. R. Ambedkar, himself a Dalit, made efforts to transform the hierarchical structures of Indian society for the restoration of equal rights and justice to the neglected lot by building up a critique from within the structure of Indian society. His was not a theoretical attempt but a practical approach to the problems of untouchability. He tried to seek the solution to this perennial problem of the Indian society not by making appeals to the conscience of the usurpers or bringing transformation in the outlook of the individual by begging but by seeking transformation in the socio-religious and politico-economic structures of the Indian society by continuous and relentless struggle against the exploitative system where he thought the roots of the untouchability lay. He thought that until and unless the authority of the *Dharamshastras* is shaken which provided divine sanction to the system of discrimination based on the case hierarchy, the eradication of untouchability could not be realised.

It was his subaltern perspective, a perspective from below which helped him to come to the conclusion that untouchability emanated neither from religious notions, nor from the much-popularised theory of Aryan conquest. He believed that it came into existence as a result of the struggle among the tribes at a stage when they were starting to settle down for a stable community living.

In the process, the broken tribesmen were employed by the settled tribes as guards against the marauding bands. These broken tribesmen employed as guards became untouchables. However, Ambedkar could not provide answer to the problem as to why only these broken tribesmen were confined to the one part of the village in the setting towards which the wind blew and the dirt of the village flowed. Ambedkar's tirade against untouchability was a tirade to make these people conscious of their rights, and to prepare them to agitate and win their rights.

Dr. B. R. Ambedkar and Indian Constitution: Dr. Ambedkar was one of the illustrious sons of the India who struggled throughout his life to restructure the Indian Society on humanitarian and egalitarian principles. He was not only a great national leader but also a distinguish scholar of international repute. He not only led various social movements for the upliftment of the depressed sections of the Indian Society but also contributed to the understanding of the Socio-Economic and Political problems of India through his scholarly works on caste, religion, culture, constitutional law and economic development. As a matter of fact he was an economist and his various scholarly works and speeches indicates his deep understanding of the problems faced by Indian

Society. From his very childhood, Dr. Ambedkar was forced to experience the evils of Untouchability. He being an untouchable by birth was forced to sit aside in classroom in the school. He was not allowed to touch his classmates. He could not mix and play with their fellows.

Owing to his academic brilliance, he won many government and private scholarships which helped him in attaining higher qualification from many Indian and foreign universities. He obtained a Ph.D. from Columbia in New York, D.Sc. from the London.

Having returned from London Dr. Ambedkar was given a high post in Baroda. When he reached Baroda no one came to welcome him. Worse still, even the servants in the office would not hand over the files to him. No one in the office would give him water to drink. He could not get a house to live in. On account of his low caste, he was refused a place on rent. He tried his best to get a room, but could find no shelter. He had to resign the post and returned to Bombay.

Dr. Ambedkar founded a Bahiskrit Hitkarini Sabha in 1924 for the upliftment of Dalits. He started Marathi fortnightly the "Mook Nayak" which means the leader of the dumb. Through this paper he awakened the dalits to fight for their rights. He arose a feeling of self respect and self confidence among the dalits and prepared for equal civil rights to the dalits.

Dr. Ambedkar launched marches to enter the Kala Ram Mandir in Nasik and drank water from the public tank at Mahad in Maharashtra. By this acts of the agitation, Dr. Ambedkar wanted to remove the mental dormancy of his people on an all India level. Dr. Ambedkar asked dalits to resist boldly all the acts of social tyranny" Goats! Lions are not sacrificed. Strengthen the organisation of the depressed classes all over the country as it is the only way for salvation." In 1946, Dr. Ambedkar entered into Constituent Assembly. He was taken into the Drafting Committee and there after he was elected as the Chairman of the drafting Committee. He was also taken as the Minister for law.

Dr. Ambedkar knew the difficulties for his illiterate, gullible, resourceless and helpless people to carry on the massive struggles.

The "orphans of the world" he resorted to the constitutional method to solve all the social, political and economic problems.

In the constitution, Dr. Ambedkar provided an inspiring preamble ensuring justice, social, economic and political, liberty, equality and fraternity. He provided comprehensive chapters of fundamental rights and opportunities without discrimination and for securing all freedom and for reducing economic inequalities. He also provided in the constitution safe guards for the protection of rights and interests of the dalits and minorities and equal rights to the women.

Dr. Ambedkar advocated his economic doctrine of "State socialism" in the draft constitution which he prepared and submitted to the constituent Assembly. He proposed state ownership of agriculture with a collectivised method of cultivation and a modified form of state socialism in the field of industry. Dr. Ambedkar also proposed that the above scheme of state socialism should not be left to the will of the legislature and it should be established by the law of constitution so that it will be beyond the reach of the parliamentary majority to suspend, amend or abrogate it. This guarantees state socialism while retaining parliamentary democracy. "It is only by this that one can achieve the triple objectives namely to establish socialism, retain parliamentary democracy and to avoid dictatorship".

Dr. Ambedkar also believed that this plan of state socialism was essential for increasing productivity without closing every avenue to private sector and also distributing wealth equitably. "The main purpose behind the clause is to put an obligation on the state to plan the economic life of people on lines which would lead to highest point of productivity without closing every avenue to the private enterprise and also provide for the equitable distribution of wealth." In other words his model of Economic Development was based on mixed economic system where state has to play active role while opening avenues for private sector.

Further Dr. Ambedkar also argued that if democracy was to live up to its principle of one man one value, it was essential to define both the economic structure as well as the political structure of the society by the law of constitution.

Thus it follows from the above analysis of Dr. Ambedkar's strategy of development that the state has to play very active and crucial role in accelerating the growth with justice through democratic methods. The foundation of democracy would be feeble and shaky if the contradictions between political democracy, enshrined in the constitution, and social and economic inequalities, existing in our society, are not resolved. And the shape and form of economic structure should be defined and prescribed by the law of the constitution without leaving it to the will of the legislature along with that of the structure of the political democracy so that social and economic democracy consistent with political democracy is established.

But due to the strong opposition of the constitution assembly, Dr. Ambedkar could not incorporate his scheme of state socialism under fundamental rights as a part of the constitution. Having failed to achieve his target by adopting such constitutional provisions for a free India, he resorted to the different mode to annihilate or at least weaken the caste system. He took a lengthy process of counter reservation.

The Constitution of India, the world's lengthiest written constitution was passed by the constituent assembly on November 26, 1949. It has been in effect since January 26, 1950, which is celebrated as Republic Day in India. Dr. Ambedkar said in the constituent assembly, "No matter how good a constitution may be, if the means to implement it are no good, then the constitution proves no better. If we want to establish democracy, then we must implement our social and economic ideal by means of peaceful and constitutional measures. Democracy's life is based on liberty, equality, and fraternity. There is a total lack of equality in India. We have equality in politics, but inequality reigns in the spheres of society and economics.

Dr. Ambedkar's knowledge in the constitutional law was extensive varied, profound and encyclopedic. The role played by Dr. Ambedkar in the making of the Constitution received the appreciation of all the members of the constituent Assembly.

On 26th November, the Constituent assembly approved the draft Constitution Bill. Then the first President of India Dr. Rajendra

Prasad praised the services rendered by Dr. Ambedkar in the making of the constitution and said:

> *"I have carefully watched the day to day activities from the Presidential seat. Therefore, I appreciate more than others with how much dedication and vitality this task has been carried out by the Drafting Committee and by its chairman Dr. Bhimrao Ambedkar in particular. We never did a better thing than having Dr. Ambedkar on the Drafting Committee and selecting him as its chairman."*

Columbia University as its Special convocation on 5th June 1952 conferred the LLD. degree (Honours Cause) on Dr. Ambedkar in recognition of his drafting the constitution of India. The citation read: "The degree is being conferred in recognition of the work done by him in connection with the drafting of India's constitution". The University hailed him as "one of India's leading citizen, a great social reformer and valiant upholder of human rights." The same university has already conferred the Ph.D. degree on Ambedkar thirty five years before.

Gautama Buddha fought to eradicate poverty, the Dukkha. He advocated the principle of no private property. He applied this principle of no private property within the limited campus of Sanghas. He advocated the doctrine of "Majjim Patipada" or the middle course. Men should neither accumulate nor enjoy too much or too little of wealth or privileges. That became the cause of "Dukkha" for the rest of the society.

For the last and the latest social revolution Dr. Ambedkar himself adopted and advised his followers to adopt, Buddhism, the spirit of equality and justice. He took refuge in Lord Buddha on 14th October, 1956 at Nagpur along with 5 lakh of his followers. Baba Saheb, Ambedkar was planning to organise a mass conversion in very near future, but they were found dead on the night of 6th December 1956.

Important Events in His Life

- Birth, 14th April 1891
- Witness in South Barrow Commission, 1917
- Untouchables' conference, Nagpur, 1918
- Bahishkrit Hitkarini Sabha Formed 20th July 1924

- Nominated as MLC, Bombay Province, 1926
- Mahad Satyagraha, December 1927
- Witness in Simon Commission, May 1928
- Nashik Kala Ram temple Satyagraha, 2nd March 1930
- Representative at Round Table Conference, 1930-32
- British Communal Award, 20th August 1932
- Poona Pact, 20th September 1932
- Yewale District, Nasik Conference, 23rd October 1935
- Mahar Parishad, Bombay Province, 31st May 1936
- Independent Labout Party Formed, August 1936
- Elected MLA, Bombay Province, January 1937
- All India Scheduled Caste Federation Formed at Nagpur, April 1942
- Appointed as Labour Minister in the Viceroy's Executive Council, July 1942
- People's Education Society Formed, July 1945
- Elected to Constituent Assembly from Bengal, November 1946
- Law Minister in Independent India, 15th August 1947
- Appointed as Chairman, Drafting Committee of the Constitution of India, 29th August 1947
- Resigned from Union Cabinet, September 1951
- Elected to Rajya Sabha, March 1952
- Buddhist Society of India Formed, May 1955
- Embraced Buddhism, 14th October 1956
- Parinirvan (Death), 6th December 1956

Dr. Babasaheb Ambedkar and his Writings

- The National Dividend of India, 1916
- Small Holdings in India and Their Remedies, 1917
- Weekly 'Mook Nayak', Started 31st January 1920
- Provincial Decentralisation of Imperial Finance in British India, June 1921
- The Problem of a Rupee—Its Origin & Its Solution, March 1923

- The Evolution of Provincial Finance in British India, 1925
- Weekly 'Bahishkrit Bharat', Started 13th April 1927
- Weekly 'Janata', Started December 1930
- Annihilation of Caste, December 1935
- Federation Vs Freedom, January 1939
- Thoughts on Pakistan, December 1940
- Mr. Gandhi & the Emancipation of the Untouchables, December 1942
- Ranade, Gandhi & Jinnah, January 1943
- What Congress & Gandhi have done to the Untouchables, June 1945
- Who Were the Sudras?, October 1946
- States & Minorities, March 1947
- The Untouchable, October 1948
- Maharashtra as Linguistic Province, October 1948
- Thoughts on Linguistic States, December 1955
- Buddha & His Dhamma, Published 1957

22 Vows of Dr. Ambedkar

Dr. B.R. Ambedkar prescribed 22 vows to his followers during the historic religious conversion to Buddhism on 15 October 1956 at Deeksha Bhoomi, Nagpur in India.

The conversion to Buddhism by 800,000 people was historic because it was the largest religious conversion, the world has ever witnessed. He prescribed these oaths so that there may be complete severance of bond with Hinduism. These 22 vows struck a blow at the roots of Hindu beliefs and practices. These vows could serve as a bulwark to protect Buddhism from confusion and contradictions. These vows could liberate converts from superstitions, wasteful and meaningless rituals, which have led to popularisation of masses and enrichment of upper castes of Hindus.

The famous 22 vows are:

- I shall have no faith in Brahma, Vishnu and Mahesh nor shall I worship them.

- I shall have no faith in Rama and Krishna who are believed to be incarnation of God nor shall I worship them.
- I shall have-no faith in 'Gauri', Ganapati and other gods and goddesses of Hindus nor shall I worship them.
- I do not believe in the incarnation of God.
- I do not and shall not believe that Lord Buddha was the incarnation of Vishnu. I believe this to be sheer madness and false propaganda.
- I shall not perform 'Shraddha' nor shall I give 'pind-dan'.
- I shall not act in a manner violating the principles and teachings of the Buddha.
- I shall not allow any ceremonies to be performed by Brahmins.
- I shall believe in the equality of man.
- I shall endeavour to establish equality.
- I shall follow the 'noble eightfold path' of the Buddha.
- I shall follow the 'paramitas' prescribed by the Buddha.
- I shall have compassion and loving kindness for all living beings and protect them.
- I shall not steal.
- I shall not tell lies.
- I shall not commit carnal sins.
- I shall not take intoxicants like liquor, drugs etc.
- I shall endeavour to follow the noble eightfold path and practise compassion and loving kindness in every day life.
- I renounce Hinduism which is harmful for humanity and impedes the advancement and development of humanity because it is based on inequality, and adopt Buddhism as my religion.
- I firmly believe the Dhamma of the Buddha is the only true religion.
- I believe that I am having a rebirth.
- I solemnly declare and affirm that I shall hereafter lead my life according to the principles and teachings of the Buddha and his Dhamma.

DEATH

Since 1948, Ambedkar had been suffering from diabetes. He was bedridden from June to October in 1954 owing to clinical depression and failing eyesight. He had been increasingly embittered by political issues, which took a toll on his health. His health worsened as he furiously worked through 1955. Just three days after completing his final manuscript 'Buddha And His Dhamma', it is said that Ambedkar died in his sleep on December 6, 1956 at his home in Delhi. Some of his supporters doubt his natural death and think death may not have been natural and put forward different theories. Try to draw parallel between his and Gandhi's death and blame Caste Brahmins.

A Buddhist-style cremation was organised for him at Chowpatty beach on December 7, attended by hundreds of thousands of supporters, activists and admirers. Ambedkar was survived by his second wife Savita Ambedkar, born as a Caste Brahmin and converted to Buddhism with him. His wife's name before marriage was Sharda Kabir. Savita Ambedkar died as Buddhist in 2002. Ambedkar's grandson, Prakash Yaswant Ambedkar leads the Bharipa Bahujan Mahasangha and has served in both houses of the Indian Parliament. A number of unfinished typescripts and handwritten drafts were found among Ambedkar's notes and papers and gradually made available. Among these were *Waiting for a Visa,* which probably dates from 1935-36 and is an autobiographical work, and the *Untouchables, or the Children of India's Ghetto,* which refers to the census of 1951.

A memorial for Ambedkar was established in his Delhi house at 26 Alipur Road. His birthdate is celebrated as a public holiday known as Ambedkar Jayanti. He was posthumously awarded India's highest civilian honour, the Bharat Ratna in 1990. He is the namesake of many public institutions, such as the Dr. Babasaheb Ambedkar Open University in Ahmedabad, Gujarat.

A large official portrait of Ambedkar is on display in the Parliament building. Jabbar Patel directed the Hindi-language movie "Dr. Babasaheb Ambedkar" about the life of Ambedkar, released in 2000, starring South Indian actor Mammootty as Ambedkar. Sponsored by India's National Film Development Corporation and Ministry of Social Justice, the film was released after a long and controversial gestation period. Dr. Ambedkar was the main architect of the Indian Constitution. He was born in a very poor low caste family of Madhya Pradesh. In U.S.A., he did his M.A. in 1915 and Ph.D. in 1916. From 1918 to 1920, he worked as a Professor of Law. Dr. Ambedkar set up his legal practice at the Mumbai High Court.

A number of unfinished typescripts and handwritten drafts were found among Ambedkar's notes and papers and gradually made available. Among these were Waiting for a Visa, which probably dates from 1935-36 and is an autobiographical work, and the Untouchables, or the Children of India's Ghetto, which refers to the census of 1951. A memorial for Ambedkar was established in his Delhi house at 26 Alipur Road. His birthdate is celebrated as a public holiday known as Ambedkar Jayanti. He was posthumously awarded India's highest civilian honour, the Bharat Ratna in 1990. He is the namesake of many public institutions, such as the Dr. Babasaheb Ambedkar Open University in Ahmedabad, Gujarat. A large official portrait of Ambedkar is on display in the Parliament building. Jabbar Patel directed the Hindi-language movie "Dr. Baba Saheb Ambedkar" about the life of Ambedkar, released in 2000, starring South Indian actor Mammootty as Ambedkar. Sponsored by India's National Film Development Corporation and Ministry of Social Justice, the film was released after a long and controversial gestation period.

EFFORTS TO END INJUSTICE

There was no cast system during the Vedic age. There was no 'untouchability'. When and how did this system creep into the Hindu society? We do not know for certain.

Did no one try to wipe out this injustice? Buddha admitted may 'untouchables' to his religion. Ramanujacharya, Basaveshwara, Chakradhara, Ramananda, Kabir, Chaitanya, Ekanath, Tukaram, Raja Rammohan Roy and other great men preached that no one is high and no one is low among God's children. Mahatma Phooley and his wife dedicated their lives to the education of the 'untouchables.' Sayyaji Rao Gaikwad, the Maharaja of Baroda, established a school for the 'untouchables' as early as in 1883. In this way many thoughtful leaders of the

Hindu Society have been trying for hundreds of years to wipe out 'Untouchability'. Both before and after India became free, many great man have sacrificed their lives for the truth and the principles they believed in. Ambedkar was one of them.

Ideas of high and low had crept into the Hindu Society; Ambedkar suffered because of this; he also fought hard against such differences; later he became the first Las Minister in free India. The credit for making a law and creating the necessary atmosphere to wipe out 'Untouchability' goes to Ambedkar.

Should Not Hindu, Who Seek Justice, Give Justice?

The 'untouchables' are Hindus. Therefore, the doors of temples should be open to them. If the Hindus can touch the Christians and the Muslims, why should they not touch the people who are themselves Hindus and who worship the Hindu Gods? This was Ambedkar's argument. He gave a call that people who practise and support 'untouchability' should be punished. Some people argued that the 'untouchables' were not yet fit for equality. The Hindus say that they want independence and democracy. How can a people who have temple upon all the libertise of a backward group aspire to democracy? Ambedkar argued like this and thundered that these people had no right to speak of justice and democracy.

In 1927 there was a big conference. It resolved that there should be no cast differences in the Hindu Dharma and that people of all castes should be allowed to work as priests in temples. The Chowdar Tank dispute went to the court. The court decided that tanks are public property. The 'untouchables' who have been subjected to humiliation for hundreds of years should find justice. For this purpose Ambedkar indicated a few clear steps. No section of the Hindus should be kept out of temples.

There should be more representatives of the 'untouchables' in the legislatures. These representatives should not be nominated by the government. They should be elected by the people. The government should employ the 'untouchalbes' in larger numbers the army and the police department.

A Fearless, Firm Mind: Those who suffer in the Hindu Society should get justice.

This was Ambedkar's rocklike decision. He was prepared to oppose anybody to reach his goal. The British Government invited several Indian leaders to discuss the problems of India. The conferences were held in London; they were called the 'Round Table Conference'. Gandhiji also took part in them. At the Round Table Conference Ambedkar spoke angrily against the government. He said that the backward sections did not enjoy equality with other sections, even under the British Government; the British had just followed the ways of the other Hindus.

This was a time when Gandhiji was very popular in India. Millions of people followed his footsteps with devotion. Ambedkar openly opposed Gandhiji's views on how justice should be secured for the 'untouchables'. He supported the views which seemed right to him. Ambedkar secured for the Harijans (the 'untouchables') 'separate electorates' at the Second Round Table Conference in 1931. As a result, the Harijans could elect their representatives separately.

AFTER RESIGNATION AS A MINISTER

In 1952, he was defeated by a Congress candidate in the election for the Lok Sabha. The entire country was shocked by his defeat.

Later he was elected to the Rajya Sabha. Whenever he felt that the government had not done justice to the Harijans he criticised it sharply. In 1953 the government brought a bill before the parliament. According to this bill those who practised 'untouchablity' would be punished; imprisonment, imposition of fines, dismissal from employment and withdrawal of licence to follow a profession – these were the forms of punishment.

To the Path of the Buddha: Soon after the framing of the Constitution, Ambedkar's mind turned towards Buddha. His mind was thirsting for peace and justice. He attended the Buddhist Conference in Ceylon (Sri Lanka) in 1950.

The bitterness of his mind was ever on the increase. In spite of it, he was not willing to embrace the Christian or the Muslim faith. Finally, Ambedkar decided to become a Buddhist. This was a great decision in his life, a decision taken after deep thought.

A NEGLECTED MESSAGE FROM DR. AMBEDKAR TO OBCS

An article was published recently in Marathi local magazine by Suhas Sonwane based on daily Loksatta. The following is a gist of it, translated from Marathi. Mr. Baba Saheb Gawande, the founder president of an Organization of Marathas from Bombay called "Maratha Mandir" was a close friend of Dr. Ambedkar. Mr. Gawande asked Dr. Ambedkar, who was then a Law Minister in Nehru Cabinet in 1947, for a message for the Maratha people to be published in the Souvenir of "Maratha Mandir". Ambedkar declined saying that he had no relation with the Organization or the Marathas, but on persistent insistence, a message was given and published in the souvenir on 23rd March 1947. Unfortunately that special issue is not available in the office of the Organization today, but was made available by Shri Vijay Survade recently and was undocumented till now. Dr. Ambedkar said:

> *"This principle will apply not only to Marathas but all Backward Castes. If they do not wish to be under the thumb of others they should concentrate on two things, one is politics and the other is education."*
>
> *"One thing I like to impress on you is that the community can live in peace only when it has enough moral but indirect pressure over the rulers. Even if a community is numerically weak, it can keep its pressure over the rulers and create its dominance as is seen by the example of status of present day Brahmins in India. It is essential that such a pressure is maintained, as without it, the aims and policies of the state can not have proper direction, on which depends the development and progress of the state."*
>
> *"At the same time, it must not be forgotten that education is also important. Not only elementary education but higher education is most essential to keep ahead in competition of communities in their progress."*
>
> *"Higher education, in my opinion, means that education, which can enable you to occupy the strategically important places in State administration. Brahmins had to face a lot of opposition and obstacles, but they are overcoming these and progressing ahead."*

"I can not forget, rather I am sad, that many people do not realize that the Caste system is existing in India for centuries because of inequality and a wide gulf of difference in education, and they have forgotten that it is likely to continue for some centuries to come. This gulf between the education of Brahmins and non-Brahmins will not end just by primary and secondary education. The difference in status between these can only be reduced by higher education. Some non-Brahmins must get highly educated and occupy the strategically important places, which has remained the monopoly of Brahmins since long. I think this is the duty of the State. If the Govt. can not do it, institutions like "Maratha Mandir" must undertake this task."

"I must emphasize one point here that middle class tries to compare itself with the highly educated and well placed and well to do community, whereas lower class all over the world has same fault. The middle class is not as liberal as upper one, and has no ideology as lower one, which makes it enemy of both the classes. The middle class Marathas of Maharashtra also have this fault. They have only two ways out, either to join hands with upper classes and prevent the lower classes from progress, and the other is to join hands with lower classes and both together destroy the upper class power coming against the progress of both.

There was a time, they used to be with lower classes, now they seem to be with the upper class. It is for them to decide which way to go. The future of not only Indian masses but also their own future depends upon what decision the Maratha leaders take. As a matter of fact it all should be left to the skill and wisdom of the leaders of Marathas. But there seems to be a lack of such wise leadership among the Marathas."

What he said about Marathas, equally applies to all OBCs, and still holds true after half a century. Dr. Ambedkar wrote much to educate the OBCs. It is only now that OBCs are awakening gradually. It must not be forgotten that the future of this country depends on them.

7

Jawahar Lal Nehru

In the heart of the Himalayas lies the lovely land of Kashmir. "Learning, lofty houses, saffron, icy water and grapes: things that even in heaven are difficult to find are common there." So wrote the chronicler of Rajatarangini, a Sanskrit record of the early and fabulous days of Kashmir. In the late sixteenth century, in 1588, Akbar, the great Mogul Emperor of India, incorporated Kashmir in his domain. Earlier Hindu and Buddhist monarchs had ruled the land until about 1294 when it passed into Muslim hands. Of the Mogul rulers, the wayward, unregenerate but sensitive Jehangir, Akbar's favourite son and successor, was drawn strongly towards this mountain land. Jehangir loved nature, and Kashmir's birds and flowers, its green valleys and streams with their majestic background of mountains and glaciers enchanted him. "Wherever the eye reaches," he wrote in his autobiography, "there are verdure and running water. The red rose, the violet and the narcissus grow of themselves; in the fields there are all kinds of flowers and all sorts of sweet scented herbs, more than can be calculated."

Nehru's ancestors came from this land of enchantment. They were, as are the vast majority of Kashmiri Hindus, Brahmins enjoying the honorific of Pandit, which means Man of Learning. The original family name was not Nehru but Kaul.

Around 1716, some nine years after the death of the Emperor Aurangzeb, who was Jehangir's grandson, a Sanskrit and Persian scholar, Raj Kaul, migrated to the imperial capital of Delhi, probably at the instance of the then Emperor Farrakhsiar who during a visit to Kashmir had been attracted by his scholarship. Raj Kaul was granted a jagir (piece of land) with a house by a canal The Persian term for canal is nahar, and it was from the accident of living alongside a nahar that the name of Nehru is derived. For a long time the family was known as Kaul-Nehra. Later the Kaul was dropped.

Although scholars, Jawaharlal's ancestors were mostly in government employment. His great-grandfather, Pandit Lakshmi Narayan Nehru, was a lawyer, and in this capacity was attached to the East India Company at the phantom court of the dying Mogul Empire. His grandfather, Pandit Ganga Dhar Nehru, was kotwal, or police officer-in-charge, of the city of Delhi. This was some time before the Indian Mutiny of i8$j? Fair-skinned like most Kashmiris, Ganga Dhar is depicted in an old painting as a red-bearded man with reflective blue eyes. He died in 1861 at the age of thirty-four. Around 1858 the Nehru family joined the fugitive caravan fleeing Delhi in the turmoil following the Mutiny, and migrated to the neighbouring town of Agra, which contains the famous Taj Mahal.

There on May 6, 1861, Nehru's father, Motilal, who was Ganga Dhar's youngest son, was bom. He was a posthumous child, Ganga Dhar having died three months earlier. By an interesting coincidence he was born on the same day, month and year as the poet Rabindranath Tagore. Commenting on the coincidence many years later Nehru remarked that apart from Gandhi and Motilal, Rabindranath Tagore had "a very considerable influence over me." The major influences, he admitted, were those of his father and Gandhiji. "I came into contact with Tagore rather in the later years when I had been conditioned more or less by my father and Gandhiji" Nehru explained. Nevertheless, Rabindranath had a very considerable influence over me." Motilal had two brothers, both very much older than he, Bansi Dhar and Nandlal. On their father's death the infant Motilal became their responsibility. Not long after, the eldest brother, Bansi Dhar, took employment with the British Government and as a member of the judicial department was transferred to various places. The care and education of Motilal thus devolved on his second brother Nandlal, to whom he was deeply attached. Nandlal was for a while the Diwan or Prime Minister of a princely estate called Khetri in Rajputana. After this he practised as a lawyer in Agra, and when the High

Court was transferred from there to Allahabad he moved to the latter place. Since then Allahabad has been the home of the Nehrus. Young Motilal was a lively, high-spirited lad not greatly addicted to formal learning but naturally intelligent. As a boy his education was confined to Persian and Arabic, but he studied English later. He went through school and college in Kanpur and Allahabad, although he never graduated. This lapse came about in a curious if typical way. Motilal took his first examination but thought he had fared badly. Thereupon he decided to skip the rest and, playing truant, spent his time looking around the Taj. Actually, he had done quite well in his first paper.

At the Muir Central College in Allahabad, Motilal came under the influence of British professors who liked his youthful independence and initiative. Jawaharlal recalls how even in his later years his father would reminisce affectionately about the English principal of his college one of whose letters he had carefully preserved. From this time date MotflaTs Westernized habits and dress and his genuine liking and admiration for Englishmen. Faced with the choice of a career Motilal decided to emulate his favourite brother and become a lawyer. He appeared for the High Court Vakil's examination and topped the list, winning a gold medal. The law at that time was one of the few professions open to Indian talent.

After three years of apprenticeship in the district court at Kanpur, Motilal moved to the loftier realms of the High Court at Allahabad and settled to legal practice at that centre. About this time Nandlal died. To Motilal, who had grown up under Nandlafs affectionate care, his brother's sudden death was a heavy blow. He had loved him greatly. Aside from their mother, a woman of imperious personality and tremendous will, much of whose strong-mindedness Motilal inherited, there was hardly any other personal influence in his life.

The burden of supporting his brother's family now fell on Motilal He plunged into work. As a lawyer he was more effective in the role of advocate than in that of jurist, being impatient of the smaller niceties of the law but quick to grasp the broad essentials of a case. His mind was keen and resourceful. He was by temperament combative. He loved nothing better than a fight;

and his assertive advocacy aided by the vigour of his personality cut a quick swath to success. Politics had then very little appeal for him, and in the India of those days political aspirations were limited to the removal of minor grievances and to pleas for larger representation in the administrative services and local government. Motilal was twenty-four when in 1885 the Indian National Congress in which he and his son were later to play a dominating part met for its first session in Bombay. The Congress owed its inception to a Scotsman, Alan Octavian Hume, who was a former member of the Indian Civil Service. At this session Hume called for "three times three cheers for Her Majesty the Queen Empress," and the delegates responded enthusiastically. Exactly forty-four years later, in 1929, the Congress party met at Lahore under the presidentship of Jawaharlal Nehru to proclaim complete independence as India's political goal.

According to the custom then prevailing in India, marriage was contracted at an early age. Motilal was married twice. He was around twenty when he married a Kashmiri girl of a family settled in Lahore, but she died shortly after the birth of a son who in turn did not survive his mother for long. MotilaFs second wife, Swaruprani, was only a little over fifteen when she entered the Nehru household as a bride.

Her husband was seven years her senior. Like her husband, Swaruprani was the last child of her family, also Kashmiri Brahmins, settled in Lahore, and of a younger stock than the Nehras. The family name was Thussu. She was tiny, being hardly five feet tall, smalled-boned, dainty and exquisite, like a porcelain figurine. Her son writes of her "amazingly small and beautiful hands and feet" Notwithstanding her doll-like delicacy, Swaruprani was a person of considerable fortitude and character. In the coming years she was to have more than a woman's fair share of tribulation. Married to a man even then well set on the road to fame and fortune, she lacked nothing of the material adjuncts to comfort, ease and happiness. For thirty years Swaruprani knew the splendour and luxury of an affluent home until along with her husband she voluntarily shed the past and all that went with it to follow the Mahatma. The Nehru household, when she entered it; was a typical Hindu joint family comprising

Motilal, Nandlal's sons and a considerable cohort of cousins, children of his father's sisters, all living under one roof and presided over by the strong-willed matriarch who was Motilal's mother. It was no easy thing for a young bride of near sixteen to adjust herself to this environment, the more so since she was not mistress of the household. Motilal lavished on her the love and care of a devoted husband, but it is doubtful whether, until she reigned in her own household, which she did a few years later, Swaruprani felt any different from a bird in a golden cage. Motilal, already a successful lawyer but still to reach the fabulous heights he achieved later, was then living in a house standing in a lane in one of Allahabad's more congested localities.

The entrance to the lane was said to be haunted. Here, on November 14, 1889, Jawaharlal was bom, and here he lived for three years. In 1889 a twenty-year-old Indian, Mohandas Karamchand Gandhi, who was studying in London to be a barrister, called on Cardinal Manning to congratulate him on his attitude to the London dockers' strike. In that year Bernard Shaw published his Fabian Essays, and Gustave Eiffel confounded his critics by completing the Eiffel Tower in Paris. Japan was granted a constitution, and the Suez Canal was neutralised. A would-be dictator, General Georges Boulanger, fled from France. In India the Congress party's fourth annual session in Bombay was presided over by an Englishman, Sir William Wedderburn. Another Englishman, Charles Bradlaugh, the atheist Member of Parliament, addressed it.

Jawaharlal's boyhood was lonely. Although the household was full of children, they were considerably older than he. Portraits of those days show him as a boy with wistful eyes, and dressed in a variety of costumes from embroidered pantaloons and coat with jewelled slippers, to a sailor's rig and a Scots kilt. A fervent admirer of the British character, Motilal was determined that his son should be brought up in Western ways.

Until the age of sixteen when he went to Harrow, Jawaharlal never attended school He was educated at home by a series of English governesses and private tutors, but of these only one, a part Irish theosophist of the name of Ferdinand T. Brooks, made any impression on the boy.

Brooks had been recommended to Motilal as Jawaharlal's tutor by Dr. Annie Besant His father was Irish, his mother was Belgian and he was born on board a steamer bound for South America. As a young man Brooks was attracted to Indian philosophy, learned Sanskrit and translated the Bhagavad-Gita, a celebrated religious poem contained in the Mahabharata, which is the great epic poem of the Hindus. He was an ardent theosophist, of a deeply devotional nature, with a strongly religious pietist streak in him which in the eyes of his young charge must have contrasted strangely with Motilal's robust secularism.

Brooks was about twenty-six when he came as tutor to Jawaharlal, then a boy of eleven. He was to die later in tragic circumstances.

Fanatically wedded to the truth as he saw it, Brooks parted company with Dr. Besant when that lady proclaimed Krishnamurthy as the coming Messiah. He was earning a precarious livelihood when his body was found in a river, drowned in circumstances which left the cause of his death a mystery. The influence of this strongly introvert character on Jawaharlal, albeit temporary, was also considerable. Brooks developed in Jawaharlal two interests which have endured a taste for reading and a curiosity in science and its mysteries. Apart from his religious bent, he appears to have been a man of much sensitivity, imagination and understanding. Between them, tutor and pupil rigged up a little laboratory, and there Jawaharlal felt for the first time the quick stir of wonder which still seizes him when confronted with scientists and scientific matters. Here he learned his early lessons in elementary physics and chemistry. Brooks was with him for nearly three years, and in this period he encouraged his pupil's liking for English literature. Jawaharlal's reading, though wide, was haphazard and discursive. He read many of the novels of Scott, Dickens and Thackeray. He was attracted by Lewis Carroll and by Kipling's Jungle Books and Kim. Fridtjof Nansen's account of his Arctic adventures, Farthest North, excited his imagination and he followed breathlessly the exploits of Anthony Hope's hero in The Prisoner of Zenda. He came to know of Mark Twain and H. G. Wells and Conan Doyle's stories of Sherlock Holmes. He thought Jerome K. Jerome's Three Men in a Boat "the last word in humour." Two other books seem to have specially impressed his youthful imagination, and he mentions them in his autobiography. They were Du Maurier's Trilby and Peter Ibbetson. Jawaharlal gives no reason for his especial choice, but it is possible that the boy discovered there the first faint glimmerings of a philosophy of life which the man was later to embrace. "And this I know," says a character in Peter Ibbetson, "the longer and more strenuously and complete one lives one's life on earth, the better for all. It is the foundation of everything." Brooks also developed in his young charge a love for English poetry, and though his other reoccupations leave Jawaharlal little time today to indulge this taste his love for the arresting phrase and evocative thought persists. The strong streak of melancholy in his character was probably also enhanced by this association. At the height of the partition killings in 1947, an acquaintance relates how he quoted to Nehru a line from the noted Hindi poet Maithili Sharan Gupta: "The history of man is the history of the Devil" Jawaharlal, bowed with care and grief, heaved a sigh and repeated the line slowly.

A similar incident is related of a dinner party. There was a programme on the sitar after dinner, and the host, knowing that his guest had had a very tiring day, suggested that he should retire.

"Oh, no," protested Nehru. "I haven't heard the sitar for a very long time."

Thereupon a fellow guest broke in, as is often the custom in parts of the country, with an Urdu quotation from northern India's most celebrated troubadour Ghalib:

" It was love, Ghalib, that brought me to this pass. Or else I too would have been of some use"

Nehru, nodding melancholy assent, gently repeated, " It was love, Ghalib..."

As a boy he was fascinated by Gustave Dore's illustrations to Don Quixote, but his visual judgment even today is less sure than his aural. His ear is more certain than his eye, and music and song have a stronger appeal to him than the sweeping brash and broad canvas of an artist. But he can be moved, even intoxicated, by the beauty of sky and stars, by the majesty of mountains and the breathless wonder of nature stirring at dawn to new life. Brooks opened to him a window on a new world.

The only Indian tutor Jawaharlal had was a venerable pandit who was engaged to teach him Hindi and Sanskrit. An old friend of the family recalls seeing a beautifully printed edition of the Samaveda, the third of the four holy books of Hinduism, among the boy's Sanskrit texts. Nehru confesses that "after many years' effort" his knowledge of Sanskrit was about as small as his subsequent knowledge of Latin at Harrow. His Hindi is fluent but it is less proficient than his English. He probably thinks in English. During his last term of imprisonment in Ahmednagar fort, Nehru shared a cell with Maulana Abul Kalam Azad, the noted Muslim divine who is now India's Education Minister. Azad has related how Nehru talked in English in his sleep. "He not only talks in English" wrote Azad. "He dreams in English."

As Motilal prospered, the family's standard of living improved. When Jawaharlal was three the father decided to move from his house in the haunted lane of the old city to a newer part of Allahabad where he rented a bungalow in an area occupied mainly by Europeans. Jawaharlal lived here until he was ten, when Motilal moved to a residence he had bought for himself known as Anand Bhawan (Abode of Happiness).

Anand Bhawan, a large rambling house ringed with verandahs, stood in spacious grounds and had an indoor swimming pool, the first of its kind in Allahabad. Here Jawaharlal learned to swim. He recalls how on first moving to his new home he watched the labourers at work on the structures and embellishments which his father had ordered. Boy-like, he was entranced by the digging and building operations.

Anand Bhawan, donated later by Motilal to the nation and rechristened Swaraj Bhawan (Abode of Freedom), stands on a reputedly sacred spot where according to some traditions the deity Rama met his half-brother Bharata, on Rama's return from his fourteen years' exile. Nearby is the Bharadwaj Ashram where legend has it that tie sage Valmiki, author of the Ramayana, once stayed. The city of Allahabad, the ancient Prayaga, Is also on hallowed ground, for here the heavenly river Ganga meets the Jumna and the fabled subterranean stream Saraswati. At the meeting place of these three rivers known as Triveni, or "the triple braid," pilgrims foregather from all parts of India, once annually for the Magh Mela and once in every twelve years for the great Kumbh Mela, a mammoth religions festival fair which goes back to the Vedic times. In these early formative years Jawaharlal spent his time mainly between his English tutors and his mother. His cousins were much older than he, and though he often listened to their grown-up talk the gulf of years prevented any affinity or companionship between them. One can imagine the little boy listening wide-eyed and not always comprehendingly to the conversation of his youthful elders. Some of it seeped into his sensitive, highly imaginative mind and stayed there.

Much of this talk was concerned with the overbearing, often insulting behaviour of Europeans and Eurasians towards Indians. Jawaharlal heard of railway compartments being reserved for Europeans which no Indian, however crowded the train, might enter. He heard of benches and chairs being similarly labelled in public parks. Sometimes one or the other of his cousins was involved in an encounter. Jawaharlal relates how these accounts created in him a feeling of strong resentment against the alien rulers of his country. At the same time he does not recall cherishing any hostile sentiments towards individual Englishmen. His own governesses and tutors were English and his father's house was wide open to English friends. "In my heart," he confesses, "I rather admired the English."

Of his father he saw little, and much of it from a distance. Off and on Motilal took time to play with his son, putting him through his paces in cricket and tennis. Sometimes father and son regaled themselves flying a kite. Occasionally of an evening as Motilal sat talking and drinking with his friends, the boy would peep from behind a curtain, trying to take in the flow of conversation and laughter. He was tremendously impressed by his father, by his robust talk, his great echoing laugh, his vitality, strength and magnetism. He thought him clever and full of courage. Now and again the eavesdropper was noticed, and on these occasions his father would pull him into the room and seat him on his knee. Jawaharlal confesses that these occasions somewhat awed him. "I grew up," Nehru was to recall many years later, "in a rather composite environment." If he admired his father he was also more than slightly afraid of him. Motilal had charm and a sense of humour, but his temper was something awful to behold. "Even in after years" writes Jawaharlal, "I do not think I ever came across anything to match it in its own line/' The patria potestas was very much in evidence in Motilal's attitude to his household. By nature overbearing, he was inclined to be somewhat feudal in his treatment of servants.

When moved to wrath by a domestic's ineptitude he thought nothing of rising from the table and then and there thrashing the unfortunate man with his own hands. A youthful Indian friend of the family, fresh from Cambridge, recounts one such incident at the breakfast table at Anand Bhawan. He describes the episode as "odd and inexcusable." On Jawaharlal his father's attitude to his servants undoubtedly made an impression. The boy's fear was mixed with resentment, and something at least of his instinctive sympathy for the helpless underdog is traceable to these early years. On one occasion Jawaharlal himself felt the weight of his father's wrath. He was about six years old when, wandering into his father's study one day, he noticed two fountain pens on his table. Two, he argued, were not necessary for one man at the same time. He helped himself to one. When the loss was discovered he was too terrified of his father's wrath to confess. But the missing pen was traced to him, and his father beat him severely. "Almost blind with pain and mortification at my disgrace, I rushed to my mother, and for several days various creams and ointments were applied to my aching and quivering little body."

It was on his mother that Jawaharlal leaned in those early years. She doted on him, and the boy, aware of her excessive, indiscriminating love, tried, as he confesses, to dominate her a little. She was his confidante, and to her he told some of his dreams, disappointments and yearnings. Loneliness gave an edge to his imagination. He used to dream of astral bodies, and imagined himself flying vast distances high up in the air without any appliance, alone and dominant. This escapist fantasy was to haunt him in later years. "This dream," he writes, 'has indeed been a frequent one throughout my life; and sometimes it has been vivid and realistic and the countryside seemed to lie underneath me in a vast panorama." From his mother and aunt, the widow of Nandlal, Jawaharlal heard, as Indian children of his age do, the old, old tales of Indian mythology and folklore. His mother told him of the adventures of the great Rama which form the theme of the oldest of Sanskrit epic poems, Valiniki's Ramayana. From her too he learned the story of the Mahabharata detailing, among other things, the war between the Kauravas and the Pandavas for a kingdom, the rains of whose capital, known as the "elephant city," are faintly discernible on an old bed of the Ganga about sixty miles northeast of Delhi.

Another of the boy's early confidants was Munshi Mubarak Ali, a patriarchal-looking Muslim who served as a sort of major-domo to the household. Often the companionless lad sought the old man's company and, snuggling up to him, listened to tales from the Arabian Nights and to stories of the Indian rebellion of 1857. Mubarak Ali's family had been ruined by the Mutiny, during which some British soldiers had hanged his father before his mother's eyes. Sorrow, as it sometimes does, had made Mubarak gentle and understanding, and the boy, looking at the lined face, the white locks and beard of his old friend, thought him the epitome of human wisdom. "The memory of him," Jawaharlal wrote many years later, "remains with me as a dear and precious possession."

Some at least of the brooding melancholy which is part of Nehru's nature might be traced to this solitary boyhood. With no companions of his own age at home, he sought instinctively the company of his mother and of sympathetic elders such as his aunt and Mubarak Ali, He was left very much to himself, and this isolation sharpened his thought and imagination. The sense of living a life apart, alone and sure, is reflected in his dream of flying high up in an empyrean void.

But always there was the earth below.

Although Jawaharlal saw little of his father, and feared him, his admiration and affection for him remained as strong as ever. On his side Motilal, though never as demonstrative as the mother, loved his son intensely. His work absorbed him, and Jawaharlal's education was a matter which he felt could be left safely to the hands of competent tutors. The mother was never in the best of health. Since her son's birth she had suffered from a number of intermittent ailments, and her health was indifferent. Life with an ailing mother and later with an ailing wife was to iniuence Nehru profoundly. He learned to value good health. Fitness became a fetish with him.

Motilal's masculine assertiveness appealed to the feminine streak in his son. The father's attitude to women, particularly to his own womenfolk, was one of amused toleration. He dismissed family squabbles as the creation of women's folly. He was not particularly religious, and was inclined to treat religion half humorously as a woman's affair.

"My father was not exactly a religious man," Nehru once remarked. "But he respected the Hindu religion since he had been brought up in it."

Jawaharlal's own ideas on religion were hazy, and his tutor, Brooks, a determined theosophist, had therefore little difficulty in influencing his pupil his way. He instilled in him an interest in theosophy by introducing him to tie works of Madame Blavatsky and by exposing him to discussions on the more esoteric aspects of this creed. Jawaharlal, then thirteen, was fascinated. He decided to join the Theosophical Society.

Motilal had been a member of the Society when Madame Blavatsky was in India, and was initiated into it by her. Founded by this formidable personage in 1875 in New York, the Society had been transferred to Madras in India in 1882. With the advent of Dr. Annie Besant, friend of Bradlaugh and Bernard Shaw, theosophy began to have an appeal for the urban Indian intellectual who was attracted and intrigued by its references to the Hindu and Buddhist scriptures. Mrs. Besant, perhaps the greatest natural orator of her day, was in wide vogue, and, hearing some of her speeches in Allahabad, Jawaharlal was thrilled. He asked his father's permission to join the Society, and was hurt when Motilal laughingly assented, displaying more amusement than interest in the affair. Motilal himself had ceased his association with theosophy within a short time of joining the Society. Mrs. Besant presided at Jawaharlal's ceremony of initiation. Not long after, the thirteen-year-old boy attended the Theosophical Convention at Banaras where he saw the bearded Colonel Henry Olcott.

His interest in theosophy, like that of his father, was short-lived. It did not long survive BrooJb's departure from the household, but while this spiritual fever seized him he went about, as he recalled later, in an aura of pallid piety. Significantly his interest in theosophy palled not because he saw anything wrong in its tenets but because many of the persons associated with the movement seemed to him to live in an impractical, unreal world and priggishly regarded themselves as the elect.

Two years earlier, when Jawaharlal was eleven, a daughter was born to his parents. His father at the time was away in England, and the boy, sitting anxiously in the verandah of his house, learned of the new arrival from the doctor. That somewhat cross-grained individual amused himself by remarking that the advent of a sister need not disturb the brother unduly. Had it been a son he would have had a share in his father's patrimony. Jawaharlal was not amused. But he was exhilarated by the thought of having a baby sister. She was named Sarup (the Beautiful One) and grew up to be the celebrated Mrs. Vijayalakshmi Pandit.

Motilal, with his wide circle of English friends, had always been impressed by the products of British public schools. He decided to send his son to one, and was fortunate to find a vacancy at Harrow.Jawaharlal was then sixteen, slightly above the normal age for entering a British public school.

A year before an event had occurred which absorbed the attention of India's educated middle class and was to affect Asian nationalism deeply. This was the Russo-Japanese War of 1904-1905. In one of his letters 10 to his daughter Indira, Nehru writes: "Early in the twentieth century an event occurred which had a great effect on the mind of Asia. This was the defeat of Tsarist Russia by Japan. ... I remember well how excited I used to get when news came of the Japanese victories.

I was about your age then." In a later letter n to his daughter he describes the Japanese triumph as "a great pick-me-up for Asia."

About the only war which Jawaharlal had followed before this was the Boer War between 1899 and 1902 in which his sympathies were with the Boers, possibly a reflection of his latent antipathy to British rule in India. For the first time he read newspapers avidly in an effort to follow the news. The Russo-Japanese conflict excited his interest more keenly, for Japan symbolised an Asian country in conflict with a European power. He bought a number of books on Japan and delighted in the exotic prose of that literary exquisite, Lafcadio Hearn, The war stimulated his imagination. He dreamt of himself, sword in hand, fighting like one of Lafcadio Hearn's knightly heroes for the freedom of his country. In May, 1905, Jawaharlal sailed for England with his father, mother and his four-year-old sister Samp. On the train between Dover and London he opened a newspaper and read of Admiral Togo's decisive victory over the Russian fleet at Tsushima. "I was in high good humour" he notes. It was in this mood that he entered upon his life in England.

8

LALA LAJPAT RAI

Lala Lajpat Rai was an Indian author and politician who is chiefly remembered as a leader in the Indian fight for freedom from the British Raj. The freedom fighter was popularly known as *Punjab Kesari* (Lion of the Punjab). He was also the founder Punjab National Bank and Lakshmi Insurance Company.

EARLY LIFE

Rai was born on January 28, 1865 in village Dhudi Ke, in present day Moga district of Punjab, India. He was the eldest son of Munshi Radha Kishan Azad and Gulab Devi, Aggarwal Banias. His father had a chequered relationship with Hinduism - having converted to Islam and then reverted back to Hinduism, which had a lasting effect on Rai's attitude towards religions other than Hinduism. He spent much of his youth in Jagraon, district Ludhiana, Punjab. His house still stands tall in Jagraon and houses a Library and museum.

POLITICAL CAREER

He was one of the three most prominent Hindu Nationalist members of the Indian National Congress, who fought for, and gave their lives during the Indian independence movement in the first half of the twentieth century. The other two were Bal Gangadhar Tilak of Maharashtra and Bipin Chandra Pal of Bengal. Collectively, they were dubbed *Lal-Bal-Pal*, and formed the extremist Hindu faction of the Indian National Congress, as opposed to the moderate faction led first by Gopal Krishna Gokhale and later by Mahatma Gandhi. Rai was also a member of the Hindu Maha Sabha, a forerunner of the current day Hindu nationalist party, the Bharatiya Janata Party. It was the Partition of Bengal in 1905 that aroused their robust nationalism and set them firmly on the path to fighting for freedom. The repressive measures of the British Government against the growing nationalist movement inspired them to infuse greater national pride and self-respect into the populace. The trio wanted a degree of self-government that was considered radical at the time. They were the first Indian leaders to demand complete political independence.

Rai presided over the first session of the All India Trade Union Congress in 1920. He also went to Geneva to attend the eighth International Labour Conference in 1926 as a representative of Indian labour. He had an opportunity to watch the labour movement in the USA and England where he was required to prolong his stay for political reasons.

Rai led the Punjab protests against the Amritsar Massacre (1919) and the Non-Cooperation Movement (1919 - 1922). He was repeatedly arrested. Rai however disagreed with Mohandas Gandhi's suspension of the movement due to the Chauri Chaura incident, and formed the *Congress Independence Party*, which was particularly pro-Hindu in voice and policy.

He was not only a good orator but also a prolific and versatile writer. His journal *Arya Gazette* concentrated mainly on subjects related to the Arya Samaj. *Bande Mataram* and *People*, contained his inspiring speeches to end oppression by the foreign rulers. He founded the Servants of the People Society, which worked for the freedom movement as well as for social reform in the country. He also wrote an autobiography in English titled *The Story of My Life*.

SIMON COMMISSION PROTESTS

A strong believer in leading by example, he himself led a procession with Pandit Madan Mohan Malaviya to demonstrate against the Simon Commission, which was to prove fatal for him. He was made the target of a brutal lathi charge in which he was injured badly. A meeting was held the same evening where he spoke with such vigour that his words, *"Every blow aimed at me is a nail in the coffin of British imperialism"*, became historic. Though he recovered from the fever and pain within three days his health had received a permanent setback and on November 17, 1928, he succumbed to the fatal injuries.

AUTHOR

Lala Lajpat Rai wrote extensively, among them - Josiah Wedgwood - The Man And His Work, The United States of America: A Hindu's impressions and a study, History of the Arya Samaj, Swaraj and social change, England's Debt to India: A historical narrative of Britain's fiscal policy in India, The Problems Of National Education In India and Unhappy India: Being a reply to Katherine Mayo's "Mother India", published in 1928. (Mother India was a polemical account of India's self rule by American historian Katherine Mayo.)

INSPIRATION AND MEMORIAL

Lajpat Rai was one of the most important nationalist leaders from the Punjab, where he is remembered reverently by Hindu nationalists today. He was a key mentor of nationalists like Bhagat Singh and Chandrasekhar Azad.

The Lala Lajpat Rai Memorial Trust was formed in 1959 on the eve of his Centenary Birth Celebration, to promote education - a cause very dear to his heart. The trust was founded by a group of Punjabi philanthropists (including R.P Gupta and B.M Grover) who have settled and prospered in the Indian State of Maharashtra.

Lajpat Nagar and Lajpat Nagar Central Market in New Delhi, Lala Lajpat Rai Hall of Residence at Indian Institutes of Technology (IIT) in Kharagpur and Lala Lajpat Rai Institute of Engineering and Technology, Moga are named in his honor. Also many institutes, Schools and Library in his hometown of Jagraon, district Ludhiana are named after him.

BIBLIOGRAPHY

Agarwal, Beena : *The Plays of Rabindra Nath Tagore : A Thematic Study*, New Delhi, Satyam Pub., 2003.

Atri, Ajit : *Gandhi's View of Legal Justice*, New Delhi, Deep and Deep Pub., 2007.

Bakshi, S.R. : *Rabindra Nath Tagore and the Challenges of Today*, New Delhi, Om Publications, 2001.

Balan, K. : *Mahatma Gandhi and Jawaharlal Nehru : The Two Stalwarts Who Shaped India*, Delhi, Authorspress, 2002.

Barman, Suren Deb : *Rabindranath Tagore and Tripura*, Kolkata, Minerva, 2006.

Bhattacharya, Sabyasachi : *Vande Mataram : The Biography of a Song*, New Delhi, Penguin, 2003.

Bose, Aurobindo : *Later Poems of Rabindranath Tagore*, New Delhi, Rupa & Co., 2002.

Bourai, Himanshu : *Gandhi and Modern Indian Liberals*, Delhi, Abhijeet Pub., 2004.

Chakrabarti, Mohit : *Rabindranath Tagore : A Miscellany*, New Delhi, Kanishka Pub., 2003.

Chatterjee, Indira : *A Thematic Study of Tagore's Novels*, Gurgaon, Shubhi Pub., 2007.

Colussi, Luciano : *Universality in Tagore : Souvenir of a Symposium on Rabindranath Tagore*, Calcutta, Firma KLM, 1991.

Dalton, Dennis : *Gandhi's Power : Nonviolence in Action*, New Delhi, OUP, 2001.

Datta, P.K. : *Rabindranath Tagore's The Home and the World : A Critical Companion*, Delhi, Permanent Black, 2003.

Desai, M.T. : *Jawaharlal Nehru, Rabindranath Tagore & Aurobindo Ghosh : A Comparative Study in their Internationalism*, 1999.

Desai, Mahadev : *Gandhi and Indian Villages*, New Delhi, Mohit Pub., 2002.

Ganguli, B.N. : *Gandhi's Social Philosophy : Perspective and Relevance*, New Delhi, National Gandhi Museum and Radha Pub., 2006.

Gupta, S.P. Das : *Rabindranath Tagore : Thought Relics: New Expanded Version*, Kolkata, Sadesh, 2007.

Howlader, Chinmoy : *Influence of Kalidasa on Rabindranath Tagore*, Delhi, Bharatiya Kala Prakashan, 2003.

Jain, P.C. : *Gandhi in Stamps : The Courier of Truth and Non-violence*, New Delhi, Aravali, 2002.

Krishnan, Anita : *Gandhian Satyagrah in South Africa*, New Delhi, Alfa Pub., 2008.

Lal, Ananda : *Rabindranath Tagore : Three Plays*, New Delhi, Oxford University Press, 2001.

Mahmud, Jafar : *Mahatma Gandhi : A Multifaceted Person*, New Delhi, APH, 2004.

Mohit Chakrabarti : *Religion and Rabindranath*, New Delhi, Kalpaz Pub., 2008.

Mukherjee, Kedar Nath : *Rabindranath Tagore's Concepts of State, Nation and Nationalism*, Kolkata, Punthi Pustak, 2003.

Pandey, Janardan : *Gandhi and 21st Century*, 1998.

Ray, Sibnarayan : *Gandhi, Gandhism and Our Times : An International Symposium*, Kolkata, Renaissance, 2003.

Sanyal, Bandana : *Achalayatan : The Petrified Place, Rabindranath Tagore*, New Delhi, Rupa, 2006.

Sharma, Rashmi : *Autobiographical Writings of Mahatma Gandhi*, New Delhi, Deep & Deep Pub., 2004.

Sharma, S.R. : *Life and Works of Rabindranath Tagore*, Jaipur, Book Enclave, 2003.

Singh, Ramjee : *Gandhi and The New Millennium*, Delhi, Commonwealth, 2000.

Sinha, Biswajit : *Rabindranath Tagore*, Delhi, Raj, 2003.

Sukanta, Chaudhuri : *Rabindranath Tagore : Selected Short Stories*, Delhi, Oxford University Press, 2000.

Tagore, Saumyendranath : *Rabindranath Tagore : Philosophy of Life and Aesthetics*, Kolkata, Aparna Book, 2006.

Yeats, W.B. : *Gitanjali : Song Offerings/Rabindranath Tagore*, New Delhi, Mahaveer, 2005.

INDEX

■■■